Praise for *The Chris Farley Show*

New York Times and *Los Angeles Times* Bestseller
★★★★ *People*'s "Pick of the Week"

"*The Chris Farley Show* shows that Farley's simplicity was in fact a tremendously complex construct. . . . Like *Live from New York*, another popular recent *SNL* book, *The Chris Farley Show* is an oral history, patched together out of scraps of interviews with Farley's friends, family, and colleagues. . . . The form [an oral history] seems particularly appropriate in the case of Farley, whose comedy was aggressively social and who was always obsessed with what people thought of him. The result is satisfyingly complex." —*New York*

"It digs beneath the buffoonish exterior and uncovers a complex human being. . . . The Chris Farley we meet here is both funnier and more lovable than the typical celebrity drug casualty, which makes *The Chris Farley Show* both sadder and more frustrating than the typical just-say-no cautionary tale." —*The New York Times Book Review*

"The most unexpected insights come from the perspectives provided by Farley's non-celebrity friends, like the Rev. Matt Foley (the namesake of the motivational speaker character), who provides a glimpse into Chris's spiritual side." —*Los Angeles Times*

"What you'll love: The book's intimate accounts give as much time to Farley's sensitive nature and generosity of spirit as they do to his ugliest moments, such as a disastrous near-death gig hosting *Saturday Night Live*." —*The Washington Post*

"Farley has no shortage of support and admirers. . . . The compilation of direct quotes from his loved ones makes for powerful reading and provides a more forceful reminder of how terrifying addiction can be." —*Playboy*

"As with any good oral history, *The Chris Farley Show* moves briskly and the reporting is deep."   —*Entertainment Weekly*

"[A] rip-roaring memory mosaic. With talents such as Mike Myers, Chris Rock, Conan O'Brien, and David Spade analyzing his humor and detailing Farley's escapades and hijinks, this is a boisterous book the comedian's fans will want to buy, borrow, or steal."   —*Publishers Weekly*

"The editors deserve credit for eliciting such heartfelt remembrances (not all of it positive) from an impressive list of celebrities—Alec Baldwin, John Goodman, Lorne Michaels, Conan O'Brien, Chris Rock, David Spade, Kevin Nealon, Rob Lowe, Al Franken, Penelope Spheeris, and many more—but readers should also pay close attention to Farley's family and friends, who get right to the heart of this flawed but humble, remarkably compassionate and enormously talented performer. Essential for Farley and *SNL* fans, and a sterling example of oral biography—well-structured, consistently engaging, and simultaneously heartwarming and heartbreaking."   —*Kirkus Reviews* (starred review)

CONTENTS

CONTENTS

INTRODUCTION

I rish brothers share one of the strangest relationships on earth. We fight like hell among ourselves on a daily basis, but one word or action against one brother brings the wrath of God down upon you from the others. That was Chris and me. We were always competing, whether it was driveway basketball, touch football, or Monopoly. Most of the time, those games would end in a brawl. Nothing bloody, mind you. Drawing blood would bring the fury of Mom or Dad down on all of us. No, most of the time we'd strike a few blows and then run like hell. And let me tell you, nothing was more terrifying than being chased through the neighborhood by a crazy, mad Irish sibling who outweighed you by twenty-five pounds and had a brick in his hand!

But rare was the time that I wouldn't come running if Chris was in trouble. I was the older brother; that was my job. And, Chris being Chris, it was a job that put me in harm's way more times than I would have liked. One such time, when I was in eighth grade and Chris was in sixth, he got into a fight with a classmate. He tackled the kid and threw him to the ground, landing on top of him and breaking his collarbone. Word got around school that the kid's seventh-grade brother was gunning for Chris. Naturally, I had to step in. I put the word out that the brother would have to get through me first. I found out later that day that the kid's brother was named Rocky. No shit: Rocky! The guy was massive (a future all-city lineman in high school, no less). No fight ensued, but I did learn that I possessed a real gift of what the Irish call "the gab." I talked my way out of it. It was my only defense, without which Chris would have certainly gotten me killed several times over. Life with Chris was exciting; he brought drama and danger into our lives. But no matter what he put you through, he could always just give you a look and make you laugh. Boy, did he make us laugh.

We always loved to tell "Chris stories." I've heard them from friends, relatives, teachers, coaches—even priests and nuns. You could be the funniest guy in the room just by describing some of the stuff Chris did. For every hilarious thing he did on camera, there were twenty things he did offscreen that just blew it away. He lived to make others laugh, and he was fearless about it. In the years since Chris passed away, there have been countless times when Chris's buddies would find themselves huddled together, sharing these crazy stories. At one time, I even thought that a collection of those stories would make a fantastic book. I still do. But I now believe that those funny stories alone would not paint the right picture of who this kid was. Chris had far too much depth and way too much pain. We all enjoyed Chris so much, and it's hard to put those things into words.

I began this project by listing all the people who either knew Chris the best or were there at the important moments in his life. I spoke to most of them and gave them assurances that this was a project that our family was behind all the way. I wanted them to be open and honest about their memories, opinions, and feelings about being part of what, for most, was an unforgettable relationship. I'm not sure I was totally prepared for the story that Tanner and I ended up with. The funny stories and outrageous moments are definitely in there, but what emerged was this amazing picture of the multifaceted character traits that Chris possessed. He was hilarious, yes, but he was also a very religious, very caring—and very troubled and addicted person. It's a sad story, no question about it. But it's Chris.

Soon after Chris died, I told my wife that my greatest fear was being sixty years old and trying hard to remember this kid who was my brother. I guess anyone who's lost someone close can say that. Being able to watch the fun movies and video clips only gets you so far; it's not the full picture. I'm pleased that this book will be something I can pick up when I'm older, remember Chris and his wild life, and be once more amazed that I had such an unbelievable person in my life.

The Chris Farley SHOW

ACT I

CHAPTER 1

A Motivated Speaker

MIKE CLEARY, *friend, Edgewood High School:*

Freshman year of college we're heading out on a road trip to Milwaukee to see a big game. We're in the car. We've got the fifth of vodka, the gallon of orange juice. We're ready to get loaded and party. Just as we start to drive, Chris says, "Stop!"

We stop the car, and he pulls out a rosary. We have to sit there in the car and say one decade of the rosary—ten Hail Marys and an Our Father—before we can leave. Then he balls the rosary up in his hand, tosses it in the glove compartment, slams it shut, looks at all of us, and says, "Well, it's in God's hands now." And we hit the road.

On June 24, 1994, life for Chris Farley was good. He had just finished his fourth season on NBC's *Saturday Night Live* and was coming into his own as one of the most promising stars in American comedy. As the earnest, sad-sack Chippendales dancer and the swaggering, van-dwelling Motivational Speaker, Chris was bringing a kind of energy and anarchy to the show not seen since its seventies heyday.

Dana Carvey, Mike Myers, and Phil Hartman were stepping down as the show's reliable go-to players, and Chris was leading the charge—alongside Adam Sandler, Tim Meadows, David Spade, and Rob Schneider—in the next cycle of revitalizing and redefining the late-night institution for a new generation. Chris was also about to take on his first starring role in a feature film, *Tommy Boy*. The following year, *Tommy Boy* would open at the top of the North American box office and solidify Chris's status as a bankable movie star.

From his very first days onstage—starting in plays at summer camp and eventually at Chicago's Second City—Chris had possessed a singular talent for capturing and relating to an audience. In the words of *SNL* creator Lorne Michaels, "People liked Chris Farley, they trusted Chris Farley, and they thought they knew Chris Farley." In his lifetime, that likability translated to a huge following on television and three straight number one box-office hits. And since his death at the age of thirty-three, Chris's appeal persists. In the past ten years, *Saturday Night Live*'s *Best of Chris Farley* DVD has sold over a million copies, making it the second-best-selling title in the show's entire history. *Tommy Boy*, for its part, has gone on to become one of Paramount Studios' top-selling DVDs of all time.

But Chris's success had not come easily. His rise at *SNL* had been marred by a constant struggle with alcohol and drug addiction. High school and college drinking had given way, eventually, to cocaine and heroin use. Through the intervention of friends and family, Chris had attempted several different recovery programs, all of them eventually ineffective.

But on June 24, 1994, Chris was clean and sober and standing onstage in a large auditorium at Hazelden, a nationally renowned drug rehabilitation facility in Center City, Minnesota. Chris had visited Hazelden twice before, both times as a rather unwilling and uncooperative resident. This time he walked through its doors of his own free will, as a guest, invited to share his recovery experience with other addicts struggling in their own battles with the disease.

Chris's presence filled the auditorium; he knew how to work a room.

Only this time, abandoning his popular, manic persona, he held the audience captive by simply standing at center stage and speaking in calm, measured tones. It was a Chris Farley that only a handful of close friends and family members ever knew. Dressed in a blue button-down shirt and stone-colored khakis, he paced a small circle, nervously fidgeting with his hands and running them through his slicked-back hair. At no point did he fall down or remove his pants. And there, alone on the stage that day with no crazy characters to hide behind, no wild-man stunts to impress, Chris gave a "motivational speech" quite unlike any he'd ever delivered on television.

CHRIS FARLEY:

Good to be here. Um, pretty nervous. I was here a couple times, so I know what it's like to be sitting where you are, full of fear and anxiety. Kinda how I'm feeling tonight! Heh heh heh!

Anyhoo.

I'm supposed to share my experience, strength, and hope with you, and so I'll start. I remember my first drink. I was seventeen years old, almost eighteen. My friend Patrick was a year above me and I admired him quite a bit, looked up to him. He was a great football player, all-state and everything like that. I went to a party with him one night. We went down in the basement. The guys started drinkin', and they went, "C'mon and take a drink, Chris."

So I took a shot, and I remember going, "Man, this sucks. I can't believe you do this."

"Just take it down like medicine," they said.

So I wolfed down about ten of 'em, no problem. And I remember hearing stuff like, "Man, I thought he was wild before, and now he's *really* gonna be a *wild* man!"

So that kind of planted in my cranium what I'd always wanted, and that was to fit in, or to be liked. Everyone seemed to love it. When I went upstairs, I remember the girls were like, "Great! Chris, *finally*!"

And I was like, "Yeah! Maybe I'll even get a chick now!"

So that night I got blind drunk and threw up in my bed. Then I called Patrick the next day and said, "Man, this was great! When are we gonna do it again?" And I got blind drunk every weekend until I graduated high school.

Then I went on to college at Marquette University. I was away from home and that meant I could party every night. I did. Each year I got worse and worse. Freshman year I'd party Thursday, Friday, and Saturday. Sophomore year it'd be Wednesday, Thursday, Friday, and Saturday. Then it started on Tuesdays, and by the time I was a senior it was every night.

Every drug that I tried I couldn't wait to try more. Sophomore year I tried marijuana and fell completely in love with it. I went home and watched *Love Connection* and was like, "Ooooohhhh man . . ." You know? I couldn't understand why everyone wasn't getting high. It was the best way to live. My God, how boring it must be for you poor sober people. So I got high every day from that day on. I'd try psychedelics and I'd have a really bad trip and still couldn't wait to do it again. "Maybe this one'll be different." And that was the way it was. I just wanted to escape.

And so I remember reading about John Belushi in the book *Wired*. A lot of people read *Wired* and thought, "Man, that poor guy! I never wanna do drugs again!" But I was like, "Yeah! If that's what it takes, I wanna do it!" 'Cause I wanted to be like him in every way, like all those guys from that show. I thought that's what you had to do.

When I got outta school, I didn't know what I was gonna do with my life. I knew I didn't have much in the grades department, and so I was very fearful. A whole lot of fear. I remember drinking was the only time I felt, you know, good. I went and worked for my dad after school. I'd show up late and stuff like that. He was the boss, and so I was his screw-up son. I didn't get in too much trouble. He'd let it slide.

The one thing I knew was that I wanted to go into acting. I went down to Chicago to try to go into a place called Second City. I auditioned for that and got in pretty quickly, but I couldn't stop partying. They gave me a warning: "If you do it again, we're gonna kick you off the main stage."

I wanted to continue performing, so I only got high for the performance, on marijuana. Then afterward I couldn't wait to get ripped. I remember one time my director was giving me notes, and I drank a pint of Bacardi in about ten minutes, before he was done talking. He asked me a question, and I was slurring my words. He said, "Oh, you're no good. I'll talk to you tomorrow." But it was kind of tolerated. My lifestyle cradled it, because I didn't have to wake up in the morning. I could get blind drunk every night, and that's what I did.

Then I went to New York and started working on *Saturday Night Live*. That was, I thought, a dream come true. I'd read all about my idols and how they partied back then. I thought, man, this is gonna be great! I am gonna get *ripped*!

Well, that just wasn't the case. It wasn't hip anymore. I stuck out like a sore thumb, taking my clothes off at parties and making a fool of myself, which I had learned to do pretty good because I thought people would like me. Nobody's afraid of the fool. "Hi! C'mon, idiot! C'mon aboard!" I was totally full of fear. I'd do anything for you to like me, including doing things that I didn't want to do. As long as I had my substance, I was okay.

I went back to Second City after my first year on *Saturday Night Live* and took a bunch of acid and cocaine and a ton of liquor and went onstage and made a complete ass of myself. They booed. I remember during a blackout between scenes someone yelled, "Get the drunk off the stage!" That kinda rang true.

I had to cover my ass so they'd hire me back at *SNL* again next year. So I came here to the Shoemaker Unit at Hazelden. I hated every minute of it. I complied and kissed ass until the counselors went home and then screwed around and tried to make everybody on the unit laugh, and didn't take it serious one bit. Got outta there and thought I was cured. "All right, I did twenty-eight days sober, no problem."

So I got outta here, didn't go to meetings, didn't get a sponsor, didn't do anything that they told me. And guess what? I got back to New York and started doing a lot of drugs. I thought, if I don't drink in front of people, they're not gonna know I'm high. I thought I was fooling everyone, and I was fooling no one.

That Christmas, after a real bad bender, my apartment was just totally ripped out. I'd ripped apart drawers, everything was on the floor, because I'd been looking for something. "Oh, what's this? Is it in here? No?" *Crash!* "Where's this?! What's that?! Oh fuck!" So Christmas, coming home to surprise my parents, what a lovely gift I was. They put me in a detox for a couple of days.

The whole rest of that season I did the outpatient thing, which was a complete joke. I would comply with them and say, "I'm really trying hard." Meanwhile I always had a thing of urine in my pocket just in case they tested me. God, what an ass, asking my friends for their urine. "Kevin, yeah, you got that, uh, urine?" Jesus. Everyone knew I was using. I just remember a horrible dismay. I was crying all the time, because I could not stop. I couldn't imagine a life with sobriety, because drugs and alcohol were the only thing that was my friend. I knew I was in trouble.

I came back to Shoemaker. I decided to make sure they *knew* that I was trying. "By God, I'm your boy, boss. I'm *trying*. Pluggin' away!" So I screwed around and complied in treatment again, and didn't take it serious. I wasn't listening, and that's what you gotta do about this disease, because it's hell to stop.

I got outta there thinkin' I was cured. La di da! Didn't last even as long as I did the first time out, and by that time I had almost thrown in the towel. I went out to California to do some work the next summer. I got into another rehab out there. It was like every time I turned around I was in friggin' rehab. God, it sucks! But I kinda started takin' this one serious, because I was like, "I don't wanna come back here, man." The door was open just a little bit. I was sick of using, and I knew I was gonna be fired very soon. I didn't want that because *SNL* was everything I'd worked for.

They told me to go to Fellowship New York, a halfway house that had just opened. So I went there and this time I was gonna finish it, you know, give it a real shot. I was frightened of going to recovery meetings. Because what if I couldn't do it? That's what would really suck.

I was glad to be sober, but after ninety days people weren't patting me on the back anymore, sayin' "Good job on that sobriety! Go get 'em!"

People just expected it. And why shouldn't they expect me to be sober? I'm working for them. But I wanted the pats on the back, and they weren't doing that.

That ninety-day mark was a real tough one for me. After a bad day at read-through, the writers didn't write me into the show, and I was going back and forth. I used. I did five bags of heroin. Then I came back and told my boss. I thought if I was honest with him, you know? That's another manipulating tool. "I'm being honest with you, so you won't fire me, right? Because I'm *trying*. Can't you see I'm trying?" All that bullshit.

So, I lost my job for about a week. I kept begging and crying, the same manipulative things. Finally he gave me my job back, but he sent me to this place in Alabama, which was kind of like a boot camp. It was exactly what I needed, a good kick in the rear end. They told me stuff like "You're arrogant. You're complying." They made me cry every single day. They'd say that if you pick up drugs and alcohol, you're a baby. I didn't like to be called a baby. I didn't like to be called arrogant. I didn't like to be called all those things that I was.

It was around Christmas time, too. Man, what a horrible place to be over Christmas, you know? Hearing "Have yourself a merry little Christmas . . ." when I'm in a stinky hospital ward. But I did things in this treatment that I didn't do before, like making sure I made my bed every day. I practiced what I would be doing on the outside. I prayed to God in the morning to please keep me sober that day, and then I'd thank Him for keeping me sober every night.

So I got outta that thing in Alabama. I got a sponsor. I got a home group. I was reading from the Big Book. I went to a morning meeting every day at seven-thirty. I got involved, because I know I can't stay sober without these things, without going one hundred percent. But I can stay sober when I do. And sobriety's good, man. Sobriety's not carrying around urine jars—that's a real treat. It's not waking up in a horrible apartment with everything broken in it. I have a nice apartment now that's all taken care of. I make my bed every day. I do the things that I did in treatment. I have a very healthy fear of getting high, and I have to take it serious, man. Because if I don't, I'm gonna use, and I cannot use again. I hate that shit. God, I hate it. I hate being a slave to that shit.

The ninety-day mark was a real kicker for me, again. I remember it was on St. Patrick's Day. I like to have an icy cold Guinness on St. Patrick's Day. I'm Irish! I have to drink, right? And I remember pacing back and forth in the rain outside a bar, crying. I was so scared, and I was just crying and crying and praying to God to help me. Then I stopped. I remembered that I don't have to drink. I called the halfway house, went to a meeting, and I did what I had to do. And today I have one year, six months, and six days. That's the most time I've ever had. And I can do this. I know I can do it.

We all can do it.

CHAPTER 2

Madison, Wisconsin

GREG MEYER, *friend:*

We were all sitting in the library one afternoon—me, Chris, Dan Healy, Mike Cleary, a bunch of guys. We're sitting at this table, and Chris is just cracking us up. Finally, he gets up to go to class, and as he's leaving somebody says, "He's going to be on *Saturday Night Live.*"

Everyone at the table just nodded. "Definitely."

Chris Farley's grandfather Donald Stephen Farley worked as an executive with the A&P supermarket company in Philadelphia, Pennsylvania. He lost everything he had in the 1930s Depression and returned to his family's home in Madison, Wisconsin. There he joined his brothers in a hardware business that sold machine parts and services. One of those services was laying asphalt roads, a lucrative field in the booming infrastructure build-out following World War II. Hanging out their shingle as Farley Oil, the brothers bought and sold road-paving contracts. They were middlemen, salesmen. They bid on contracts with state and county officials and in turn brokered the services of the crews that laid the actual roads.

Donald's son Tom Farley, the second-youngest of six, applied for a special driver's license and began driving for the family business at the age of fourteen. Later, at Georgetown University in Washington, D.C., he discovered his calling in the game of politics. He soon found himself president of the campus Young Republicans and a frequent dinner guest of Wisconsin senator Joseph McCarthy.

During his senior year, Tom met Mary Anne Crosby, the daughter of an established Boston family and a student at Marymount College. Upon graduation, he moved back to Madison to attend law school at the University of Wisconsin, the first step in his plans to seek a career in law and a future in elected office. Mary Anne followed him to the Midwest, and they married in 1959.

The following year, Donald Farley suffered two massive heart attacks. He could no longer run the family business or support a family. With two parents, several siblings, a wife, and a new daughter depending on him, Tom had little choice. With only one year of law school remaining, he quit, shelved his dreams, and for the next thirty years plowed his expensive East Coast education and considerable personal charm into selling asphalt.

He sold a lot of it.

As a partner in Farley Oil—and later owner of his own company, Scotch Oil—Tom Farley was very successful. He became well known across the state, thriving in a business run entirely on his boisterous laugh and hearty handshake. His success gave him the means to provide for his family, which in the Irish Catholic tradition would soon grow quite large. Tom and Mary Anne's daughter, Barbara, was born in 1960; Tom Jr. a year after that. Two years later, on February 15, 1964, at 3:34 P.M., Mary Anne gave birth to her second son, Christopher Crosby Farley. He weighed eight pounds, fifteen ounces. Next came Kevin Farley in 1965, and then finally John, the youngest, in 1968.

Although Tom Farley, Sr., had grown up in a middle-class pocket of

Madison proper, when it came time to make a home of his own, he moved to the Village of Maple Bluff. Maple Bluff was, and is, an idyllic slice of affluent twentieth-century suburbia. Clustered on the eastern shore of Madison's Lake Mendota, it is home to the governor's executive mansion as well as the stately residence of one Oscar Mayer, proprietor of a local luncheon meat and hot dog concern. There, among Maple Bluff's tree-canopied lanes and rolling green lawns, Tom and Mary Anne raised their children. Over the next fifteen years they lived in four different homes, each one bigger than the one before. The last had a commanding lake-front view. Growing up, Chris would lack for little in the way of material comfort. The Farleys lived well. On paper, at least, it looked like the American Dream.

TOM FARLEY, *brother:*

When Chris came along, my grandmother insisted that my mom wasn't going to be able to handle three kids at once, so this Spanish woman came to help the family. My first memory is this woman coming into our lives because of Chris. I always remember that Chris got special attention.

KEVIN FARLEY, *brother:*

Maple Bluff was a great neighborhood. We were always outside playing, jumping in the leaves, riding our bikes, like kids do.

Chris was always popular, right off the bat. He always wanted to start up a game, get everyone together. We'd play kick the can or ghost in the graveyard, which was what we called hide-and-seek. I was the shy kid, and I was amazed at how he could make friends so easily. We changed schools a good bit, but no matter what school Chris went to, he always instantly had a new group of friends. Making people laugh was just instinctive. And also he looked to Dad. Dad was very outgoing. My parents always had parties, were very involved in the community. A lot of that carried over for Chris.

What I remember most from the earliest years are the Christmases we used to have. That was always a big event. Whenever the relatives came over we were sort of made to dress up and look nice, basically put on a show for the rest of the family, talking to all the aunts and uncles. Dad insisted on that.

TOM FARLEY:

It's been explained to me by more than a few therapists that we exhibited a typical Irish Family Syndrome. The father is the bullhorn and the head of the family, but not really the head of the family. It's really the mother who keeps everything together, and Mom always did. Our life was straight out of *Angela's Ashes*, only, you know, with plenty of money. Dad always drove the big Cadillac. We were certainly well off by Wisconsin standards, or at least gave the impression that we were. There was a point when we were all taken out of the parochial schools and sent to public schools for a year. Dad had some excuse that, looking back, didn't really hold water. But this was 1974, and Dad was in the oil business. He'd had a bad year and couldn't keep up with the tuition. But he always kept up appearances that everything was fine.

KEVIN FARLEY:

Dad loved politics. He ran for school board at one point, but didn't win. That was probably because he had all his kids in private school. They sort of hammered him on that. But we went out and put up signs for the race. Dad joined the board for Maple Bluff. It was a subdivision, but it had its own councils and so on. He enjoyed that immensely. He was a conservative man, politically, and very civic-minded.

TOM FARLEY:

Dad's voice was a sonic boom. All he'd say was, *"It's time to go to mass! Everybody in the car!"* and you'd scramble like it was a DEFCON 4 siren from the Strategic Air Command. You didn't want to get on his bad side. He was very lenient, but with four hyperactive boys, somebody's got to crack the whip sometimes. And when the whip would crack, it would crack hard.

KEVIN FARLEY:

He was very strict, but if you could get a laugh out of him, you were okay. And Chris knew that. One time Chris walked into Mrs. Jennings's class at Edgewood Grade School and said, "Excuse me, Mrs. Jennings, where do I 'shit' down?"

She hit the roof and called my dad in for a conference. She told him what happened, and said Chris needed to be suspended. Chris was like, "I didn't say it, honest."

And Dad said, "Well, Chris says he didn't say that. And if my son says he didn't do it, then I believe him. You must have heard him wrong."

So she backed down. Then, on the way home, Dad turned to Chris and went, "You said it, didn't you?"

"Yeah."

"I knew it."

They both had a laugh over it, and that was it. He knew Chris had done it, but it was okay to laugh as long as nobody got hurt. Those kinds of incidents cropped up all the time.

As strict as Dad could be, when he decided it was time to have fun, it was time to have fun. We would pile into the station wagon and go shopping or out to mass. Sometimes we'd go out to the apple orchards to pick apples. The church bazaars my dad loved. He'd come in and say, "There's a church bazaar out in Lodi!"

And we'd go, "Aw, jeez . . ."

And then we'd all get in the car and go all the way out to Lodi for homemade pies and such at this bazaar out in a farm field somewhere. The rituals of our house when we were young all centered around the family. There was never a time when we wanted to rebel and get away from it.

JOHN FARLEY, *brother:*

Family dinners were very important. We had a dinner bell. Anything we were doing anywhere in the neighborhood, we could hear this giant bell outside our kitchen. We'd stop what we were doing—setting fires, whatever—our heads would pop up like deer and we'd run home.

There were actually two bells. There was our dinner bell at six-thirty, and there was also a giant whistle that would blow through the entire neighborhood at five o'clock. It wasn't from a factory. It wasn't the emergency broadcast system. It was just a whistle that the town of Maple Bluff had. Why it went off every day at five we still don't know. We assumed it meant it was time for all the families to start their cocktail hour.

KEVIN FARLEY:

Other than family, the one thing that was important to my parents was education, in particular a Catholic education. Some parents are really hard on good grades, but our parents cared more that we learned how to be good people, that we had big hearts and were kind. I don't know of any better guy in the world than my dad, just in terms of being a strong, moral person. He always stressed that in us.

TOM FARLEY:

If Dad instilled anything in Chris it was this love of the underdog, for the kid that's getting picked on. If we were driving down the road and you made a joke about some strange-looking homeless person out on the sidewalk, man, he'd lock those brakes up and the hand would come back. You didn't dare do that.

My dad was very Catholic, and in Catholicism that whole idea of right and wrong, good and evil is very important. Chris was very aware of that from an early age. It all stemmed from *The Exorcist*. The mere fact that we'd seen that movie brought the devil into our house, and that started this whole superstition in Chris, not just of good and evil, but the literal, physical devil. He and I shared a bedroom for a time, and he was next to the closet; that just freaked the hell out of him. "Tommy, we gotta change beds," he'd say. "Tommy, please. The devil's in the closet."

KEVIN FARLEY:

Every night for months after *The Exorcist* came out, he'd just show up in our room with a sleeping bag and crash on the floor between Johnny and me. It was sort of an unspoken thing. If you asked him why, he'd say, "Shut up, okay? I'm just sleeping here." Chris was afraid of the dark, and he hated sleeping alone.

He was a very spiritual person, instinctively spiritual, and he'd always talk about it, so much so that he'd scare the crap out of you. As you grow up, even though you still call the devil by name, you begin to understand him as a spiritual idea, and a lot of people stop believing in the devil altogether, which, of course, is exactly what the devil wants. But Chris, he believed in the devil. He believed in hell, and it scared him.

TOM FARLEY:

He prayed to St. Michael the Archangel every night, because Michael was the one who'd thrown Lucifer out of heaven. It was more superstition than spirituality, to be honest. He read something once about the different ways your shoes land after you take them off means different kinds of luck. If your shoe was to one side, it was bad luck. If it was upright it was good luck, and so on. So every night I'd kick off my shoes, not caring where they landed, and Chris would say, "Tommy, pick up your shoe and set it right."

"No."

"C'mon."

"No."

"Please."

"Do it yourself."

And he'd get out of bed and go and move my shoes; he felt that strongly about it.

KEVIN FARLEY:

Growing up, Chris was wild and crazy and liked to have fun, and Tommy was more reserved. It really reflected, more than anything, the two sides of our dad. Dad would carry himself as this very professional gentleman, but he could also be this boisterous, crazy, laugh-out-loud kind of guy. And Tom and Chris were the two sides of that personality. To the extreme, really. John and I are somewhere in the middle.

TOM FARLEY:

Kevin was very focused, got decent grades. We called him Silent Sam, Steady Eddie. He just did his thing and did it well. John was the gopher. He was so much younger than the rest of us. He was always pleasing people, doing what it took to tag along. Still is to this day. As for myself, I was the brains in the family, which is really kind of sad. But I was Tom Farley, Jr., and everything that that entailed. My dad went to Georgetown, and so from day one the pressure was on me as the oldest son to live up to Dad's expectations.

The expectations for Chris were that there were no expectations. He just kind of marched to his own drummer. One day Chris said, "I want to join the hockey team." The next day he had a brand-new set of hockey gear, never mind that he couldn't really skate that well. So there was full support for him in whatever he wanted to do, but no real expectation that he should fail or succeed.

Chris and I were always together, but I was trying my best to toe the line and he was effortlessly crossing over the line, trampling it with no consequences; it annoyed the crap out of me. And because he was always so funny, my friends would want him to hang around. I hated that.

KEVIN FARLEY:

What was most important to Chris, really, was that he made people laugh. Chris was always the fat kid. Kids can be pretty mean, and humor was his only weapon, from grade school on. He wanted to be a football player, and that meant being part of the popular crowd. He used his humor to do that.

TED DONDANVILLE, *friend, Red Arrow Camp:*

I met Chris at summer camp, with all the other brothers. Tom was actually my counselor, and Johnny wound up being my best friend. You didn't forget Chris. Even if I'd never seen him again after camp, I'd remember him. During mass, if the priest made the mistake of asking for audience involvement, Chris was right there. His hand would shoot up, and then he'd figure out whether or not he had something to say.

DICK WENZELL, *play director, Red Arrow Camp:*

Red Arrow Camp was established in 1922, and was named after the Red Arrow Army, Second Division, from Wisconsin. It had originally been built as a logging camp in the nineteenth century. Some of the cabins date back to that time. It was a resident seven-week camp.

TIM HENRY, *friend, Red Arrow Camp:*

Chris always had some kind of stunt going. On Sundays they'd load all us Catholic boys into this old school bus and drive us into town. The girls' camps would come to Sunday mass, too. Now, you're never allowed to have candy at camp, but somehow one Sunday Chris has gotten ahold of these white tic tacs. He fills his mouth with them, and he's walking up the aisle for communion so prayerfully, and when he gets in front of the girl campers he rolls his eyes back like he's going to pass out and then he falls and hits his mouth on the side of the bench and spits out all the tic tacs. They go clattering across this wooden bench, and Chris is yelling, "Oh my God! My teeth!" The girls were just aghast. We were all laughing hysterically.

HAMILTON DAVIS, *friend, Red Arrow Camp:*

It was anything for a laugh, absolutely anything. They gave away all these awards for good behavior and accomplishments and such. Chris didn't care.

TOM FARLEY:

He was our windup toy. You said it. He did it.

KEVIN FARLEY:

He didn't win a lot of the awards, but because he was so funny they'd put him in the camp play, and he was the star. Chris would always credit Dick Wenzell with encouraging that in him.

DICK WENZELL:

Chris was strictly a jock, but he had a lot of charisma. Once I got him onstage, his connection with the audience was unbelievable. Not only could he project to the audience, he could also receive from them. Chris could take whatever the audience gave to him and build on it. He just did it naturally. Visiting parents would comment on how magnetic he was. And this was when he was ten years old.

TED DONDANVILLE:

The camp play was really a bunch of skits strung together. One year they did a takeoff on *Snow White and the Seven Dwarfs*, and Chris played the villain. When they caught him, he told them they could do what they wanted to him as long as they didn't step on his blue suede shoes. Then he launched into this Elvis impersonation that brought the house down.

HAMILTON DAVIS:

Whatever the story was, they'd just drop him in there. He was such a crowd-pleaser that they didn't even have to have a part for him. Just put him up onstage. One time he did "Hound Dog" dressed up like Miss Piggy.

FRED ALBRIGHT, *counselor, Red Arrow Camp:*

When people ask "Where did Chris Farley get his start?" I say he got it at Red Arrow Camp. As a kid, he was just a miniature version of what he would become. Dick Wenzell used the expression "He was always on-stage." And that was the case. A lot of it was a diversion, because down deep Chris was one of the most sensitive guys you'll ever meet. Even though he came across as this kind of rough, gruff, jovial guy, you could hurt his feelings with just a word or two. Incredibly sensitive guy.

MIKE CLEARY:

Chris was the very first guy I met at Edgewood. I grew up in Scarsdale, New York, and moved to Madison in high school. Edgewood can be a little clubby. For days, the rest of the kids didn't even come near me. Then one day I was sitting in the commons, getting ready for football practice. Chris came up and said, "You're the guy from New York? Hi, I'm Chris Farley." He was the first person to make me feel comfortable being there.

ROBERT BARRY, *friend:*

At school you always wanted to be around Chris. He was a blast, but his focus was always on you, talking *you* up, making *you* feel better. "This is my buddy Robert," he'd say. "He's all-state basketball." He's this. He's that. He's the greatest. It was never about himself.

TODD GREEN, *friend:*

We had the closest thing to what I would call a dream high school situation, where six or seven guys were as close as brothers and laughed their asses off every single day, and Chris was the glue that kept us together. He was such a pivotal part of our high school experience. Chris was the type of person who didn't see social class, or ethnicity, or anything like that. He came from a lot more money than most of us, but you would never know.

MIKE CLEARY:

One time I was visited by an old friend of mine from back east. He'd been a big football player, but he'd had this horrible car accident, and now he was in a wheelchair. A lot of kids could be uncomfortable around that, but Chris just embraced him. He spent the entire day making this kid feel welcome and totally at ease. And the thing is, he did it with no effort. His generosity was so commonplace that it was utterly unremarkable.

DAN HEALY, *friend:*

Chris made people feel good about themselves. Everyone was on a pedestal for some reason or another. He drew people together, naturally, and it was cathartic to be around him. To me, Chris would bat his eye and I would lose it laughing so hard my sides would hurt.

GREG MEYER:

People ask me what it was like going to school with Chris Farley, and I say, "You've seen him on *SNL*, right?"

"Yeah."

"Well, crank that up times ten."

JOHN FARLEY:

With the birth of the VCR, we memorized *Animal House*, *Stripes*, *Caddyshack*, *Meatballs*, *History of the World*, *High Anxiety*, and *Blues Brothers*. And I'm not talking about memorizing the lines. We memorized everything, every inch of footage. The foreground, the background, we memorized it all. And Chris pulled from that constantly.

One of Chris's favorite bits to do was to put his arms out like Frankenstein and make this monster voice, "Urgggh duugggh!" That was from an obscure scene in *Meatballs* with Spaz introducing himself to the cabin where, in the background, some fat camper was doing that Frankenstein thing. The whole thing was maybe half a second of film, maybe. But even that we had down. Take the original cast of *Saturday Night Live*, add in Mel Brooks, and you have our childhood.

NICK BURROWS, *guidance counselor/assistant football coach:*

Every time you'd walk down to the cafeteria, packed full of three-hundred-plus kids, all you had to do was listen for the roar of laughter and you'd know where Chris Farley was sitting. As I remember, Chris didn't really tell jokes. It was just who he was. He just *was funny*, being himself. People just liked hanging around him. I was his guidance counselor, and I liked hanging around him.

JOEL MATURI, *dean of discipline/head football coach:*

His antics were never mean or destructive. Chris did a lot of crazy things, but most of the stories of Chris being in trouble at Edgewood are, unfortunately, fabricated. I say "unfortunately" because they sound very entertaining many years later. There is one hilarious story about Chris and a nun that I know for a fact just isn't true.

NICK BURROWS:

We had a geometry teacher named Colonel McGivern. He was a retired air force colonel. Back then we had a lecture hall where all the kids would go for these huge group lectures while the colonel did equations and theorems on this big overhead projector. Well, one day Chris gets down in the aisle and belly-crawls up to the front of the room. He gets to the stage stairs, waits for Colonel McGivern to turn back to the projector, and then sneaks up and around, behind the curtain.

Now, Colonel McGivern had this thing called the Groaner of the Day, a really bad, corny joke that he'd use to end each day's lecture. He'd tell it, and the kids would all groan because it was so lame. So Chris waits, and just as Colonel McGivern delivers his punch line, Chris drops his pants and moons the entire audience, sticking his rear end out between two folds in the curtain. Well, the whole place erupts with laughter, and the colonel—who can't see Chris—stands there scratching his head, going, "Jeez, I didn't think it was that funny . . ." And then of course everyone really loses it.

Some sophomore girl gets offended, and she rats Chris out. I get a call from Joel Maturi, telling me that Chris has done this thing and needs to be punished.

"Nick, uh, are you familiar with the term 'hung a moon'?" he asks me.

"Sure, Coach."

"Well, that's what he did, and we need to get his parents over here and sort this out."

So I call Mr. and Mrs. Farley, and they come down to the office. I tell the Farleys about Chris hanging a moon and the colonel and the Groaner of the Day, the whole story. And Mrs. Farley just busts out laughing. She can't stop. Then I start laughing. Then Mr. Farley starts losing it, too. So here we all are dying laughing, waiting for the dean of discipline to come down.

Now, Joel Maturi is a real straight-arrow, buttoned-down kind of guy. We all straighten up as he comes in with his yellow legal pad where he's got the incident written down. "Mr. and Mrs. Farley," he says, very businesslike, sitting down, reading from his notes. "Ahem. Yes, it would appear, Mr. and Mrs. Farley, that your son has 'hung a moon' in his geometry class."

Mrs. Farley loses it again. She gets me laughing. Mr. Farley busts out again. And finally Maturi, as stiff as he is, he starts laughing. We're all roaring in my office. Finally, Maturi takes the legal pad, chucks it on the table, and says, "We're just going to forget about this one."

It should have been a suspension, but he threw it out because, quite frankly, we all thought it was too funny.

TOM FARLEY:

Chris would show up in Room 217, the detention hall, on a fairly regular basis, and Coach Maturi always seemed to be laughing under his breath, saying, "... *dammit, Farley.*"

When Chris was sorry, he was genuinely sorry. He'd be so guilty and remorseful, and he would always take his punishment. He knew it was the price to pay for getting the laugh. But before that apology would come, he had to get a laugh and you had to admit that it was funny.

Chris's bedroom was at the other end of the hallway from the bathroom, and lots of times he was just too lazy to get up and go. So what he did was he kept glasses in his bedroom. He'd pee in those, and then take them down to the bathroom and empty them out once he was ready to get up. Well, one time my mom found one of the glasses. We were all sitting at the dinner table the next day, and she had told my dad about it.

Dad was so furious he didn't know what to do. I mean, here was Chris peeing in our drinking glasses. Chris knew that Dad knew, and Dad knew that Chris knew that he knew, and there was dead silence at the table. Everyone was waiting for the other shoe to drop. Finally, Dad reaches over to take a sip of his water, and Chris goes, "You're not gonna drink out of *that* glass, are you?"

"*Goddammit!*"

Chris knew what was coming, but he had to get the laugh first.

KEVIN FARLEY:

Chris was such a natural talent that he was always being asked by the teachers to try out for the school plays. But he wouldn't have any part of it. "That's for pussies," he'd say.

DAN HEALY:

Madison is sports crazy. They'll watch anything played with a ball. It wasn't cool to do drama. In a perfect world I think Chris would have been about six-foot-three and played in the NFL. I remember when we started freshman football. It was a big deal at Edgewood. You knew making the football team was a key part of fitting in. After one of those first practices I heard this voice behind me say, "Well, my brother told me that if I can start on 'O,' then I'll probably start on 'D.'"

I turned around, and there was Chris. He was already pretty over-weight, and he was wearing these saggy gray wool socks with his football uniform. Everyone else was in bright white athletic socks, and here's this chubby kid dressed kind of funny. I just thought, this poor kid actually thinks he's gonna play? But he did. And he was great.

KEVIN FARLEY:

Chris would play noseguard, and because I was his brother he'd want to hit me pretty hard in practice. My God, he hit me good. A couple of times I think I practically blacked out. "God, you really nailed me," I'd say.

"I know," he'd say. "I wanted to."

We were really competitive, and he was a really good football player. You couldn't move him because his legs were so powerful and he was so low to the ground. He was a really good interior lineman. He just didn't have the height or the NFL build that he needed.

JOEL MATURI:

Chris was like Rudy in that way, the kid in that story from Notre Dame. I mean that very honestly. He was all hustle. Chris would be the first one to jump into a drill, first one to volunteer for anything. We were not a great football program. I think his junior year we went 5–5, and his senior year we went 6–4. But Chris always thought the glass was half full. When other kids might have said something was impossible, Chris thought it was possible. He always *believed*. And that's why you loved him.

MIKE CLEARY:

Around Madison you played against teams with these huge, enormous guys who went on to Division One teams. They'd just steamroll right over you. It was so demoralizing. But with Chris on the field, you'd never let that get to you. He'd never let you forget about having fun, even when these future NFLers were grinding your face into the mud.

PAT O'GARA, *friend:*

When we played football, all the guys would go in to take showers. And of course all these sophomores and freshmen were nervous about showering with the older guys. Chris would be in there, in the showers, buck naked, curling his finger with a come-hither look at these kids going "Want some candy?" It'd scare the crap out of them. It was always an interesting time when Chris would hit the showers. He had a reputation of, well, exposing himself. All the time.

GREG MEYER:

He was naked a lot.

PAT O'GARA:

Wasn't ashamed at all. So, junior year, I was sitting in typing lab, practicing, and Chris was sitting next to me. I said to him, "Chris, I dare you to whip it out in front of this girl here."

I'm typing away, and Chris just pulls his pants down and lays it out. I don't think twice about it. To me, I'm just like, "Jesus, what a sick bastard."

And that was the end of it. Nothing happened. Then, about a month later, Coach Maturi says to me, "I understand that you dared Chris Farley to expose himself to this girl."

"Yes, sir," I said. "I said that."

"Well, she's been in therapy for about a month now because she keeps having flashbacks and has had a lot of psychological problems."

A prank like that would normally just get you disciplined somehow, but this girl and her parents were making a real issue out of it. Chris wound up getting expelled.

TOM FARLEY:

Dad, typically, said the school was overreacting. It was the school's fault, not Chris's. So rather than demoting him down to public school, he was sent off to private boarding school, La Lumiere in LaPorte, Indiana, for the rest of the semester. Senior year they let him back in.

GREG MEYER:

Chris was really, really pissed at himself, very disappointed to be leaving Edgewood. He'd do that thing out of nowhere where he'd smack his head and go, "Fuck! *Idiot!* Can't believe I did that."

KEVIN FARLEY:

When he would get into trouble, even as a kid, it was like something would take control of him that he couldn't help but cut up and make people laugh, even though he knew he'd get in trouble for it. And he'd look back at whatever stupid thing he'd just done and be like, "Why did I do that? Why did I get myself in detention just to get a laugh out of Dan Healy?"

NICK BURROWS:

The thing is, he was accepted by his friends and the other kids without all the crazy behavior. Quite frankly, he didn't need it. But he felt that he needed it. Someone at Marquette told me a story about a time on a Monday morning on campus. It was a dreary winter morning, and Chris all of a sudden just broke out running, dove into a snowbank, and started kicking his legs out in the air. Now, why would he feel compelled to do that?

GREG MEYER:

He was always insecure about his weight. He'd project this attitude of not caring to everyone, but among the inner circle of guys, he talked about it quite a lot. He said it was the worst thing in his life.

TOM FARLEY:

At some point, Chris started getting into his share of fights. We were at a basketball game in Stoughton, Wisconsin. I was there with a girl, and word came up through the bleachers that Chris was down, just beaten and bloodied. Someone had called him a fatty, and that was enough for Chris to go off. We took him to the hospital and patched him up. Ruined my date.

HAMILTON DAVIS:

He was always fighting his weight, and I mean bad. He wanted to get with the guys who were lifting weights, would play any sport. He just wanted that weight off him so bad. We were both big guys. One summer he was a cookie, working in the kitchen, and I was a counselor, and we went on this diet together. We lost a bunch of weight, thirty pounds or so. He looked great. Chris always wanted to be mainstream, getting a girl and all that.

KIT SEELIGER, *girlfriend:*

I met Chris freshman year in high school. We had a lot of classes together, and we were pals. For Valentine's Day, Edgewood would do carnation sales. You could buy them for your girlfriend or whatever, and sophomore year Chris bought me one and gave me a box of candy. I think, as far as high school goes, we were boyfriend and girlfriend then. I was a late bloomer. I didn't have boys beating down my door, by any means, and maybe I felt safe to him. I'm sure that probably had something to do with it.

We talked on the phone a lot. Then as we got a little bit older we'd go out on dates and so forth. Chris was pretty insecure when it came to dating and girls, but the fact that we were friends beforehand made it a little bit easier. When his parents took him out of Edgewood and sent him to La Lumiere, that's when our relationship was probably the most serious. We talked on the phone probably every single night. We wrote long letters, back and forth to each other once or twice a week. We'd end each letter by writing, "I miss you so much," and it was a game to see how many o's you could put in the word "so." It was all pretty innocent, really. For the most part, we were just good friends. I know he told me things that he never told his guy friends. He would say he loved me, and things like that, things I know he never admitted to his friends that he'd said.

Then, the summer going into senior year, Chris broke up with me. I was shocked. But it was after a time when he had started standing me up. My mom couldn't stand Chris. She'd get so angry at the thought of my waiting around for him. But around the time we broke up, things were really taking a turn for the worse.

PAT O'GARA:

Toward the end of Chris's junior year, we were at a party one night at Pete Kay's house. Chris and I were downstairs in the basement all alone. I was drinking something. Chris had a bunch of beers, and he was just slamming them. I was like, "What are you doing? Slow down. This is ridiculous."

But he went and got drunk. I remember the next football practice on Monday he kept telling everyone, "O'Gara got me drunk!" He actually told one of the assistant coaches, who was like, "What the hell'd you do to Farley?"

That's how it all started.

TODD GREEN:

For the first two and a half years of high school, Chris was adamantly against drinking or doing drugs of any kind. Totally and completely.

ROBERT BARRY:

Chris didn't drink until he was a junior, but the minute he did it was all over. I don't ever remember a time when I could sit down with Chris and have "a beer" and have a conversation. It was balls to the wall, all the time.

KEVIN FARLEY:

The first time he got drunk, he came in, woke me up, and got into a fight with me. Then he woke up in the morning and didn't remember it, and I was like, "Whoa. What's wrong here?"

It was the first sip he ever had, and there was a complete personality change. Everybody was drinking in high school, but nobody I knew had the kind of reaction he had. Chris was a fun guy, an outgoing guy, and it turned him into kind of a monster. It was like pouring gasoline on a fire. And I don't think he liked it. He didn't like being that guy, but at the same time he craved it.

And nobody talked about it. You don't narc on your brother. All I knew was that everyone went out to the football games and went drinking. That's what you did. We just thought, hey! Chris is *so* crazy! And there were other guys just as hard-core as he was, passed out at parties and all that.

He got in trouble a couple of times, but for the most part it just slid by. We had these bedrooms downstairs where it was real easy to sneak out of the house. You could come and go, and you had plenty of time to clean yourself up before you went upstairs and saw the folks. I don't know how much they knew what was really going on. They didn't know. They didn't want to know.

TOM FARLEY:

Drinking was okay in our house. There was alcoholism on my mom's side of the family. On my dad's side, well, it was Wisconsin. You drank first and asked questions later. Our father was "a couple of tumblers of scotch a night" guy. From early on, we all knew what five o'clock meant. It was all right out there in the open.

The drinking age was eighteen, which effectively made it sixteen, so for us to go out and drink in high school was no big deal. All you did in Madison on Friday nights was cruise around, eat, drink, and then everyone would end up at Rocky's Pizza. Whenever we went out, Dad would call us into the living room and dole out twenty-dollar bills to all of us. "C'mon in here!" he'd say. "Here you go. Buy a round for the boys on me!"

"But we're only seventeen."

"Be careful!"

We'd all walk out the door, head right down to Vic Pierce's liquor store, and charge a six-pack on Dad's account. You were ready to go. Chris was very generous, and Dad always made sure we had the means to be generous. It was part of being a Farley.

TODD GREEN:

Mr. Farley always made you feel like a million bucks as soon as you walked in the door of that house. It was always, "Hey! How ya doin'?!" All the Edgewood guys, we loved Mr. Farley, loved him.

DAN HEALY:

You heard all these stories about Mr. Farley being friendly with Joseph McCarthy and all these very powerful, conservative people in Wisconsin. He talked it and walked it.

TOM FARLEY:

My dad created an image for himself. He was always dressed in a custom-tailored blue blazer and slacks, perfectly starched shirt and tie. It was always, "Hey, Dad looks great! Check out his new blazer!" And, of course, no comment that the blazer was a size sixty-five because Dad was hitting four hundred pounds.

ROBERT BARRY:

He was an overwhelming personality. Just a loud, gregarious guy. His whole business was going around schmoozing people all over the state, and he was very good at it. The Farleys had this image they projected, living in Maple Bluff, having the status symbols. They would do a lot of different things to cover their problems up. But when you look at the family now, you can see how much of a façade it all was.

JOHN FARLEY:

Maple Bluff was a fantasyland, a place where there weren't any consequences. What we'd do in the Farley household, back in the eighties, back when everyone drank, was we had *fun*. We'd party and laugh. We'd put on little comedy sketches with each other. We weren't trying to be comedians; we were just doing what came naturally and what we liked to do, just joking around. Didn't know drinking was bad for you. Didn't have a clue. We grew up in a time and a place where at five o'clock every day, everyone would break out the cocktails. We thought it was normal. Put a gun to our heads, we thought it was normal.

TOM FARLEY:

We lived in a make-believe world. We were living with the elephant in the room—the literal elephant in the room—that no one wanted to talk about. My dad weighed six hundred pounds by the time he died. But Dad wasn't overweight. Dad didn't drink too much. Dad was just Dad. We didn't talk about it among ourselves, and we certainly didn't talk about it with anyone else.

Mom was really the only one to acknowledge what was going on with Chris. She was the voice in the wilderness, and for years there was nobody else on board with her.

"What's wrong with Chris?"

"Your mother and I are handling it."

And that was as far as it went for a long, long time. Nobody was willing to face the truth. Nobody confronted Chris about his problem, because doing so would have meant acknowledging that Dad had a problem—that we all had a problem.

CHAPTER 3

An Epiphany

DICK WENZELL:

As an actor, it took me a long time to learn how to let the character take me over, to lose myself in it. I think Chris figured that out
very early in life, and he could hide himself by being anybody else
that he wanted to be.

After Chris's expulsion and subsequent stint at La Lumiere prep
school, he was allowed to return to Edgewood for the whole of
his senior year. He graduated in the spring of 1982 with little direction beyond a vague sense that he might one day work in the family
business. But Chris's father firmly believed that all of his children should
receive a Catholic education, and so Chris found himself enrolled at Marquette, a Jesuit university in Milwaukee, Wisconsin.

Though Chris's grades did not make the cut for admission, they did
qualify him for the university's Freshman Frontiers Program, a prelimi-
nary summer school in which students could earn their way into the in-
coming class. Together with high school friend Dan Healy, Chris entered
the program, passed, and began regular course work in the fall.

It has been said that college is less a place for academic achievement and more a rite of passage through which to discover oneself. By that standard, Chris's years at Marquette were a ringing success. As always, he won friends easily, especially among the Marquette rugby team—the gung-ho, gonzo athletes who would become his ad hoc fraternity. Given the preferences of his father, and lacking any clear ones of his own, Chris started out in the business studies program. Bored and disinterested, he did not do well. However, as his understanding of his talents grew, he changed course and dedicated himself to a career in acting and comedy. Though his early attempts at performance were frequently clumsy, Chris kept at it with a dedication he had previously shown only in his football uniform.

As a Jesuit institution, Marquette teaches its students to pursue knowledge and personal growth not only for their own self-advancement but also for the glory of God and service to others. Chris's four years in Milwaukee would give him the opportunity to do precisely that.

JIM MURPHY, *friend:*

When he first came to Marquette, he was a very preppy guy. Super preppy. He would always have his hair combed and always had polo shirts and khakis and Top-Siders. Then over time he would take those Ralph Lauren button-down oxfords and he'd rip the sleeves off. Then, in the next phase, the khakis became army fatigues and the oxfords turned into flannel shirts. It was the same thing everyone did in college. We all kind of came in as one thing and left as another.

FR. MATT FOLEY, *friend:*

The first time I saw Chris was on the rugby pitch. I was the president of the rugby team, and a sophomore. He was a freshman. He was wearing some kind of obnoxious chartreuse-colored polo shirt with argyle shorts and gym shoes. I was drawn to him right away because I thought, oh, this poor soul is going to get his ass kicked. The guys on the rugby team are a little rough, and here comes the preppy, portly kid. But he hustled and made many friends in no time because he was such a classic character.

One of the great things about Chris was that he was so very generous. Marquette would play Madison every year in rugby, so we went out there that fall. We'd been drinking all day, and Chris was like, "Let's all go over to my place!"

We get there, and Mr. Farley and Mrs. Farley are just the most gracious hosts. All these drunk, dirty rugby guys are running around their house—this is around one in the morning—and Mrs. Farley is going, "Oh, you boys! Let me make some sandwiches." And she just brought out all these beautiful sandwiches.

We rode back to Milwaukee in the back of a pickup, freezing our asses off. It had a camper top on it, but it wasn't very warm. The bars in Madison closed at one, but the bars at Marquette didn't close until three. You could close the bars in one town and still make it to close the bars in the other. That's the rugby mentality at its finest.

KEVIN FARLEY:

When I got to Marquette, Chris had only been there two years, and he was already a legend, flat out the funniest guy on campus, and that really grew out of the rugby parties. The Avalanche was a typical Milwaukee bar. That's where the rugby players would go party after their games. It had a great jukebox and a couple of pool tables. They had fifty-cent Red, White and Blue beers. When you finished your bottle, you threw it against the back wall of the bar.

Chris started doing this thing after the games: naked beer slides. Everyone in the bar would pour out their beer and he'd take off all his clothes and take a running start and slide across the bar like Pete Rose coming into home base. The Avalanche is long gone, but people still do it. It's something of a Marquette tradition. People have built a legend around it.

JIM MURPHY:

It got to a point where every team coming in to play Marquette had heard about the beer slides and wanted to see them. Chris would start to take his clothes off, going, "Aw, man. Why do I always have to do this?" But he'd kind of set the tone early, and he always had to live up to himself.

PAT FINN, *friend:*

Any time during a game that there was a lull, or any opportunity for a laugh, you'd just look over at Chris. One game, we file in for this line out. Everyone is waiting for the inbound pass. Chris kind of looks over and then pulls up his pants into his ass like a thong. The whole other team just turns and stares, like, "What the hell's with this guy?" Then, with the whole team distracted, Chris takes the pass and gets about twenty yards on the play. He was always hilarious.

DAN HEALY:

Freshman year of college, a group of us had done a road trip for some winter festival. It was freezing, snow everywhere, and we were goofing around, diving and playing in the snow. And while we were all screwing around, Chris just stopped cold. He stopped, and he turned to me and said, "I think I can make people laugh."

He'd had an epiphany, literally. He was starting to realize that he had this ability, a calling in life.

FR. MATT FOLEY:

He saw his talent as a gift from God—there's no doubt about that. I went away to seminary after his freshman year, but one thing I found fascinating about him in those two semesters was that he had a tremendous faith life, devoted and disciplined. He was not evangelical; he didn't preach about it, but it was something in the fiber of his soul.

At Marquette, there's the Joan of Arc Chapel, this beautiful chapel brought over stone by stone from Europe, and they have a daily mass. Inevitably, you would find Chris there, disheveled and partied out and just sort of scruffy. There's not a doubt in my mind that he was in church more than any other student on that campus, at least three or four times a week.

PAT FINN:

After I met Chris, we signed up for a class called the Philosophy of Humor. We thought, could there be an easier A? I don't know why we thought that, since we'd never gotten an A before. Truth be told, Chris got a D. But Father Nauss, who taught the class, gave us each a copy of "A Clown's Prayer." The last lines go, "Never let me forget that my total effort is to cheer people, make them happy, and forget momentarily all the unpleasantness in their lives. / And in my final moment, may I hear You whisper: 'When you made My people smile, you made Me smile.'" It meant a lot to us, and we kept it in our wallets.

There were times, for instance, when Chris and I'd be on the highway, going through a tollbooth. He'd do a bit in front of the tollbooth taker, and it'd make the guy laugh. At first you were kind of like, oh, that was a little weird. But on the other hand it was like, you know, he just made that guy's day. That guy's gonna go home and tell his wife, "Yeah, this big guy came through in a car today and did this thing with the steering wheel . . ."

One of the cool things about Chris, and one of the noble things about Chris, is that if he made somebody's day better, if he could ease the pain and sadness in the world just a bit, that was why he felt he was here.

MARK HERMACINSKI, *friend:*

The thing about Chris was that he always made all of us feel like *we* were the funny ones. He always listened and anything you'd throw out there, he'd bounce it back as a joke, so he made everyone feel like they were a part of what was going on. Even if you're not a comedian, it's fun to sit around and laugh together, and he could pull the humor out of you.

MICHAEL PRICE, *dean, College of Communications:*

I was going through the student registrations for the spring semester of his sophomore year, and I saw that Chris hadn't preregistered. I called him in. He said he really didn't want to be there anymore. He didn't want to be in school, period. I said, "Chris, what do you want to do?"

"I want to be at Second City," he said. "It's a comedy company in Chicago."

"Well, I can certainly see you doing that," I said, "but why don't we talk it over with your folks? See what they say."

He seemed a little reluctant to even bring this subject up with them. His father wanted him to go into business. But Chris and his parents came down to my office. We talked about what Chris wanted. I said, "You guys talk it over, and I'll be right outside."

When I came back in, the decision was made. Chris would remain at Marquette. He could drop the business studies major, and he'd major in communications studies and minor in theater. Then, if he graduated, they would support his wishes to do what he wanted. Onward he went.

PAT FINN:

Chris and I took this professional speaking class together. The teacher would give you a topic, like a how-to speech or a "talk about a relative" speech. Then you would have to write a three- or eight-minute talk.

The first one was fine, but we both thought it was a little easy. We were sitting at lunch right before the next class, and one of us said, "Hey, why don't we make up each other's topics and go improvise it?"

So that's what we did. Our speech was supposed to be on our summer job. Chris decided that I'd spent the summer repairing air conditioners. I told Chris that he'd been a carny in the circus.

Chris got up with nothing but a blank sheet of paper and said, "Hi,

I'm Chris. This summer I spent three months as a carny with the circus." And he just started telling stories. How he fell in love with the fat lady, made out with a midget. The class stared at him. It was amazing to watch, because you knew it was complete fiction.

After those speech classes, Chris and I were determined. We wanted to "do comedy," but what that meant we didn't actually know. If you want to be a lawyer you go talk to somebody's uncle. But it wasn't like we could call up Bob Newhart and ask him. We'd sit and listen to *National Lampoon* albums. We'd watch *Saturday Night Live*, David Letterman. We'd do everything we could to see anybody do anything funny.

JIM MURPHY:

Chris and I both had these things that we were pretty passionate about, art and comedy, but we were at a Catholic liberal arts school in Wisconsin, not the place most conducive to learning these things. Fortunately Marquette actually did have a healthy theater program. The big thing for Chris was when he got a part in the school play. It was Sam Shepard's *Curse of the Starving Class*. It kind of got him going.

TOM FARLEY:

Growing up, we didn't have a lot of choices: you played sports. But at Marquette a dean said to Chris, "Why don't you try out for one of the plays?"

Chris was like, "Guys don't do that."

But he did it anyway and eventually found out that he wasn't an athlete who happened to be kind of funny. He was an actor who happened to be very athletic.

MICHAEL PRICE:

Dance was a part of the theater requirement. If you're going to be a theater minor or major, you gotta do that. So Chris took ballet. You know, he moved well. He was large, but he was not a slouch. He was great. Sheila Reilly, the ballet teacher, had a dress code and it was pretty stringent, and I think Chris got by without having to abide by that. He may be one of the first students she ever allowed to wear sweats instead of tights.

KEVIN FARLEY:

It was a very formative time for him. After he moved out of the dorms, he and a bunch of his rugby pals lived in this big piece-of-shit house up on Nineteenth Street. They called it the Red House. It was a hellhole.

JOHN FARLEY:

Whenever I'd walk into the Red House I'd say, "Well, well, well. Looks like somebody forgot there's a rule against alcoholic beverages in fraternities on probation." It was just disgusting. Dad refused to go in for basic sanitary reasons. Everything had a touch of something on it. Odd smell, too.

JIM MURPHY:

One of our roommates was the Budweiser rep on campus, so everything was Budweiser, signs and cups everywhere. Chris's room was at the top of the stairs. Any time your parents would come, it was the first room they'd see. He was such a slob, food and clothes everywhere. There'd be all these fruit flies and it was, well, let's just say it was college.

MARK HERMACINSKI:

We put Farley close to the bathroom, but that didn't help much.

KEVIN FARLEY:

The bathroom was unspeakable. One of the things that made Chris a legend on that campus was his room, simply the fact that a human being could survive in there. People would come over just to look at it.

JIM MURPHY:

We were pretty poor, so we didn't turn on the heat until after Thanksgiving to try and save money. It was so cold. We had a rugby awards banquet there. We kind of cleaned it all up and everyone brought dates. The girls all came in dresses, and they were freezing. We had a bucket for ice so we could make cocktails. We put it out on Friday night. By Sunday night, the ice hadn't melted.

The other thing I remember about the Red House was every couple of months Chris's mom and dad—this being Wisconsin—would send him a twenty-five-pound summer sausage and a twenty-five-pound wheel of cheese. Any time you'd look in the refrigerator there was never anything inside it except this gigantic sausage and this huge wheel of cheese.

MARK HERMACINSKI:

The kitchen was all infested with flies and maggots. After two months we just closed the door. But we had a lot of fun. Since we had the campus Budweiser rep, they'd pull up the truck with ten, fifteen kegs and we'd have a party with five hundred of our closest friends. Chris always drew a crowd. Wherever he was, in Madison, on a rugby road trip, he'd have a crowd around him in minutes.

TOM FARLEY:

The place where Chris really learned how to be this galvanizing figure was at Red Arrow camp. It was like a graduate school in male bonding. Every summer in college we all went back as counselors, and every summer all the kids and the other counselors, they'd rally around Chris.

FRED ALBRIGHT:

The kids loved him. How could you not? Every year, he was one of the most popular counselors. Chris had this very sensitive, sweet side to him, an empathetic side that helped him communicate with kids in this amazing way.

DICK WENZELL:

He could take any old boring activity and make it a fun, exciting experience. If you were eight years old, digging for earthworms with Chris was the most fun you ever had. He'd just hypnotize these kids. "We're digging for monsters, boys! Oh! Hey! I found a big one!" And he'd lead them off on this grand adventure. And that's the same thing he did with an audience.

RANDY HOPPER, *counselor, Red Arrow Camp:*

Chris came to life around those kids. He was the biggest kid there. We had this flag-football game called the Salad Bowl. When it was time for the big game, Chris would get up there in front of the boys and give them a pep talk that convinced them that this was the game of their lives. He'd get them all riled up. He'd be waving fistfuls of bacon, going, "Sooweee! Love them Hogs!" doing his big, high-school-coach motivational speech. In ten minutes, he'd have thirty kids so riveted and excited to be playing in this game that the Super Bowl would pale by comparison. His ability to connect with people was uncanny.

FRED ALBRIGHT:

He couldn't talk to girls, though. Around girls, Chris'd hide behind his jokes. He'd start flexing and doing this jokey, deep-voice, macho-man thing to try and hit on them. One night we're out at a bar near the camp and he goes up to these women and says, "Well, which one of you little ladies is gonna go home with me tonight?"

And one of the women looks at him and says, "Well, it can't be me, because you're my son's counselor."

Chris felt so small after that you just about could've balled him up and put him in a thimble.

He had one girl that he had met up north in Minocqua during the summer. She really adored Chris. They'd kid around, and it was like they were buddies, but Chris had this greater attraction to her. He would talk to me every day about how he'd had some moment with her. I see her now fairly often, and she didn't even realize that he was so completely enthralled with her.

TIM HENRY:

Being a camp counselor was all about working the girls from the other camps. If you played your cards right you could go out several nights a week, but the girls were only allowed to go out one night a week. So you always had one little honey from each camp.

RANDY HOPPER:

We'd all go out in the woods, have a big bonfire, and it was all about trying to score. That was the game. Chris was not too adept at that, not usually. But he would entertain everyone.

TIM HENRY:

It would always piss Tom off, because Chris didn't know when to stop. We'd be out in the woods, Tom would be working his magic on some girl, about to close the deal, and Chris would come barreling through the campsite fucking around. Then Tom would have to tell me to fuck off because I was laughing so hard.

TOM FARLEY:

One night, these two girls I knew from Georgetown had come all the way up from Chicago to visit. Chris was so out of control, and he wouldn't turn it off. These were nice girls, and one of them I was really trying to get serious with. They were getting annoyed, really offended. He wouldn't stop, and I couldn't take it anymore. I lost it. He was acting up and running around, and I grabbed him and I beat the shit out of him, just whaled on him, punching him in the face. He was crying so hard he couldn't even fight back. He was so scared. The next day he showed up at mass black and blue and bloodied all over.

TIM HENRY:

Chris so wanted to be with one of those girls, but he would always go back to what was safe. He would revert to the guy who's had too many beers and got silly. Most nights the parties would go really late. As the hours wore on, everybody would start to drift away and pair off out in the woods, and there would be Chris, alone by the campfire.

DAN HEALY:

I only stayed at Marquette for a year. After that, I transferred to University of Wisconsin. That sophomore year was a crucial time for Chris. I started to hear stories about him drinking alone in his room, which was weird. We were always big social drinkers, but never the sit-alone-in-your-room kind of drinkers. The Marquette rugby team came into Madison one time. We all went out and drank, and then afterward I made a point of saying to Chris, "What's going on? I hear you're really going off the deep end." He backed away immediately. He didn't want anything to do with that conversation.

JIM MURPHY:

Then, during our junior year in the Red House, Chris read that book about John Belushi, *Wired*.

MARK HERMACINSKI:

Wired was the only book that Chris Farley read in college. The only one.

JIM MURPHY:

For our spring break that year, me, Chris, and this other guy went to L.A. We had a couch to crash on, and Chris was really developing an appetite for this career he wanted. We went around doing all the Hollywood tourist stuff, and the whole time Chris was like, "Jimmy, I really think I can do this."

I'm a huge fan of Buster Keaton and all those early physical comedians. One time I was trying to turn Chris on to Fatty Arbuckle. So I made him sit down and watch one of Arbuckle's films. At the end of it, the only thing Chris said to me was, "Wow, Jimmy, he did all of his own stunts." He fixated on this one thing about Arbuckle, and that was all he really took away from it. And that's sort of what happened with Belushi. When Chris read *Wired*, he just took completely the wrong thing away from it. You could tell that what he saw in Belushi and what you and I saw in Belushi were two different things. Chris wasn't blindly imitating Belushi, but reading that book validated all the addictions and impulses that Chris already had inside him.

Chris didn't smoke pot freshman or sophomore year, didn't do any drugs at all, other than drinking. Then all of a sudden that year it clicked. I have this vivid memory of him in his room one day. While everybody else was going to class, he sat in this chair with a big red bong. He sat there doing bong hits and chugging Robitussin cough syrup. Back and forth. One after another.

At that point you could see where it was going. I'd try to explain to him, you know, that you can only get so high. It's like pouring water into a glass. You can pour in all you want. After a while, it's all just spilling over the sides. But it was the same thing no matter what he did. It was the same when he tried pot, or when he tried mushrooms, or when he tried comedy.

PAT FINN:

The first place Chris and I ever got up and performed together was during our senior year in a skinny bar in a bad neighborhood in downtown Milwaukee. It was called Wimpy's Hunt Club, and it had an open-mike night at midnight. The stage was literally twelve milk crates turned over in the corner. There were about nine people in the audience, all factory workers on break from the brewery. Tough crowd.

Chris and I went up there, and it was like when you're in middle school and you go on a date and you don't really know what you're supposed to do. It was that awkward, and that bad. We *bombed*. We signed up to do it again the next week. Then we found out that a bunch of Marquette students were going to be there. We chickened out and didn't go. Everyone got real mad at us.

Finally we signed up for the Follies, the school talent show. We got an actress, and we decided we'd do a parody of *The Dating Game*. Jim Murphy was the host, and another friend of ours, Seamus, was the third bachelor. We kept on meaning to get together and work, and we'd talk about it every once in a while, but we never had any idea what we were doing. Then about a week before the show the girl quit school and moved to Chicago, and we figured we'd just blow the thing off.

But the night of the Follies, I was over at Chris's house and we were hanging out. About fifteen, twenty minutes into it, and we get a phone call from the stage manager. "Where the hell are you guys? You better get down here. People are pretty pissed. They want to see you—and they're screaming for Farley."

We hopped on our bikes and rode over. It was way bigger than we thought it was going to be. There were at least a couple thousand people there. The show had three more acts to go before it ended. "You're goin' after this singer," the stage manager told us.

Chris just goes, "All right, Jim, you're the emcee." He looked over at Seamus, who had overalls on. "Seamus, you're farmer guy." Then he flicked my collar up on my shirt, unbuttoned a button, and said, "And Finner, you're cool guy."

"Okay. What about you?" I asked.

He pulled out these nerdy glasses and said, "I'll be nerdy guy. Let's go."

Jim went out, made up some intro, brought out Seamus, and they did a funny little Q&A. Then I went out, doing this "cool guy" walk, hopped on my stool, and answered some questions. There was no girl, mind you, just the host and three male contestants, but that became part of the gag.

Then Jim said, "All right, let's bring out the next guy." The spotlight hit Chris coming out of the curtain. He ran as fast as he could and then tripped and slid across the entire length of the stage. The place went berserk. Then he went over to his stool, clumsily knocking it over. He finally clambered on and then fell right off. It was insane. The audience loved it.

As soon as it was over, Chris and I ran backstage, and I remember he just grabbed me by the shirt and he looked right in my eyes and said, "We're gonna be doing this for the rest of our lives. That was the greatest high I've ever felt in my life."

MICHAEL PRICE:

In the spring of Chris's senior year, we got one of those rare days when you can open windows, be outside, and throw a ball around. There was this white house on Kilborn Avenue where all these girls lived. Chris had a cherry smoke bomb. He lit it and put it on the open windowsill, thinking the smoke would drive everyone out and it'd be a good prank. But he forgot that when you light those things they twirl around and spin out of control. Well, it spun off and landed on their couch. And it burned. I mean, it really burned. Pretty soon the house was on fire, and it was spreading to the second floor. Chris figured he'd better get the heck out of there. So he took off with a friend, and they went down to Illinois, just across the border.

The next morning I got to work about seven, my phone rang and it was the police department. They were wondering if Chris was around. I called the Red House, and they said Chris wasn't there. I hung up, and then, about fifteen minutes later, two of the Red House guys showed up at my office. They said they couldn't talk to me on the phone because their line had been tapped. I said, "Oh, come on. You guys are outta your mind."

They told me where he was. I called him in Illinois. I talked to him and told him to come back. Then I called his folks in Madison. They asked me to give them the name of a lawyer in Milwaukee, so I did. Between the lawyer and his parents it was decided that Chris would come to my office, we would all meet there, and then he would go and turn himself in.

I called the police department, and I told them what the lawyer told me to say, that I knew where Chris was and he would come down there on his own the next day. Chris came back. The attorney took care of things. And after many weeks of delayed hearings and so on, Chris came away from it with a "dangerous use of firearms" charge, or something like that. He ended up with about thirty hours of community service, but he couldn't get his diploma.

* * *

In *Tommy Boy*, Chris's partying, rugby-playing alter ego graduated from Marquette in seven years. In the real world, Chris squeaked out in four and a half. As a result of the smoke-bomb incident, he was put on probation, and university policy did not allow students on probation to graduate. However, he was allowed to walk in the graduation ceremony with his classmates, complete his course work at the University of Wisconsin in the fall, and receive a Marquette diploma the following December.

Forced to return to Madison for school, Chris moved into an apartment downtown, close to many of his high school friends who had never left. Between finishing his classes and performing wherever and whenever he could, Chris took the only job offer he had. He went to work for his father.

MIKE CLEARY:

To understand Chris you have to understand something about Madison. Madisonians tend to be very educated, very literate, and upwardly mobile, but I would say that seventy-five percent of them have never seen the ocean. And I'm not kidding. Madison's got everything you need—that's the default mentality here. And Chris came back in large part because the family discouraged him from doing anything else.

TOM FARLEY:

Dad always wanted all of us home. It was almost like, "You can't make it out east, and so you don't need to try it." Kevin bought into that at first, and Chris did for a while, too. Dad had tried it with me. After I left Georgetown, I said, "Hey, all my buddies are going up to New York. That's where I want to go."

Dad sat me down and said, "You'll never make it."

"Watch me," I said. And I left.

Dad and I butted heads throughout our lives. If he said something was blue, I said it was red. Chris was the opposite. Everything he did was to please Dad. At that point, he had done the plays at Marquette, but he really had no idea of how to go about making that into a possible career. Dad just said flat out, "No one's going to offer you a job. You'd better come work for me." So Chris went to work for Dad, but it wasn't a two-man job, so there wasn't a whole lot for him to do. The job was really a joke.

KEVIN FARLEY:

When Chris finally left and I came in to take over the job, we opened up the drawers of his desk and there was nothing in it but *Cracked* and *Mad* magazines.

JOHN FARLEY:

What did Chris do for my dad? Hell, what did my dad do? No one really knew. He'd take people to dinner, entertain them, and they'd buy stuff from him. That was our notion of work. Dad didn't really have to sell his product. He was selling roads. Everyone needs roads, and all roads are basically the same. Oil plus gravel equals road. The funniest, nicest, coolest guy was going to get the bid from the county, and there was no better guy to hang out with than my dad. Add Chris to the mix and they could sell anybody anything.

My grandfather was a salesman, and some days he had to go on four breakfasts, going town to town to town. Then he'd have to go to all these lunches, and then come home and have a dinner. It was the same for my dad. My dad knew every restaurant, every bar in Wisconsin. You'd drive by some place way the hell out in the middle of nowhere, and Dad would be like, "They can sauté a mushroom like nobody's business. Good cheeseburgers."

My dad's clients were these farmers, these down-home guys from rural towns who just happened to sit on the county highway commission handing out multimillion-dollar contracts to pave roads. The big thrill of their month was when Tom Farley would drive out from Madison and take them out for a schmooze and a steak dinner. You know those square pats of butter they keep on the table? Farmers in Wisconsin eat those like appetizers, like a predinner mint. Just open 'em up and eat 'em. Sweet Jesus that's insane, but it's a very Wisconsin thing.

Sit. Eat. Talk. Drink. That was the business. It was about putting on a show, buying the round of scotches, prime rib for everyone. That's the key to who the Farleys are. We'd rather see a smile on someone's face, even if it meant hurting ourselves. I don't know why we did, but we did.

TOM FARLEY:

Chris was a great entertainer of clients, but for Dad to keep paying him twenty grand a year just to go to lunch was a bit much. So Chris started doing these open mikes at the student union. He bombed, failed miserably. He was getting up at the liberal, progressive University of Wisconsin and telling crude lesbian jokes. That went over like a fart in church. He'd get heckled and booed. Then he found improv at the Ark.

TODD GREEN:

Chris, Greg Meyer, and me all lived near each other downtown. And one night Chris said, "Guys, we gotta go to this thing, the Ark."

All through our childhood we always knew that Chris was going to do something. We just didn't know what. That night they were doing some skit and they needed audience participation. Chris started to get into it, and he completely stole the show from the performers. That was the start of the whole thing.

DENNIS KERN, *director, Ark Improvisational Theater:*

Chris always spoke fondly of his days at the Ark, and I was always very appreciative of that. We sort of took him in off the street—quite literally—and gave him a home. He showed up at the theater one night after a show and stumbled in through the door. He was so drunk he could barely even form coherent sentences. He was just going on, like, "Wanna do . . . comedy . . . improv, I wanna—gotta do this . . ."

I could barely understand him. To be honest, I thought he might be retarded. I didn't think he'd remember anything that I told him, so I said, "Look, we're having a rehearsal tomorrow. Why don't you come by and join us then?" Then I showed him out the door, thinking that was the end of the whole episode.

The next day I got a call from my wife, who was at the theater. "Did you tell some big guy that he could come to our rehearsal today?" she asked.

"Yeah," I said, "but I didn't think he'd actually show up."

"Well, he's here. And he brought a case of beer."

CHAPTER 4

Attacking the Stage

BRIAN STACK, *cast member, Ark Improvisational Theater:*

Keith Richards said that the first time he heard rock and roll it was like the whole world went from black-and-white to Technicolor. That's how Chris always seemed to describe finding comedy.

As a city, Madison, Wisconsin, has something of a split personality. On the one hand, it's a typical Midwestern town with no shortage of beer, football, and competitive bratwurst eating. On the other hand, thanks largely to the University of Wisconsin, Madison carries with it a long history of liberal, even radical, politics. Wisconsin governor and U.S. senator Robert LaFollette launched his left-wing Progressive Party in Madison. And in the late sixties and early seventies, the university itself saw some of the country's most violent antiwar protests, culminating in the bombing of the school's Army Mathematics Research Center at Sterling Hall.

In such a hothouse political environment, a small but vibrant arts community was bound to spring up as well. It would still be a few years before enterprising UW students hatched the *Onion*, the satirical newspaper that eventually found its way to Internet fame and glory. In Chris's day, if you lived in Madison and had a notion to seek a career in comedy, you went to the Ark.

Dennis and Elaine Kern founded the Ark Improvisational Theater in Madison in 1982. Both professional actors and directors, they had left New York City determined to do theater on their own terms and, God forbid, actually make a living at it. For its first two years, the Ark staged weekly shows at a local bar, Club de Wash, and offered classes in improv and acting. It quickly became recognized as a stepping-stone for those on their way to greater opportunities in neighboring Chicago. Joan Cusack, who had joined the cast of *Saturday Night Live* in 1985, was among the Ark's alumni.

As the theater grew more established, the Kerns purchased a defunct downtown building that had once housed a Brinks truck garage. They gutted it and installed a small one-hundred-seat theater. It was that converted garage that Chris Farley stumbled into late one night in August of 1986. For over twenty years, he had been a performer in search of a stage. He had finally found it.

JODI COHEN, *director/cast member, Ark Improvisational Theater:*

I was there the day that Chris came to audition. I forget what the scene was, but as part of it he fell out of his chair and—*smack*—landed on the ground. I thought he'd really had a heart attack. My first reaction was: Is the theater insured for this? What's going to happen? That's how convincing this fall was.

Elaine and I didn't want him in the company. He seemed like a wild card, and he didn't seem very focused. But Dennis said, "This guy is really talented. He should be in the group." We formed a company called Animal Crackers, and Chris performed with them.

BRIAN STACK:

I had never met anyone like him before. He had such incredible enthusiasm in everything he did. One thing that gets lost a lot is that when it came to the work, he was always very serious about it. He was always on time for rehearsal. In fact, he was usually there before everybody else. I never, ever remember him being late for a show.

I don't know if Chris had ADD, but people who have a lack of focus, when it comes to something they're passionate about, they hyperfocus. Chris was certainly like that when it came to acting. Our group's shows were mostly short-form, game-oriented improv with a lot of audience suggestions. But we also did some sketch-type stuff, and Chris was great with both of them. He was just a blast to work with from day one.

One thing that always amazed me was his ability to do things that if I had done them would have put me in the hospital, and then he'd get right up from them. He could slam into walls and slam down on the stage. He was such a natural athlete. He was almost like a ballet dancer. Even though Chris is known for being a great physical comedian, some of my favorite things were the subtle little characters he would do.

DENNIS KERN:

The Motivational Speaker appeared onstage for the first time at the Ark. It wasn't the same as on *Saturday Night Live*, but it was there in its infant form.

PAT O'GARA:

The Motivational Speaker actually started back in high school and was based heavily on our coach, Joel Maturi, who would go off on these inspirational speeches. He'd be prepping us for the game, briefing us on the other team's defense and all that, and Chris would be right there behind him, imitating him, making all these faces and forcing us all to laugh.

JOEL MATURI:

The Motivational Speaker is based in part on me; there is some truth to that. Mostly some of my mannerisms, the hiking up the pants, the spreading the legs and crouching down to get serious. I was pretty vocal with the pep talks and the Knute Rockne speeches. Those kinds of things. I think the more philosophical side of the character was actually based on his dad.

DENNIS KERN:

We taught Chris the basics of improv and scene work at the Ark, but the natural talent he had was already present. As a performer, he was just there in the moment, like Johnny Carson used to be on the *Tonight Show*. What Carson was so brilliant at was just reacting and responding naturally to the environment around him in a way that made you laugh. Chris had those same instincts. He just knew what to do.

BRIAN STACK:

He could do the same thing fifty times and somehow always make it funny. If a pretty woman walked by he would drop and start doing push-ups, starting out "... 198 ... 199 ... 200." I'd seen him do that lots of times. It shouldn't have been funny to me anymore, yet it always was. It's hard to explain why it was; it just was. You could videotape it and analyze it with a computer, like you would a golf swing, but you still wouldn't understand it, and you could never hope to replicate it.

One night after a show we went to this bar, and Chris was making this middle-aged couple in the bar laugh. He was dancing with the guy's wife and doing these cat-eye things with his hands. The husband was laughing so hard that he was actually falling off his bar stool, and he eventually said to Chris, "What's your name? I want to be sure and remember it. I've never laughed like this." It was strange. Everyone sort of sensed that there was just something unique about him. Chris wasn't famous, but it was the same reaction he would get years later after he left Madison and became a movie star.

DENNIS KERN:

Chris and Brian Stack had just started rehearsals on *Cowboys No. 2*, a Sam Shepard play that we were going to put on. And Chris, meanwhile, had been taking trips down to Chicago here and there with his father. Then it became clear what all those trips to Chicago were for.

BRIAN STACK:

When Chris decided to leave, it was pretty upsetting. He loved the Ark, but he was bursting at the seams to get out, and Chicago was the first step. I think Dennis was happy that Chris was leaving to pursue his dream, but he seemed kind of angry on his last night.

DENNIS KERN:

I was happy for him, but at the same time I thought it was too soon. I thought that he needed to be more in contact with the source of his creativity before he went to try at the professional level. I always knew he would make it, but I don't know that he was grounded enough in the technique of acting to have something to hold on to. He was immensely talented, but that talent was sort of at the whim of whoever needed the next laugh.

TOM FARLEY:

The experience he had at the Ark told him he had to get out of Madison. Plus, he couldn't take the job at Scotch Oil anymore. As much as he wanted to please Dad, after a year of selling asphalt even Chris was like, "I gotta get out of here."

JOHN FARLEY:

Dad had made the ultimate sacrifice. He would have been a great lawyer, smartest man you ever met. Dreamed of going into politics. But he had given all that up to raise a family. And so he wanted everyone to stay in Madison, because that was what he'd sacrificed everything for. Years later, Chris had to cry for this scene when he filmed *Black Sheep*. So he turned to me and he said, "Johnny, make me cry."

I said, "Well, Dad's all alone in Wisconsin with two ladies. All his boys have gone and moved on with their lives."

"*Shut up.*"

He really got angry that I had said it. Somehow it had triggered the wrong emotion.

MIKE CLEARY:

When Chris was working for his dad, he called me up one day and said, "I gotta talk to you about something."

"What's that?"

"Well, I have an opportunity to go to Chicago to study at Second City. What do you think?"

I really wasn't sure about taking risks like that. I said, "Chris, you need to just work with your dad. Establish a solid career and maybe do this stuff on the side." That was totally my mentality. Finally, I said, "Well, what does your dad say about it?"

And his exact words were, "My dad says I should definitely take the opportunity and go for it. He's gonna back me one hundred percent."

I said, "Well then there's no conversation here. You have to go."

TOM FARLEY:

We thought Chris would come running home in six months, and he never came back.

*   *   *

In June of 1987, Chris left for Chicago. He moved into a small apartment off Armitage Avenue, just north of Chicago's Old Town neighborhood. There he rejoined his Marquette rugby and acting friend Pat Finn.

The yellow porch light of Second City had led Chris to Chicago, but he quickly found that the doors of the renowned comedy institution did not immediately open for untrained unknowns fresh off the bus from Wisconsin. Forced to look elsewhere for a place to learn and perform, he found it at ImprovOlympic.

Today, ImprovOlympic has become an industry mainstay in its own right, producing a steady stream of bankable film and television stars, among them Mike Myers, Vince Vaughn, John Favreau, Andy Richter, Tina Fey, Steven Colbert, the Upright Citizens Brigade, and director Adam McKay, not to mention a healthy chunk of the writing staff at *Late Night with Conan O'Brien*.

But when Chris arrived, ImprovOlympic was still a fledgling outfit of vagabond comedians looking to make the funny anywhere they could. Teacher and director Charna Halpern had founded the group in 1981 with several goals in mind. Second City used improv as a means to create sketch comedy. Halpern wanted a curriculum in which improvised performance was the end in itself. At Second City, only a handful of seasoned performers trickled up to the main stage. Halpern gave ImprovOlympic a communitarian ethos, allowing even new and less-experienced students the chance to practice and learn in front of a paying audience.

In 1984, comedy guru Del Close joined Halpern's cause. As a director in Second City's early heyday, Close had trained and mentored a who's who of comedy, from John Belushi to Harold Ramis to Bill Murray. He was instrumental in shaping the forms and conventions of the Chicago school of improvisation. Perhaps his most notable contribution was the Harold, a long-form, fully improvised performance in which a whole cast works together off of a single audience suggestion to create a cohesive, continuous series of scenes.

For Close, the goal of improv was not to get laughs but rather to find the real, emotional truth of the characters that created those laughs. He found the perfect instrument for that in Chris Farley. With Halpern's instruction and Close's inspiration, Chris began his comedy education in earnest. Some expressed doubts about his raw, unschooled talents, but those doubts quickly vanished. Chris, performing full throttle at night and bumbling through a comical parade of semiemployment by day, proved to everyone that he was destined for a life onstage.

PAT FINN:

After I graduated from Marquette, I went down to Chicago. Chris followed about a year behind me. We had no jobs, and we had no idea what we were doing. He moved into his place off Armitage, and we went from there down to Second City one day around two in the afternoon. We just kind of paced around in front of the theater, back and forth. In our minds, the scenario literally went something like this: Somebody up on the second floor would say, "What? We need two more people for the Second City main stage? Where are we going to find— Oh, wait! What about these two people out front? They look *hilarious*."

That was about how far we'd thought things out. Then, after about ten minutes of pacing around, Joel Murray—Brian and Bill Murray's brother—walks by. He was at Second City at the time, and he and I had gone to the same grammar school, so I knew him a little.

Chris said, "There's Joel Murray. He's Bill's brother. You should talk to him."

"I don't know, Chris."

"You got to! C'mon. That's why we're here."

So Joel walked up, and I said, "Joel. Hi. I'm Pat Finn, from St. Joe's."

"Yeah. Little Finn," he said. "What's goin' on?"

"Um, nothin'. This is my friend Chris. We wanna get into comedy."

He just kind of looked at us. Chris's eyes had this look like the next thing out of Joel's mouth was going to be the keys to the kingdom. And, actually, it turns out it was.

JOEL MURRAY, *cast member, Second City:*

So one day here's Pat Finn, who I haven't seen since high school, standing there with this big guy. I could tell that the big guy was restraining all of his energy to just listen and be attentive to what I was saying. But I basically told them, "Go find Charna Halpern and Del Close at the Improv-Olympic and study with them, and then see if somebody'll let you paint the bathroom at Second City."

It was funny, knowing Chris later, just to watch him holding it in, trying not to be an idiot.

CHARNA HALPERN, *director/teacher, ImprovOlympic:*

ImprovOlympic didn't even have an actual theater at the time. We performed at Orphans, this bar on Lincoln Avenue. We had to be out by ten o'clock so the band could come on. We got kicked out of Orphans, and we moved around to like fourteen different spaces. It was an insane time. But I kept attracting these really brilliant people—Farley and Pat Finn, Mike Myers, Vince Vaughn, Jon Favreau, Andy Richter—and the shows kept getting better and better. But even though we were getting thrown out of these places, the audience was following us. It just kind of kept snowballing, getting bigger and bigger, and that was what it was like when Farley showed up.

BRIAN STACK:

I went down to Chicago to visit him at ImprovOlympic. He was taking classes, but Charna hadn't let him go up onstage to perform yet. After the show, he was pacing outside, and I could just see he had all this pent-up, frustrated energy that had nowhere to go. You could see how he was bursting at the seams, how he *needed* to get up onstage.

CHARNA HALPERN:

One night after a couple of weeks, Chris came up to me with Pat Finn and said, "Let me go onstage! Let me play tonight!"

"You?" I said. "God, no. You're definitely not ready."

He started getting violent. He was banging his fists on the wall above me, like, "Let me go! Let me go onstage! I'll be great! You'll see!"

"I'll tell you when you're ready to be onstage," I said.

He was just not hearing it. After a good seven minutes of his badgering, I finally got fed up myself. I said, "All right, I'll tell you what. You can go onstage and play tonight, but if you're bad you will never ever get on my stage again. Do you wanna take that chance?"

Before I even finished my sentence, he was bounding out into the room to tell the guys he was going on. Everyone was looking at me like, "Are you crazy?" But he got up there and was absolutely hilarious.

The good thing about it was that when he got back to class, he started to calm down. Once I'd let him go onstage, he'd lost that need to prove something. From then on he was really willing to learn and get better.

PAT FINN:

From that point on, he just committed a hundred and ten percent. We took classes with Charna. Then we got classes with Del. There were two improv teams that got assembled around that period. One was very cerebral—that wasn't us. We were the physical group, called Fish Shtick. People wanted to watch them because they were so smart and heady, but then they'd want to watch us because we were just off the wall.

BRIAN STACK:

Chris once said that Del Close told him to attack the stage like a bull and try and kill the audience with laughter.

NOAH GREGOROPOULOS, *cast member, ImprovOlympic:*

He was so big and emotional, very physical. He gave one guy a permanent scar on his forehead when he dove from the bar onto the stage in this overblown ninja thing. He landed on him, smashing his glasses into his head. His commitment was just past the point of safety.

TIM MEADOWS, *cast member, Second City:*

I was already touring for Second City, and I used to go back and perform at ImprovOlympic every now and then. One night I went up there and did a Harold with Chris's team. It's difficult when you're the new guy in a group, because they already have their dynamic and you don't know how you'll fit into it. But the very first time we performed together Chris was right there for me. I started a scene where I was hanging something up, and it was obvious to everyone in the audience that I was hanging up laundry on a clothesline. But Chris came out and said, "Doctor, what does the X-ray say?"

I just looked at him and said, "Well, it's not good."

And it got a big laugh because it was such a change from where people thought it was going.

PAT FINN:

When you get a suggestion in an improv set, usually one performer goes out and sets the stage based on the idea. And sometimes that person is out there for a while, just fumbling around. He doesn't know where he's going, and because he doesn't know, it's really difficult to step in and help him.

One night this girl walks out and puts a pretend briefcase down and goes, "I had such a great day today, honey. They made me partner at the law firm and they love me and somebody's gonna be interviewing me for *Newsweek* . . ."

And on and on and on. It was this long exposition, just going no-where. We're all standing there at the back of the stage, thinking, how do we even enter this scene? She's giving us nowhere to go.

This goes about a minute or so. She's droning on and on, and finally Chris storms out of the back line and goes, "Sweet Lord, would you just shut up and bowl?!"

His instincts were near perfect. With one line he put the whole scene in a place and a context and established what the joke was. "My God, every time you bowl it's something different. You're a doctor. You're a lawyer. 'Look at me, I discovered something!' Bowl the *goddamned* ball."

JAMES GRACE, *cast member, ImprovOlympic:*

He was an amazing processor of information. He wasn't great at getting things started, but if you gave him anything, he would take it, internalize it, have a perspective on it, be affected by it, and ride it out for the scene.

CHARNA HALPERN:

He was an amazing listener onstage, like a sponge. You could just see him reflecting your idea through his facial expression and taking on your mood. He totally got it.

And he was in incredible shape. That always surprised people. I remember one football sketch he was in where his teammates were making fun of him for being out of shape. They'd say, "All right, fatty, drop and give me twenty." And Chris could do it, with no problem, clapping his hands in between each push-up, even. He was all muscle under there.

TIM HENRY:

We're at a bar in Chicago one night. It's ten degrees outside. Chris has got his English driving cap on, Timberland boots, and some cutoff sweat-pants, and he's sporting these huge muttonchop sideburns. The after-work crowd is there. A bunch of little honeys are at the bar, and Chris starts chatting them up. "Hey, how are you? What do you guys do?" he says.

They work in advertising or insurance or whatever, and they ask him, "So what do you do?"

Chris is standing there, sweating in ten-degree weather, and he goes, "Me? What do I do? I'm an aerobics instructor."

We're all laughing, 'cause we know he's winding up to have fun with them.

"Aerobics instructor?" they say. "Are you kidding me?"

And Chris, with one hand on the bar and one hand on the stool, defying all laws of physics, goes from standing stock still, leaps into a perfect backflip, and lands back right on his feet. Hat doesn't even come off his head.

"Yeah," he says. "You know, aerobics instructor."

TED DONDANVILLE:

I got hooked on Chris's shows very early. When I went back to Red Arrow Camp to be a counselor, Kevin and Johnny told me Chris was down in Chicago. I'd been thrown out of the University of Denver; I wasn't having a traditional college experience. So I started hanging out with Chris a lot. When you'd go and see him in these bars, you'd have to sit through an hour and a half of bullshit watching these kids learn how to do comedy. But however good or bad the shows were, Chris always had that moment, that one moment where lightning would strike and he'd just kill the audience.

PAT FINN:

ImprovOlympic was very young, and I think that's what made it, for lack of a better word, romantic. There were no agents coming to see you. There was nobody pitching a screenplay. It was just about the pure love of the game, going out every night and making people laugh.

JAMES GRACE:

It was like a wave of energy. We were doing five shows a week, one on Thursday and two on Fridays and Saturdays. We were just all constantly together all the time, performing, hanging out. Everybody who was there had come because they wanted to challenge themselves and push the boundaries of comedy. People were either rehearsing or performing every night of the week. You were consuming it all the time. And when you weren't rehearsing or performing, you were hanging out with people whom you rehearsed and performed with. Once you were on a team, that was basically your fraternity.

It was very collegiate, especially when it came to the drinking. I would say that if you took a clinical definition of alcoholism, then everybody there had a huge problem. Farley always did everything bigger than everybody else, but we were all out of control. One time I saw Pat Finn fall down two flights of stairs solely to make me laugh. That's what we did, outrageous things all across the board.

PAT FINN:

Chris must have had something like forty jobs during that time. One day he and I were walking down Armitage Avenue, and he was like, "Yeah, I worked there. I worked there."

And I was like, "When?"

"Well, I worked at the butcher shop for like an hour, and they fired me. Then I got a job at the hardware store the day after the butcher shop, but I was really tired 'cause I'd had to get up so early for the butcher shop, you know? So I fell asleep on some boxes in the back."

I said, "How could you fall asleep within hours of your first day on the job?"

"I don't know, but they were really pissed."

So he lost that job. Basically he'd lost every job up and down the street. Eventually, we'd go to church and he'd pull the little tags on the bulletin board that said "Need neighborhood workers" and stuff like that.

He got a job as a bouncer, but then one day he said to me, "Hey, I think I kinda got fired from that bouncer job at the bar."

"Jeez, Chris"—this was on Sunday—"you started it on Friday. What happened?"

Apparently a fight had broken out, so he—Chris, the bouncer—had left, because he didn't know what to do. And he'd caused the fight.

What had happened was Chris was checking IDs, and, goofing around, he goosed some girl in the butt. Her boyfriend thought it was somebody else, and he started shoving people and it broke out into a real melee, so Chris just kind of slipped out the front door.

All the other bouncers came out from inside and finally settled it. Then the owners came out and said, "My God, who's on the front door?"

At that moment, Chris came back around from this alley down the side of the bar. He saw the owners, panicked, turned down this alley, and yelled *"And stay out!"*

"Where the hell were you?" they asked.

"Where was *I*? Where the hell were *you*? There were like nine guys in the alley on top of me."

"What?"

"It's okay. I took care of it. But, man . . ."

"Oh Chris, we're so sorry."

So on Saturday he went back to bounce again. I asked him how that went.

"Well," he said, "normally you get your shift drink around eleven. But the girl behind the bar really liked me, so I got my shift drink at seven. Then I had another one. She was making those greyhounds that I like. Man, I had a lot of 'em."

"Were you okay?"

"Well, that's my question. I'm not sure. I passed out on the people in line while I was checking IDs, and all the bouncers had to take me across the street and put me into bed."

"Uh-huh."

"So do I just go over there to get a paycheck, or do I ask 'em to mail it? How does that work?"

"I don't know, Chris. You probably drank more than your pay-check."

"Yeah, you're probably right. I guess I just won't go over there for a while."

He didn't seem particularly fazed by it. It just kind of reinforced to him that he needed to find a way to make a living in comedy.

CHARNA HALPERN:

We got a pilot, an improv game show, similar to *Whose Line Is It Anyway?* I picked out a bunch of our best performers, of which Chris was one, and they flew us all out to L.A. We were doing some really smart work, and the producer just wanted us to dumb it down. "It's too smart," he kept saying, "too smart." And he started firing some of the best people. He wanted to bring in all these dick-joke stand-up comics.

So, one by one, my cast was getting fired. It was just a nightmare, which Del had warned me was going to happen. Chris could see what was going on. At one point in the rehearsal he said, "Look, I'm sorry, but I don't wanna get fired."

"Do what you gotta do," I said.

And so he hiked up his shorts into the crack of his ass and started jumping around doing the monkey dog boy dance, which is when you hold your crotch with one hand and put your fingers up your nose and just start jumping around being silly. And, oh, they were on the floor laughing, because that's the kind of dumb stuff they wanted. And he saved his job.

But Chris wasn't always a caricature of the fat guy. He did beautiful scenes. When he did serious scenes, oh my God, he could make you cry.

NOAH GREGOROPOULOS:

Chris's vision of himself was that everyone just wanted to see fatty fall down, so that was what he was going to give them. But there were plenty of other guys who could fall off a chair and eat in Roman proportions.

What Del Close liked about Chris wasn't necessarily what everybody else liked about him. Del felt that Chris was in touch with genuine emotions in a way not all improvisers allow themselves. That's what Del was really attracted to in Chris. He wanted to show Chris that he could be more than just a one-note performer.

CHARNA HALPERN:

After Chris was done working with me, I couldn't wait for him to get to Del, because that was the next level. I said to Del, "I can't wait for you to see this guy. I want to see what you think."

Del watched him, and after the show he turned to me, and the first thing he said was, "Oh, that's the next John Belushi."

CHAPTER 5

Whale Boy

JUDITH SCOTT, *cast member:*

If you think of the rest of the Second City cast as flat land, Chris was something that fell out of the sky and gave us shape. He might blow out a huge crater, like a meteor, or just collide with the ground, becoming this huge mountain. And by creating this landscape, he gave the rest of us the terrain on which to play.

C hris Farley spent a little over eighteen months studying and performing at ImprovOlympic. The young theater was rapidly becoming one of Chicago comedy's best-known training grounds, but at the time it remained just that: a place to learn. For actors seeking out professional opportunities and a professional paycheck, Second City was still the place to be. Since its founding in 1959, Second City had established itself as the nation's graduate school of comedy. In the early days, Robert Klein, Joan Rivers, and Alan Arkin all came across its stage. Over subsequent years, dozens of Hollywood stars matriculated there as well.

Chris auditioned for Second City's touring company in January 1989 and was offered a position. Most performers would have spent months or even years on the road before joining the main-stage ensemble; Chris made the move in a matter of weeks. Del Close had been offered the opportunity to direct Second City's spring revue, and he was given great latitude to mold the show and its cast to his own liking. The performer he liked most was Chris. Second City producer Joyce Sloane expressed reservations about the young performer's readiness and his outsized partying habits, but Charna Halpern insisted that working with Close was exactly the kind of discipline Chris needed. Sloane ultimately agreed.

And everyone agreed that Chris's potential was virtually without limit. During his eighteen months at Second City, Chris performed in three revues: *The Gods Must Be Lazy, It Was Thirty Years Ago Today*, which marked the theater's thirtieth anniversary, and *Flag Smoking Permitted in Lobby Only*. Also making the leap from the touring company at that time was Chris's friend Tim Meadows. Second City veterans David Pasquesi, Holly Wortell, Joe Liss, Judith Scott, and Joel Murray, as well as understudy Tim O'Malley, rounded out the cast. With each show, Chris's reputation grew. He created a number of characters and scenes that would go down as some of the best in the theater's history.

TIM O'MALLEY, *cast member:*

I was sitting in the main lobby at Second City. Chris came through the front door, all big and boisterous like he always did. He went upstairs and auditioned. What he did for his audition was he pretended he was late for whatever the scene was, took a running leap from stage left, and landed flat in the middle of the stage. They hired him right away, just on his energy and his commitment. Everyone was like, "You should have seen this guy's audition. He was fucking nuts."

TIM MEADOWS:

Me and Farley were the two new guys, both coming straight out of the touring company. We bonded over the fact that we didn't know what the fuck we were doing.

HOLLY WORTELL, *cast member:*

When we started rehearsals, Chris's inexperience showed. You had to come up with your own scene ideas, and he was not very good at that. One day we were throwing out these social, political, and cultural ideas, and Del said, "Chris, do you have anything?"

Chris went, "Um . . . yeah. I was thinking, um, that there's rich people . . . and, uh, there's poor people . . . you know . . . something about that."

And I was like, "What was *that*?"

TOM GIANAS, *director:*

Chris was a great writer, actually. He just worked on his feet. You gave him a premise, and he'd spin it into gold.

JOEL MURRAY:

The first time I had to improvise with him onstage, the suggestion we got from the audience was "the drunk tank." It was like, okay, there's a natural. I said to Chris, "Let's do a two-person scene where I'm your dad and I'm picking you up at the drunk tank, but in actuality I'm a drunk, too."

"Yeah," Chris said. "Let's go with that."

I didn't know anything about Chris and his father at that point; I just figured he was Irish so he'd know what I was talking about.

It was a great scene, and the emotions in it were so close to home in some ways, this drunk Irish father in his pajamas picking up his son. He's coming down on the boy, but everything he says—like "That time your mother left me after I mowed down the hedges . . ."—reveals that he's a drunk, too.

So father and son have this meaningful talk about their drinking, and Chris is defending himself, like, "But I'm really *good* at it." Like his dad should be proud of him. Of course it winds up with Chris's character offering to drive home. And the dad, who's been drinking, says, "Yeah, yeah. I think that's a good idea."

And that became Chris's big sketch in the first show. What do you do with a drunken sailor? You have him play a drunken sailor. Del Close was in the audience, and he came backstage and said, "Yeah, well, that one's ready. Script that."

NATE HERMAN, *director:*

At Second City, a lot of the performers tend to be very verbal. But every once in a while a physical comedian comes along, and when an actor has that rough physicality in such a small setting it really tends to explode.

PAT FINN:

When Chris's first revue opened, he was an instant hit. There was a scene where he played a waiter. The people eating dinner were the heart of the scene, but Chris came out and got a huge laugh with "Can I get you something to eat?" That was it. He went over to the other side of the stage to make the drinks and sandwiches in the background, and every single head in the audience slowly turned to watch Chris. It was the oddest thing. Even if he was doing nothing, you wanted to watch him do nothing.

JOE LISS, *cast member:*

His mere presence would induce laughter. Anything he'd do on top of that was gravy.

DAVID PASQUESI, *cast member:*

Crowds loved him. I don't think you can find anyone who'll refute that. That's not an opinion.

HOLLY WORTELL:

On Friday and Saturday nights, we had a break between shows. Chris and I would always dash out and get something to eat, and we'd always run into about half the audience from the first show. We'd both been onstage for the past two hours, but everyone would come right up to Chris and say, "You were so great!"

Chris would go to great pains to say, "Hey, she was in the show, too. Wasn't she good?" And that was very sweet of him, but it seemed logical to me that people would notice him more.

JOEL MURRAY:

During that first show the cast, minus Holly, went away to Joyce Sloane's place on Lake Michigan. It was the dead of winter, and we'd brought a whole bunch of "Murray Brothers' Tea," this big thing of psilocybin mushroom tea. We wrote half the show that night, just from stuff we came up with screwing around. I've never laughed so hard in my life.

JOE LISS:

We were fucking around inside the house. I started doing this crazy English character. Tim was going on about how he couldn't feel his legs. The sun was coming up, and we couldn't find Chris. "Where's Chris?" "Let's find him!" We struck out of the house on an "expedition" to track him down. We ran out, and there he was, lying out on the ice of Lake Michigan. "Look," we said, "it's a whale!" "No! It's a boy!" "*It's a Whale Boy!*"

JOEL MURRAY:

The whole lake was frozen ice, these huge glacier formations, crazy stuff. And at one point, Farley was out there, shirt open, T-shirt over his head, diving like a seal onto the ice, doing these crazy belly flops, his stomach bright red. We riffed on this Whale Boy thing for hours, high on mushroom tea, laughing our asses off out there on the frozen ice of Lake Michigan.

JUDITH SCOTT:

We came back to the cabin, and as the drugs wore off we realized that we'd written a scene.

TIM MEADOWS:

We had trouble putting it on paper. When we got back we tried to improvise with this Whale Boy character, and there was just too much information. Plus, we all remembered it differently because we'd been tripping. So Nate Herman, our new director, sat down and said, "Each of you tell me your version of the story."

We did that, and then a few days later he came in with the whole thing. The story was that we had raised this Whale Boy as a real boy and hidden his true origin from him. The scene was his coming-out party into society. But the tension underneath was that his mother couldn't stand the fact that this was not her own son. Ultimately, we have to tell Chris the truth: that he's not our son, but in fact the product of a whale impregnated by radioactive human sperm and medical waste. Once he discovers that, Chris launches into this grand song and soliloquy about reclaiming his true identity.

Tom Farley and Mary Anne Crosby at a
Georgetown University spring formal, 1956

An early portrait of Chris, 1965

Hanging stockings on Christmas
Eve, 1967, (from left) Chris, Tom Jr.,
Kevin, Mary Anne, and Barbara

A Farley Christmas card family
portrait, 1968, (from left) Kevin,
Chris, Tom Jr., Tom Sr., Mary Anne,
Johnny, and Barbara

The Farley kids on summer vacation at Sagamore Beach, Cape Cod, 1969, (from left) Chris, Johnny, Barbara, Kevin, and Tom Jr.

Chris and Kevin visiting brother Tom Jr. at Red Arrow Camp, 1971

Chris and Tom Jr. playing in a private plane owned by family friends visiting from Detroit, 1970

Chris at summer camp, 1973

Chris as a Cub Scout, photographed by den leader Mary
Anne Farley, 1973

Chris (standing, top left) and his fellow cabin mates at Red Arrow Camp, 1974

A Farley family photo, taken at their home on Farwell Drive in the Village of Maple Bluff, 1972: Mary Anne, Tom Sr., Chris, Tom Jr., and John (standing); Barbara and Kevin (sitting)

Taking flight at age eleven

Sporting a broken leg and wrist from skating, 1977

Playing the class clown
for friends in fifth grade at
St. Patrick's School in
Madison, 1974

© 2007 COURTESY OF THE FARLEY
FAMILY ARCHIVES

Posing in a new suit for
his eighth-grade graduation
from Edgewood Campus
School, 1978

© 2007 COURTESY OF THE FARLEY
FAMILY ARCHIVES

Going out for the Madison Lakers youth hockey team. He played one year.

Noseguard, Edgewood varsity football team, 1980

Getting ready for his junior year homecoming dance with Greg Meyer (center),
Robert Barry (second from right), and their dates

At a high school dance, senior year,
with Todd Green (left) and Dan Healy

Fr. Matt Foley (bottom, far left) kneeling next to Chris and the rest of the gonzo athletes of the Marquette rugby team

Becoming an actor: backstage as "The Policeman" in a Marquette production of Sam Shepard's *Curse of the Starving Class*

The intrepid inhabitants of the legendary "Red House" at Marquette, with Jim Murphy (seated, bottom left) next to Chris, Dan Healy (perched, top left), and Mark Hermacinski (looking up, top center)
COURTESY OF JIM MURPHY

Enjoying college
COURTESY OF MARK HERMACINSKI

Leading his cabin on a woodland hike at Red Arrow Camp

Announcer Fred Albright (center) interviewing Hogs coaches Randy Hopper (left) and Chris Farley (right) as they prepare to rally their team for Red Arrow Camp's annual "Salad Bowl," 1983

Performing in a Red Arrow counselor stunt night, with Fred Albright

The Farleys, minus Johnny, at Chris's "graduation" from Marquette University, 1986

Onstage at the Ark Improvisational Theater in Madison

The founding cast of FishShtick at Chicago's ImprovOlympic theater, including Pat Finn (standing, second from right), James Grace (seated, center), and Chris

The cast of Second City during Chris's first revue, *The Gods Must Be Lazy*: Tim Meadows and David Pasquesi (back row); Chris, Judith Scott, and Joe Liss (middle row); and Holly Wortell and Joel Murray (seated)
© SECOND CITY

The original stage incarnation of Matt Foley, Motivational Speaker, (from left) Chris, Jill Talley, Bob Odenkirk, Holly Wortell, and Tim Meadows
© SECOND CITY

HOLLY WORTELL:

We wanted him to be able to spout from his head like a whale, and so our stage manager took a football helmet, drilled a hole in it, and connected this water hose so Chris could squirt water out of it.

JOEL MURRAY:

He looked like a Hummel figurine. When he would come out like a choirboy and sing the Whale Boy song, the crowd would go nuts.

The last preview before opening night, he does the song and goes to exit through a door, and he pulls the doorknob off. There's nothing he can do, so he jumps into the crowd, and he breaks his foot. We're all like, "Suck it up, Farley. C'mon." But it turns out he really did break his foot, and he had a walking cast for opening night.

TIM O'MALLEY:

Ian Gomez took over, and Chris was out for a good eight weeks. But nobody could stop him from coming in and doing the improv sets. He'd come in and do those on a cast.

JOE LISS:

Chris was always "boy." He was Whale Boy. We did another sketch where he was Caramel Boy. Then of course there was *Tommy Boy*.

NATE HERMAN:

Paul Sills, one of the founders of Chicago improv, used to say, "Out there doesn't matter. This is the only place that matters. The stage is the only place you exist." So if the stage is the only place you feel real, it makes sense to make the whole world your stage.

ROBERT BARRY, *friend, Edgewood High School:*

Whatever Chris Farley did in the movies or on TV, that was just Chris Farley. He was never acting. Or, perhaps, Chris was always acting. That might be a better way of putting it.

CHARNA HALPERN:

He was always more himself onstage than off. He was more intelligent onstage. He'd step out there, and it was like a light would go on behind his eyes.

HOLLY WORTELL:

I remember we'd be in his apartment and he would be really calm. He'd talk about his feelings, things that he would never say around the guys. Then we would walk down the stairs and open that door out onto Wells Street and, literally, the second that door opened he turned into "Farley." It was like a jacket that he put on when he was leaving the house.

Chris would tell me a story about his day, like maybe a story about ordering a sandwich from the guy at the deli, and he'd do his voice and the guy's voice, acting out this little scene. But instead of just saying, "I told the guy, 'I want a tomato,'" Chris was really acting it up, like, "I *told* the guy, 'I *want* a *tomato!*'"

And so I asked him, "Chris, how come when you speak, you're imitating yourself?"

"What?"

I said, "When you tell that story about yourself, you're doing your own dialogue in a different voice. You're doing a character voice *for you.*"

And that kind of blew his mind.

TED DONDANVILLE:

Most of the people at Second City, after the show they'd all go out for drinks, and they'd just hang out with you like a normal person. But Chris and Joe Liss, they couldn't stop. The red nose and floppy shoes stayed on.

NATE HERMAN:

His greatest frustration was trying to beat that character that he was becoming. He really seemed like he was uncomfortable being the great, swaggering drunk; it didn't suit him. I always thought that inside there was this nice kid from Wisconsin going, "I'm really not comfortable doing this, but this is who I'm supposed to be."

TIM MEADOWS:

Chris used to say that he only had one character, and that was the fat, loud guy. But of course that wasn't true at all. In our last revue, we did a scene where the premise was basically that Chris and I were good friends, we're hanging out, and then his sister, played by Jill Talley, comes in. She and I really hit it off and I'm digging on her and Chris is *really* not okay with it.

JILL TALLEY, *cast member:*

The more Tim and I would milk our flirtation, the more Chris would amp up his reactions. Tim was giving me a foot rub, I was laughing at all of his jokes, and Chris was just fuming, bubbling under the surface, which he did so brilliantly.

Then Chris comes right out and tells Tim, "You can't date my sister."

"Why, because we're friends?"

"No, because you're black."

TIM MEADOWS:

The thing that I loved about Chris was that he was willing to be the racist in that scene. He starts off as my best friend, and then when I exit the stage for a moment he does this really subtle change where he confronts her and tells her he doesn't like it. Then I walk back onstage right as he says "nigger." Every night you could hear a pin drop as soon as he said it. People didn't expect that from Second City, and they certainly didn't expect it from Chris.

FR. MATT FOLEY:

When he was at Second City, he would call me late at night and I could tell he was using, that he was not doing well. He was really struggling; he was so damn lonely. He'd lost some of his anchors, and he was ashamed of his drug use.

TIM MEADOWS:

When we were in Chicago, we all drank, and we all did our share of other things. But one night after we did the first show we were getting notes from Del in the back. Farley went into the kitchen, got a bottle of wine, and just started guzzling it straight down. I remember watching him drink that bottle and thinking, holy shit.

Then, when we would go out drinking after the show, it would never end. His personality changed. He was a messy drunk. He would just get loud and in your face. I would go to one bar with him, and then he'd ask me if I was going to Burton Place, this bar that was open until five in the morning. I'd say, "No, I don't like that place." There was just a bad vibe in there, a lot of people who were involved in heavier drugs. I used to call it Satan's Den, and he would always tease me about that. "You wanna go over to Satan's Den with me?"

TIM O'MALLEY:

When you drank or got high with Chris, it was like corralling a tiger. I was doing coke on a regular basis, and I knew I was an addict. I don't know if I recognized Chris as being worse off than me, though. Guzzle and pour, guzzle and pour, slobber and puke. That was about it for us. We'd sleep all day. If we had rehearsal, we'd haul out of bed and make it there by eleven. We'd always try and get home by sunrise and get some sleep, but some days we were partying right up through to rehearsal, then try and get a nap and some food in before the show. Then, sometimes, we were just high for days.

TED DONDANVILLE:

The first hour of drinking with Chris was fun. The second hour was the best hour of your life. The rest of the night was pure hell.

DAVID PASQUESI:

He was taking it as far as someone could while still making it to work, and he was being rewarded all along the way. So there was no reason to stop.

TOM GIANAS:

Chris came in to rehearsal one day, and he was really out of it, kind of falling asleep. I took him aside and told him he had to go home. But Chris could always turn on the charm. He talked me into letting him stay. I always regretted that one moment. It was just a minor incident, but it was one instance where I had an opportunity to exert some discipline over him, and I didn't do it.

JOE LISS:

Second City sees itself as a family, and we were a pretty codependent family, too. There could have been a big intervention from the cast, but it didn't happen. We were all doing drugs.

The one thing we did crack down on was drinking during the show. That wasn't okay. One time I caught Chris in between sets. There's the greenroom backstage, and then there's another dressing room on the other side with a pass-through between them. I'm backstage, and I look down the pass-through and see Farley at his locker. He looks around, reaches into his locker, takes out a big tumbler, takes a big sip, and then hides it back in his locker.

I'm like, "You motherfucker."

So I wait for Chris to leave and go and get a big box of salt from the kitchen. I take the drink, fill it with salt, stir it up and let it dissolve, put it back, and head back to the other room and wait.

Chris comes back for the next show, reaches into his locker, gets the drink, takes another big sip of it and just does this beautiful spit take, spewing the drink all over. There was no more drinking during that show.

CHARNA HALPERN:

We had a couple of meetings with Chris where Del Close told him about the clinic where he went through aversion therapy and stopped drinking. It's a horrible process, like something out of *The Twilight Zone*. They shoot you up with this chemical and then they make you drink this watered-down alcohol until you vomit. Then they throw you back in your bed, and a couple of hours later they shoot you up and make you go through it again. They keep doing this until even the smell of alcohol makes you throw up. It sounds futuristic, but it works.

So Del told Chris about this therapy. "You need this," he said. "Try it. It works."

And Chris was like, "Nah, that's too permanent."

PAT FINN:

We were at a bar in Chicago once, Chris and me and his dad. Chris's dad goes, "Finner, you want a beer?"

"Oh yeah that'd be great, Mr. Farley."

"Christopher?"

"Uh, yeah. Thanks, Dad," Chris says.

"All right," he tells the bartender. "Two Old Styles for Finner, and a coupla Old Styles for Christopher. And I'll have a scotch. Tall glass. Rocks. Leave the bottle."

The guy just kind of stares at him. Mr. Farley stares back. Then he finally turns around to get the drinks.

I go, "Wow, Mr. Farley, really? What are we, in the Old West?"

"Look, Finner," he says. "I like scotch, and when I want a drink, and this bartender's talkin' to his gal pal down at the end of the bar, I'm not gonna wait for him. So I get a bottle, and I can have scotch whenever I want it. On top of that it's kind of fun to see what they charge me, because they never know how many shots are left in the bottle."

TOM GIANAS:

When his dad would come to the shows, they'd go to That Steak Joint, which was this steak restaurant right next door to the theater. They had this thing called the Trencherman's Cut, which was this ungodly cut of meat, just an unholy-size piece of Chicago beef. You would buy it for the table and eat it family style. When Chris and his dad would go, they'd each order one.

TIM MEADOWS:

His father used to tease him if he couldn't finish his. It was funny to see Chris when his parents came to town, because it was the only time you'd see him dressed up. The pressed shirt, the sport coat, the slacks. He'd have a haircut and a shave. He wanted everything to go right.

TIM O'MALLEY:

He was still a kid. His parents paid his rent for him. We told him to save some money and pay his own rent so he'd feel more responsible for himself. "But my dad wants to pay for everything," he'd say.

JOE LISS:

It was like they were still treating him like a kid at college, and he was embarrassed of it, or tired of it. He would get these care packages from his mother, and he would get visibly angered by them. She would send him food and slippers, new clothes from Brooks Brothers, and he'd be like, "Aw, dammit." But if you looked at his private life, you were like, "Chris, you need new clothes. You need a cleaning lady."

HOLLY WORTELL:

One time I tried to get Chris to open a bank account. He didn't have one. He would just cash his checks and have cash on hand. He was very generous, would buy everybody drinks, but he wouldn't save anything. I said to him, "Look, just walk with me up the street and open up an account."

"No."

"Chris, you can't just spend all your money. You're spending all your money on food, drugs, and alcohol. You have to put some away for rent and bills and savings."

And he wouldn't do it. He would not set foot in the bank with me.

JILL TALLEY:

We all took turns bringing him home. I remember being shocked that he didn't really have anything, nothing that you would associate with a home. It was really sparse, just a bare mattress and a big trash bag full of clothes. That was it.

JOEL MURRAY:

I had an apartment above Los Piñatas, this Mexican place by Second City. I always believed that Joyce Sloane had something to do with Farley all of a sudden having the apartment next to me. She knew that I would watch out for him.

He was like Pigpen from *Peanuts*. We had mice, too. The mice would come through my apartment and stop and give me this look, like "We're just on our way over to Farley's place."

JOYCE SLOANE, *producer:*

He always talked about how he wanted a girlfriend, and I said to him, "Do you think you could bring a girl up there? To that apartment? You gotta clean it up."

I tried to tell him that Bluto was just a character John Belushi played in *Animal House*; that wasn't what he was really like. When John's widow Judy was in town, I introduced him to her, and I said, "Do you think a lady like this would've been married to him if he was really that character that you saw?"

I thought that was a good thing to do, to let him know what John was really like. It didn't sink in, obviously. So I hired a cleaning woman for him to try and fix his place up. She came every week.

TIM O'MALLEY:

For all the trouble, everyone wanted to take Chris under his wing. The alumni that came in, like Bill Murray, would just adopt him immediately. It just oozed out of him: "Love me. Please love me." He got so much love. He got a ton of it. I don't know how he was even able to process it.

DAVID PASQUESI:

It was pretty obvious that there were problems for Chris from the word go. I don't think we realized that it was as detrimental as it was, but we could all see it. Then there was some odd behavior that was a bit obsessive-compulsive. We just thought it was weird, and we were right. That was some weird shit.

JOE LISS:

Before he put his pants on, he'd lick the tip of the belt, then the buckle, then he'd put on his pants. Before he went onstage, he'd touch the floor twice, touch the wing of the stage twice, and then go on. Every time.

BOB ODENKIRK, *cast member:*

I cannot express to you how much he licked everything. He'd open his wallet and lick everything inside it, the pictures, the money. He had to lick his shoelaces to tie them. He'd lick his finger and touch the stair, lick the finger, touch the stair, and do it all the way up the staircase. It was totally nuts.

HOLLY WORTELL:

One night I was onstage, and I said a cue line for Chris to enter. He should have been standing right at the door, but I could see him off in the green-room, and that meant he had to go all the way down the corridor back-stage and enter from the other side. I remember thinking, he's got to cover all that distance, touching every door twice, touching every stair twice, touching all the coats twice. It's going to be an hour before he gets there.

One day we were walking down the street, and he kept bending down and touching the sidewalk twice, touching the parking meters twice. I said to him, "Chris, why do you do that?"

And he said, "I'm just trying to even everything up."

JOE LISS:

He was superstitious, too. There was this Ouija board backstage. "Get that thing out of here!" he'd say. He was afraid of it. So, of course, someone took the Ouija board and put it on his pile of props in the back. "Who did this?!" he yelled. Then he took a towel—he wouldn't touch it with his hands—and he picked it up and threw it aside.

TIM MEADOWS:

I was surprised by Chris's faith. He'd go to mass all the time. I always admired that about him. I grew up in a Christian household, but once I got to Chicago I didn't go to church anymore. I just prayed whenever I wanted something.

HOLLY WORTELL:

We would do charity gigs sometimes where they would pay us a hundred dollars, which was *huge* for us; the most we ever made was $435 a week. But whenever we would do those charity shows, Chris was the only person in the cast who turned down the money. He would always say, "Please keep this and make sure it gets to the people you're helping."

JUDITH SCOTT:

He had a moral code, a sense of right and wrong. There was something in him that was correct and proper and Midwestern. If we were in a meeting and somebody's idea got shot down, Chris would immediately take up for that person and defend them.

HOLLY WORTELL:

In a show, you do the scenes, the director gives you notes on those scenes, and then you build on that the next night. I was so excited that I was going to get to work with Del Close, but what I came to learn was that Del *hated* women, didn't think they were funny, didn't want them in the show. At a certain point I was like, "What is this guy doing? He's not coming up with any ideas. He's not pushing us. He's not doing *anything*." He would say to us, "No notes after the show tonight."

Then, after several weeks, Chris came to me and said, "Holly, I know I shouldn't be saying this, but I've just got to tell you something."

"What?"

"When Del says we aren't having notes after the show, we are. We're all going over to Joel's apartment, and he's giving us notes. Del says that you and Judith are evil witches and you're trying to ruin our show."

And what was happening was that Judith Scott, Joe Liss, and myself, who hadn't worked with Del over at the ImprovOlympic, would go home every night, not knowing what was going on, and Chris, Tim Meadows, Joel Murray, and David Pasquesi were all going over and working on the show with Del. For Chris to go behind Del's back and betray him was *huge*. Chris would never go against any authority figure, but he did it because he felt what Del was doing to Judith and me was wrong.

JILL TALLEY:

Once in a blue moon I'd make it to church, and I would always see Chris there. I always got the biggest kick out of watching him come back from taking communion, because it was like he knew everyone there, all the parishioners. He'd nod and smile at them, and they all really liked him. The priests really liked him, too. He was very much a part of that community. It was just a pious, quiet side of him that you'd never know unless you saw him there. Then, fourteen hours later, I'd be carrying him home from a bar and putting him to bed.

FR. MATT FOLEY:

Chris and I would sit and talk all night. He would ask me about God, about faith. His biggest questions always related to his struggles with evil, with his addictions. Drugs were Satan, to Chris. Fighting that took a lot out of him.

HOLLY WORTELL:

When he was drunk, he might do or say something he shouldn't have done. But one day he told me, "I went to church and I confessed, and now it's over so I can do it again."

And I said, "Chris, I'm Jewish. But I'm pretty sure that's not how your religion works. That doesn't even make sense."

One night, Matt Foley came to see the show, and the three of us went out after. I said to Matt, "I have to ask you this. Chris says if you sin and go to church and confess and say your Hail Marys, then you can just do it again."

And Matt said, "No, of course you can't do it again. You have to try *not* to do it again."

I punched Chris in the arm and said, "See?"

FR. MATT FOLEY:

There are two ways to look at confession. One is to say, "I'm in a state of grace. God has blessed me, but in the midst of that greatness I have treated my brother or sister poorly and need to make atonement."

The flip side is to say, "I'm a sinner. I'm not worthy. I have to find Christ to find my way out of my natural state, which is sin."

I'm not sure which side Chris worked from, but I suspect it was the latter. "I am not worthy to receive You, but only say the word and I shall be healed." That's what Chris believed. And that's not wrong, but it needs to be balanced with an understanding of the good side.

Chris was grateful for each day of the life God had given him. He never saw himself as an equal of God, and many times we do. A lot of our humanism is very arrogant. It says, "I'm God. I'm equal to God." Chris was never like that. He stood in awe of God.

BOB ODENKIRK:

He saw things in a very simple way, good and evil, right and wrong. I was raised Catholic, too. I can remember being scared of the devil, of hell. It's real in your head.

One time at Second City, Chris was violently drunk at a party. He was picking up these chairs and throwing them across the room. Me and my girlfriend brought him back to his place, and he started throwing the furniture there, too, chucking it across the room. Then he just stopped, looked over at me, and said, "Odie, do you think Belushi's in heaven?"

It was sad, and chilling, and I didn't know how to answer him. It made me think that those myths that you live with as a kid, they don't always help you when you're an adult. They don't help you deal with grown-up things.

* * *

Even as Chris's personal troubles began to mount, his professional fortunes only grew. Every night the audience favored him more and more. His reputation began to draw interest from the talent scouts at *Saturday Night Live* as well as representatives at Brillstein-Grey, the powerhouse management firm in Beverly Hills. In the spring of 1990, Chris was signed by Brillstein's Marc Gurvitz, who would manage him for his entire career.

On March 24, 1990, *Saturday Night Live* flew Chris to New York to attend a taping of the show and to have an informal meeting with executive producer Lorne Michaels. It was the first solid indication of their interest in him and of things to come. At the same time, work had begun on Chris's third Second City revue, *Flag Smoking Permitted in Lobby Only*. For this show, producer Joyce Sloane brought in Tom Gianas, a young director from outside the Second City universe. Gianas in turn hired actress Jill Talley and *SNL* writer Bob Odenkirk to join the cast. It was a fortuitous meeting for all. At Gianas's request, Odenkirk helped Chris create the signature character that would take him to *Saturday Night Live* and beyond.

TOM GIANAS:

When you're lined up to direct a show at Second City, you just go in and watch the performers. You make notes, jot down inspirations. Night after night, I would go there to work and make notes, and every time I saw him onstage, he transformed me from a director into an audience member; I forgot to take notes. I would just sit back and laugh and laugh and laugh. That's never happened to me before or since.

I've worked with a lot of great people over the years, from Jack Black to Steve Carell, and this is something I can only say about Chris: From the moment he stepped onstage, the audience was completely invested in him. There was just a sense of "He's gonna cause trouble, and I want to be here when it happens."

When I arrived, he was doing the Motivational Speaker guy, but it wasn't as a motivational speaker yet, because that idea didn't exist. It was just *that guy,* in a million different contexts, usually a coach, or maybe an angry dad. It would destroy the audience every night. I said to Odenkirk, "We cannot open the show without that character."

And that's when Bob came back with a sketch about a family with pot-smoking kids who hire this Motivational Speaker, a guy who lives in a van down by the river, is thrice divorced, and uses the complete disaster of his life as an example of what not to become.

BOB ODENKIRK:

I sat down to write it, and the sketch came out pretty much whole the way it was done. I handed it to Chris, and watching where he took it was insane.

TIM O'MALLEY:

Chris could never remember his lines during rehearsal. He'd get so amped up with the energy of that character, doing the hips and the arm-pumping thing. He screwed it up every night for eight weeks. Odenkirk and Pasquesi sat down with him and went over and over his lines. He was like, "This is hard. This is like learning the Our Father."

Then, on opening night, we were all worried he was going to screw it up—and he nailed it. When he came offstage, I said, "Why the hell did you finally get it tonight?"

"Big game," he said. "Coach is here." Del was in the audience.

FR. MATT FOLEY:

I was in the audience that night. When he said, "My name is Matt Foley, and I am a motivational speaker!" I was probably as red as a beet. I smiled and slid down a little further in my chair.

After the show we went and hung out in a bar for a time. Chris told me that he was never going to change the name, that it was always going to be Matt Foley. I'm honored by it still.

TOM GIANAS:

To this day, it's got to be the funniest thing I've ever seen. It never stopped making me laugh, and that's rare.

NATE HERMAN:

Chris was never captured in either movies or TV as good as he was on-stage. He was too explosive. He just seems flat in all those movies. It's like watching a large wild animal in a cage.

BOB ODENKIRK:

The Matt Foley sketch was basically the same every night, but he was always on the edge of that character, forgetting his lines, making up new ones, changing the blocking. He was never content to mimic last night's performance, which a lot of actors do. Sometimes, you try to make the performance fun and surprising again for the people onstage, who might be a little tired of it. Chris was doing a great show for the audience, but he was doing a completely different show for the rest of the cast. I can picture it in my head right now like it was yesterday. Night after night I'd stand there, four feet away from him, and just watch in complete awe.

HOLLY WORTELL:

I used to have to hold my cheeks with my hands because my face hurt from trying so hard not to laugh.

TIM MEADOWS:

Just watching him adjust his tie, or hitch up his pants, was enough to make you lose it. He'd get closer and closer to your face every night when he was saying his lines. I played the son. He started picking me up and tossing me up in the air, flipping me around. Then out of nowhere he'd kiss me. He just had a ball doing it.

JILL TALLEY:

He was so into the character that he'd be swinging his head around and his glasses would go flying off. Then he'd proceed to act like he couldn't see for five minutes, stumbling around looking for his glasses, and that would become the scene. Funny things would just happen organically. Even if he did the script word for word, it felt new every night.

BOB ODENKIRK:

I just remember thinking, no one else in the world will ever be able to do this character.

TIM MEADOWS:

After Farley left for *SNL*, Ian Gomez filled in for him. Every night he tried to do a different character to make that scene work, and he could never do it. Finally we said, "We gotta cut it."

TOM GIANAS:

The night that *SNL* came to scout him, he was nervous but confident. I remember saying to the cast, "The set's yours. You can put up whatever you want tonight." I wanted Chris's strongest pieces to go up so he'd have a good shot at it.

TIM MEADOWS:

We had a great show that night. And it was great for me. Chris and I worked so well together. That helped me get noticed, and I got hired at *SNL* about six months later.

JILL TALLEY:

He was nervous about *SNL*. He went back and forth with everyone. "What should I do?" He called his parents, his priest, the entire cast. We were all like, "What do you mean, 'What should I do?' You take it."

But he went round and round on it. Chris had his apartment, his bars, his church, and Second City right in this little four-block radius. That was his world, and I don't know that he ever really left it. He was scared to leave that behind, to leave his family, to leave everything he'd ever known.

KEVIN FARLEY:

I was at the airport when Chris left. Chris was crying, and Dad was crying. It was sad to watch. When you're from the Midwest, you don't really ask for the spotlight. You just have your Sunday Packers game and that's about as exciting as it gets. But I think Dad knew, we all knew, that after this nothing would ever be the same.

PAT FINN:

I got married the Saturday of Chris's first night on the show, and he was all bummed out that he wasn't going to get to be in the wedding. He called me early in the week and was just apologizing profusely because he had to miss it. "Maybe I can make it," he said. "Get them to put me on next week."

"No! You're doin' the show!" I said.

"I know. I sorta got to. I mean, I shouldn't ask if I could skip it, right?"

"Chris. C'mon. It's *Saturday Night Live!*"

"No, but it's your wedding."

And that's the great thing about Chris: *SNL* was his dream, but if he could have skipped that first show to make my wedding, he would have.

The night of the ceremony, we were all at the Hilton. At ten-thirty, with everyone out on the dance floor and the wedding in full swing, about ten of us, including me in my tux and my wife in her wedding dress, snuck out and went over to the bar in the hotel and watched Chris make his debut on *Saturday Night Live*. It was so strange, so surreal. We'd all grown up with this show, and Chris was the first one we'd ever known to join those ranks. Just a few weeks before, he'd been hanging out in our apartments, and now he'd made it.

CHAPTER 6

Super Fan

CONAN O'BRIEN, *writer:*

When Chris first got to the show, I met him hanging out in the conference room outside Lorne's office. He was dressed kind of like a kid going to a job interview. We chatted for a bit. I liked him right away.

I came in and out of that conference room several times during the day, and Chris was still waiting. Lorne would do that to you, make you wait a long time. At the end of the day, I was feeling bad for him, so I said, "Hey, kid. I'll show you around the studio," and I led him on kind of a mock tour where I pretended to be in charge of everyone. Chris fell in and started playing along with me. After that I left and went home. I came back to work the next day, and Chris was still waiting outside Lorne's office.

He had this energy, even when he was sitting there waiting for his meeting, rocking back and forth in his ill-fitting sports jacket with his tie all pulled off to the side. He seemed really earnest about doing the show. You just had the feeling that he was going to be a lot of fun and he belonged here. It was like the show—and I don't mean this to sound condescending—but it was like the show had been given this new golden retriever puppy.

From the day he arrived at *Saturday Night Live*, Chris Farley was already suffering comparisons to the other outrageous, larger-than-life figure in *SNL* history: John Belushi. When Chris died seven years later, eerily, at the same age as Belushi, those comparisons became gospel. In truth the two men shared far more differences than similarities. Still, in life and in death, Chris has borne the accusation of trying too hard to follow in Belushi's footsteps—an accusation with varying shades of truth. Yes, Chris looked up to and admired his predecessor, but whatever influence Belushi's ghost had on a young Chris Farley paled in comparison to the truly dominant forces in his life: his father, his family, and his faith. As far as drugs and alcohol went, Chris's bad habits were very much his own, seeded in his DNA and showing up at keg parties long before Belushi's demise. And if Chris followed Belushi in more positive ways, he was hardly alone.

In the comedy epidemic of the twentieth century, John Belushi was Patient Zero. The twin blockbuster successes of *Saturday Night Live* and *National Lampoon's Animal House* fundamentally changed the landscape of being funny. Movie studios began churning out huge blockbuster comedies like *Ghostbusters* and *Beverly Hills Cop*. Stars like Eddie Murphy, Mike Myers, and Jim Carrey beat a well-trod path from sketch-comedy cult status to Hollywood fame and fortune. Second City and ImprovOlympic grew from regional theaters into multiheaded corporate enterprises, churning out hundreds of aspiring comedians every year and spawning scores of other schools and venues across the country. Chris Farley and his friends were the first generation born into and weaned on that era. Their reverence for it and obsession with it was the common denominator that bound them together.

It all began in 1975 when producer Lorne Michaels assembled the original cast of *SNL* and took to the air live from New York every Saturday night. Following his departure in 1980, producer Dick Ebersol took over the show. Ebersol presided over some difficult years but also culti-vated the stardom of Eddie Murphy and assembled the all-star cast of Billy Crystal, Christopher Guest, and Martin Short.

In 1985, Lorne Michaels returned. The show needed new direction, and he needed a job. After a rocky start, he went back to the drawing board in 1986 and assembled the cast—Dana Carvey, Phil Hartman, Jan Hooks, Nora Dunn, Jon Lovitz, Kevin Nealon, Victoria Jackson, and Weekend Update anchor Dennis Miller—that would breathe new life into the show. Mike Myers came aboard in '89, but otherwise no visible changes where made, or needed, for the rest of the eighties.

Then, in the fall of 1990, a slow transition began to take place. Nora Dunn and Jon Lovitz left; Chris Farley and Chris Rock entered. Far younger than the established cast, the two became fast friends and soon found themselves sharing an office. Farley and Rock were the only per-formers added that fall. Tim Meadows, Chris's Second City cast mate, would come on board at midseason.

Back in the writers' room, Jim Downey, a freshman writer in *SNL*'s early years, had assumed the reins of head writer and producer. At the core of the writing staff was a group that had led the resurgence from the show's mid-eighties nadir: Robert Smigel, Jack Handey, Bob Odenkirk, and Conan O'Brien. Meanwhile, Tom Schiller, Al Franken, Tom Davis, and Marilyn Suzanne Miller—also veterans of the show's original writing staff—had all come back for an additional go-round. Added to that was a very young team of stand-up comedians—Adam Sandler, David Spade, and Rob Schneider—whose age and sense of humor would ultimately bring about a generational shift at the show. Both on camera and off, *SNL* found itself with a varsity squad and a junior-varsity squad. It was an odd mix of talent, but it worked well. For a while.

Chris arrived in New York in October. His older brother, Tom, had lived in the city for many years, and together they found an apartment for Chris on Seventh Avenue, just north of Times Square and right around the corner from the show's Studio 8H in Rockefeller Center. The canyons of midtown Manhattan were a striking contrast to the cozy comforts of

Chicago's Old Town, but Chris soon discovered the Carnegie Deli, St. Malachy's Church on West Forty-ninth Street, and a fine Irish pub called The Fiddler's Green, all within a small walking radius. He had made his home again, scarcely able to believe what that new home was. As many latter-day *SNL* writers and performers have said, anyone who works at the show is a fan of the show, first and foremost. And Chris was surely that.

ROBERT SMIGEL, *writer/coproducer:*

I was a coproducer as well as a writer, and so I got to go with Lorne to Chicago to scout the Second City show. Hiring Chris was probably the easiest casting decision Lorne's ever had to make. In all the shows I scouted before or after, I'd never seen anybody leap out at you from the stage the way Chris did. Lorne hired him the next day.

JIM DOWNEY, *head writer/producer:*

There was so much buzz about Farley that our checking him out was almost pro forma. It was kind of automatic.

LORNE MICHAELS, *executive producer:*

I'd had something of a concern that maybe he was too big, personality-wise, to play on television. Theatrically, he was sort of playing to the back of the house. But after we saw him, there really wasn't much doubt.

ROBERT SMIGEL:

Lorne invited me to be in on his meeting with Chris. Chris showed up, and he was in full altar-boy mode, lots of "yes, sirs" and bright-eyed alertness. He was so transparently on his best behavior that you kind of had to laugh and wonder if it was inversely proportional to his worst behavior. Lorne talked about the show and what would be expected of him, and

Chris just kept sweetly nodding his head in agreement. Lorne had been told, at that point, about Chris's problems. I don't remember exactly what he said, but he told Chris, in so many words, that it wouldn't be tolerated. He even said something to the effect of "We don't want another Belushi."

LORNE MICHAELS:

It wasn't presented to us that Chris had any sort of problem, just that he was still a little young and liked to party too much.

TOM FARLEY:

All the cast and writers were sort of strolling in over the course of that first week. Chris immediately gravitated to this younger, newer crowd of writers and actors: Rob Schneider, Adam Sandler, and David Spade. They were coming on as writers. The only two new cast members were Chris and Chris Rock. They got all the press.

DAVID SPADE, *cast member:*

I had done four shows as a writer/performer. Then it was summer break, and when I got back Farley and Rock came on as featured players. Sandler came about six months later.

I met Chris the first day, walking over from the Omni Berkshire, where *SNL* had put us up. I saw him downstairs, and I'd heard about him. We talked and then we walked over to 30 Rock together. I thought he was funny. He was a nice Wisconsin dude, a genuine, sweet guy. I was out from Arizona. I'm not really a bad guy. We just gravitated to hanging out all the time and stayed buddies ever since.

MARCI KLEIN, *talent coordinator:*

I first met him the day he started. He was wearing this English driving cap and looking very Irish. He was very quiet and deferential, very nervous, like I was the person in charge or something, which I thought was funny, because I wasn't. He would get so nervous; that was one of the things that was really charming about him.

CHRIS ROCK, *cast member:*

We both got hired the same day, which was probably one of the greatest days of my life. We were the new guys, and they threw us together. The funny thing was that everyone was worried about *me*—I lived in Brooklyn and didn't want to move to Manhattan, because I couldn't park on the street and I couldn't get a cab. I said it in the *Live from New York* book: Two guys named Chris both get hired on the same day and share an office. One's a black guy from Bed-Stuy and one's a white guy from Madison, Wisconsin. Now, which one is going to OD?

KEVIN FARLEY:

When he got the show it was sort of strange, kind of scary in a way. Chris always liked the camaraderie of Second City, so a high-pressure situation like *Saturday Night Live* seemed mean and cutthroat. Dad was nervous. We all were. Chris could barely flush the toilet. How was he going to handle fame and television and New York City?

TOM FARLEY:

I was working at Bear Stearns in those days, at Forty-sixth and Park. Chris and I went out to lunch one day, and afterward I had to go back to work. We were standing on Park Avenue, right where it goes into the Met Life Building. Chris asked me about some good places to go shopping. I pointed him in the direction of Fifth Avenue. Then he said, "Look, I don't have any money. I'm staying at this fancy hotel, and I've got this nice, big salary, but I haven't gotten paid yet."

So I went to a cash machine, got out $160, gave it to him, and went back to work. I got a call about a half hour later. "Uh, Tommy, I had a little problem," Chris said.

"What do you mean?" I asked.

"Well, I went up to Fifth Avenue like you told me and I was walking down the street and I saw these guys playing cards."

And I was like, oh no. "What did you do?" I said.

"Well, these guys were playing cards for money, and they were winning."

"Yeah, okay."

"And the guy looked at me and he said, 'Where's the card? Take a guess. How much you got, buddy?' And I said, 'I got $160.' And he said, 'Well, put it down.' "

"Let me guess, you lost the whole nut."

"Uh, yeah . . . can I get some more money?"

So I went and met him at the cash machine and said, "Don't do that again. Stay away from the guys playing three-card monte."

He said, "But I don't understand. How were all those other guys winning?"

"They were all part of the scam, Chris."

"Oh."

AL FRANKEN, *writer:*

Chris was very shy and self-effacing when he showed up. That never really changed too much, though he did get less shy. He was also one of these guys who came in with an incredible amount of respect for what had gone before him. He was just genuinely awed to be there, and wanted to know everything about the show. I don't want to name names, but some people would come in saying, "I was destined to be here! Get out of the way, old man!" That was not Chris.

CHRIS ROCK:

You could just tell he was funny. Normally you meet a guy, and you're automatically skeptical about him. You're basically not funny until proven otherwise. But there was something about Farley where you could tell he was funny when he said hi.

TOM FARLEY:

Chris called me up the first week he was there and said, "Hey, they're going to film me for the opening montage. Do you want to come down and watch?"

I said, "Sure. Where are you doing it?"

"Well, you can pick anywhere you want," he said, "so I was either going to do the steps of St. Patrick's Cathedral or McSorley's Ale House." Two very telling choices, and no question as to which one won out.

"Which is it going to be?" I asked.

"McSorley's."

So I met him down there at like two A.M. on a Tuesday night after it closed. We kept drinking beer after beer during the shoot. "Draining our props," as we called it. We were up till five in the morning.

My parents came into town for the first show. We had a blast showing them the whole New York thing. They stayed at the RIHGA Royal. We went to Gallagher's Steak House, which was Dad's favorite. Dad stayed in the hotel. He didn't go to the show. With his weight it was just too much trouble. So we all went to the dress rehearsal and then went back to the room to watch the live show together.

KEVIN FARLEY:

We were just excited as hell. It was sort of surreal, sitting there waiting for his first scene. Kyle MacLachlan was the host, and they did this *Twin Peaks* parody. Chris was the killer. He really didn't have anything to say, any real laugh lines in the sketch, but of course he found a way to milk a few laughs by giving a look or drawing a word out. It's strange to see your brother on national television. I just sat there going, "This is weird."

TOM FARLEY:

I remember walking out of Rockefeller Plaza after the first show on our way to the after party. There were all these limos lined up. Chris said, "Wow! Look at all those limos! Ain't that something?" Pause. "I wonder if we can get a cab."

"Chris, who do you think these limos are for?" I said.

"What do you mean?"

I saw some guy with a clipboard and walked over to him. "Is one of these cars for Chris Farley?" I asked.

"Yes, sir," he said. "Right over there."

"Wow," Chris said, "How did you know that?"

"Because that's how it works here."

MIKE SHOEMAKER, *producer:*

The first show he didn't have much, because nobody knew him to write for him at that point. But that always takes a while. We knew he was going to hit big, and he did it pretty quickly. The "Chippendales" piece was only his fourth show.

JIM DOWNEY:

The thing that suggested "Chippendales" was less Farley and more Patrick Swayze being the host. You had a guy who was sort of built like—to the extent that I notice these things—like a male stripper. And he obviously could dance; that was how he'd come up in show business.

The second element was that nothing made me laugh more than the band Loverboy, whose big hit was "Working for the Weekend." So you had Patrick Swayze, male stripper, you had Loverboy—just add Farley.

KEVIN NEALON, *cast member:*

I played one of the judges, and my experience was the same as anyone who's seen it on television. I can't even think of the word to describe it. Incredulous, maybe? I did everything I could to keep a straight face.

JIM DOWNEY:

We didn't know it was going to be as popular as it was. You never do. In read-through Chris is just sitting fully clothed at the table while Lorne reads stage directions. We didn't know until he did it at dress.

MIKE MYERS, *cast member:*

I knew in rehearsal that a star was born.

DOUG ROBINSON, *agent:*

Adam Venit and I were agents at CAA. We'd known about Chris from Chicago, and we had been talking to Marc Gurvitz at Brillstein about signing him. At CAA, you have to get a consensus from the entire group of agents if you want to sign someone. All we did was show everyone a video of the "Chippendales" sketch, and it was done. We signed him right then.

BOB ODENKIRK:

I didn't like the fact that the first thing he became known for was that Chippendales thing, which I hated. Fucking lame, weak bullshit. I can't believe anyone liked it enough to put it on the show. Fuck that sketch. He never should have done it.

TOM DAVIS, *writer:*

When you get laughs like that, there's nothing wrong with what's going on onstage.

ROBERT SMIGEL:

It was a fantastic sketch—I'd say it's one of the funniest sketches in the history of the show—because of the way Downey wrote it. If the sketch had been written that a fat guy was trying out for the Chippendales and everyone was making fun of him or acting like it was crazy, then yes, it would have been just a cheap laugh at the expense of a fat guy. But the way it was constructed, with everyone sincerely believing that this guy has a shot, the judges studiously scribbling notes on his dance moves, that's what makes it original and completely hysterical.

JIM DOWNEY:

My overriding note to Chris was, "You're not at all embarrassed here. They're telling you, 'Our audience tends to prefer a more sculpted, lean physique as opposed to a fat, flabby one,' but your feelings are never hurt. You're processing that like it's good information. Like you're going to learn from this and take it to your next audition."

Of all the pieces I've done it's one of the most commented upon, and that's of course because of Farley. I can't take any credit for that except casting him. He was also very nimble and a good dancer, which made it impossible to feel like it was just a freak show.

Later in that show, Jack Handey had written a sketch about a mouse-trap-building class. It was one of those group scenes where everybody has a very small part to play. Farley had only one little bit to do, but he had so won the audience over with "Chippendales" that he got the biggest reaction in the piece. They had already adopted him as their own.

CHRIS ROCK:

"Chippendales" was a weird sketch. I always hated it. The joke of it is basically, "We can't hire you because you're fat." I mean, he's a fat guy, and you're going to ask him to dance with no shirt on. Okay. That's enough. You're gonna get that laugh. But when he stops dancing you have to turn it in his favor. There's no turn there. There's no comic twist to it. It's just fucking mean. A more mentally together Chris Farley wouldn't have done it, but Chris wanted so much to be liked.

I wanted to be liked, but I had no problem saying something was racist and I wasn't doing it. Imagine if they'd had me in that sketch and then said at the end, "Oh, we can't hire you. You're a nigger." Would I have done a sketch like that? If I had, ten years later I'd want to shoot myself.

That was a weird moment in Chris's life. As funny as that sketch was, and as many accolades as he got for it, it's one of the things that killed him. It really is. Something happened *right then*.

TIM MEADOWS:

You had to prove yourself to get airtime and to get your sketches on. It was obvious after "Chippendales" that he was going to be one of the standouts. I can't remember too many read-throughs where he didn't have something to do.

TOM DAVIS:

During the early read-throughs, I was shocked when I heard him struggle to read scripts he was seeing for the first time. He struggled with reading in the way of someone who was not schooled well. But on the stage he was brilliant, absolutely brilliant. He was a star. I saw it the first day he walked in the office. There was some quality that shone brightly. Despite his shortcomings as someone who hadn't honed his skills yet, it was clear that he had the raw talent to work on that show successfully, which he did.

ALEC BALDWIN, *host:*

In the cast of *Saturday Night Live* you have people who've come from improv troupes, and you have people who've done a lot of stand-up comedy. You can distinguish the real actors from the stand-ups, and Chris was a good actor, a very good actor. He could have had a career for the rest of his life. Fat, thin, old, young, he was a really talented guy.

JIM DOWNEY:

Farley was like an old-school cast member. The first cast was a repertory company. They weren't comedians; they were funny actors, and they were called upon to do lots of different things. In the nineties, we got those with more of a stand-up background. And that's not to knock the stand-ups. Nobody has ever made me laugh harder than David Spade. But the danger is that a stand-up can do an absolutely devastating ten-minute audition, but that might not help you two years later when you need a Senator Harkin in your congressional hearings piece. As a general rule, we've always done better with the old Dan Aykroyd types.

LORNE MICHAELS:

I used to say that he was the son that John Belushi and Dan Aykroyd never had. When Chris was a kid, he used to tape his eyebrow up to try and figure out how Belushi did it.

TOM SCHILLER, *writer/short-film director:*

It was very shortly after he arrived that he asked me about Belushi. I could tell by the gleam in his eye that he was very excited to find out as much as he could. I don't recall exactly what I told him. I guess I told him a lot. But there was an immediate bond, and he wanted to be in one of my films to take part in that heritage.

MARILYN SUZANNE MILLER, *writer:*

Chris would come up to me and say, "You knew John. What was he like? How did he dress? Just tell me everything you knew about him." He just had this reverence, and it was always about real minutiae.

MIKE SHOEMAKER:

He always idolized Belushi, but when I looked at him I saw more of Aykroyd and Murray.

TIM MEADOWS:

Chris would always throw in bits or accents inspired by the older guys, more Bill Murray than anyone. He stole his "Da Bears" character from Aykroyd. Todd O'Connor, that's basically Aykroyd's Irwin Mainway, that cheesy salesman who sold all the dangerous toys.

ROBERT SMIGEL:

I had moved to Chicago in 1982 to take improv classes with the Second City Players Workshop. Today it seems you can take them anywhere, but back then that was the only place to go.

I was always a huge sports guy, and I wanted to see all the iconic Chicago sports landmarks, so not long after I moved there I went by myself to a Cubs game at Wrigley Field. I just walked up to the box office about a half hour before game time and said, "Give me the best ticket you've got." It was right behind the dugout, so I was pretty excited.

But during the game I noticed that the fans in the crappiest seats—the bleachers—were the ones having all the fun. I got a better look at them outside the ballpark after the game. They had their Cubs T-shirts on over their collared, button-down shirts; it was like a uniform. They all seemed to wear aviator sunglasses, which had been out of style for a good five years. And they all had these big walrus mustaches, which I think to them were some sort of symbol of virility, probably passed on from Dick Butkus to Mike Ditka. They had a swagger to them, even though at the time all their teams pretty much sucked, which made the whole thing funnier.

Years later, at *Saturday Night Live*, there was a writers' strike that shut us down after February. Bob Odenkirk and I decided to go back to Chicago and do a stage show we'd talked about. The original sketch as we did it then was three of these guys sitting on a porch, talking about the Bears. It was more absurd, just guys talking about stuff and the conversation always going back to "and I'll tell ya who else will be riding high come January. A certain team known as . . . *da Bears.*" It was a hit in Chicago, but we never thought about doing it on *SNL*. Too local, we figured.

Then in 1991, Joe Mantegna hosted, and Bob suggested we do it. To make it more accessible, we set it in a sports bar and made it a parody of the Chicago sportswriters show, only with these ridiculous fans and their outrageous predictions given as sincere, cogent game analysis. Their idea of predicting an upset was to say that the Bears would only win by thirty points, instead of seven hundred.

Jim Downey is from Joliet, Illinois, and he was really insistent that the Chicago accents be dead-on. He felt that was really important to the joke. The only person in the cast who could really do the accent was Chris. Mike Myers could do a pretty decent accent, because he'd lived there awhile. Downey actually thought my accent was the best, and he wanted me to play the third guy.

So we did that original sketch with Mantegna. It did well, and that, I thought, was it. But it caught on in Chicago. A popular deejay named Jonathon Brandmeier played excerpts from it all the time. By spring the Bulls were headed for their first championship, and, coincidentally, George Wendt was hosting our season finale. It made sense to do another one. It was fine, but in Chicago it had a life of its own. "Da Bulls" was suddenly the rallying cry of the team. It's funny, because I had never thought of it as a catchphrase. In the scripts, it was always spelled "the Bulls"; the "da" just came out in the delivery.

That summer in Chicago, Michael Jordan was honored by Comic Relief. George, Chris, and I were invited to do the Super Fans onstage with Jordan at this benefit at the Chicago Theater. Jordan had a lot of fun doing it and got comfortable with the idea that he could do comedy. That led to him hosting the season opener in the fall, where we did another one. It just took off from there. I think we did eight or nine in total.

It was fun to do on the show, but we had even more fun doing things at Chicago events. Chris and I started doing predictions every Thursday night for the local Chicago NBC affiliate. We'd tape them via satellite from 30 Rock in New York. Chris's managers never liked the idea of his doing these Chicago appearances if he wasn't getting paid, so he only did a few. I always thought that was ridiculous. Some of them were once-in-a-lifetime experiences.

When the Bears made the playoffs, in December of '91, Chris, George Wendt, and I actually stood at the fifty-yard line at Soldier Field and made a pregame speech. Half the fans went nuts and half were just weirded out, I think. Then they let us stay and watch the game on the field. I felt like a moron wearing my costume out there during the game, but I wasn't going to pass up the chance to watch from the sidelines.

At halftime they had a contest where they let kids try and make a field goal from a tee on the ten-yard line. Quite spontaneously, they asked us if we wanted to participate. We said sure, and suddenly on the PA it was, "Ladies and gentlemen, we direct your attention to our additional contestants."

We let Chris take the first kick. He lined up to make the field goal, took a running start and then slipped and nosedived right into the mud. The whole stadium went crazy. George and I didn't know what to do. We'd let the funniest guy go first, and now we had no way to top it. I figured the only thing I could do was to try and actually make the kick. So, with beer in hand, I lined up and kicked the ball and somehow I made it. The crowd loved it.

Then it was George's turn, and by now he'd figured out a topper. He had Chris snap the ball to me. Then instead of placing the ball down, we ran a "fake" and I lateraled to George. I "blocked" Chris, and George ran it in for a touchdown, as the announcer called it on the PA. That was just so much fun. The stadium was packed, and everyone was cheering and going crazy for a fat guy running ten yards. It was one of those perfect moments in life, where all your hard work comes together in a way that's better than anything you could have imagined.

TIM MEADOWS:

It was a great time during those first couple of years. We were young. We all had money, we lived in New York, and we were on *Saturday Night Live*. We would always have dinner after the read-throughs. Saturday nights after the show we would hang out. We all played golf. We'd go to movies. We got invited to a lot of stuff, basketball games, baseball games. We all immediately bonded with each other.

CHRIS ROCK:

We just had fun. There was a lot of McDonald's, a lot of going out to eat, a lot of watching MTV. We'd watch the musical guests rehearse. "Let's run down and see Pearl Jam." We got to see a lot of the grunge stuff before it really took off; all those bands made their first appearance on *SNL*.

KEVIN NEALON:

More and more, the older cast members started to realize we had our own little west wing going on with Spade, Farley, and those other guys. You'd go over and there'd be *Playboy* magazines lying around and it'd be a bit of a mess. They'd all be talking about what models they'd gotten laid with, and then you went into Dana or Phil's office and they'd be talking about their 401(k).

DAVID SPADE:

We would just hang out and get in trouble. We shared an office, me and Chris. You'd have to go through our office to get to another little office for

Rock and Sandler. There was always Smigel around, or whoever else. We were all back there, screwing around and staying up late, trying to write and think of ideas and brainstorm and do whatever you gotta do to stay alive on that show.

MARCI KLEIN:

You just spend so many hours there, and so much time of your life. We were all sort of the same age. We were all always together. It's just inevitable that this group forms. We go to the party, then hang out at somebody's apartment, and the next thing I know, it's six A.M. and Chris and Adam are crashing in my living room.

TOM FARLEY:

The guys at *SNL*, they were like Chris's new rugby team. Not nearly as wild but a lot of fun, and they gave Chris that fraternity atmosphere that he always thrived in. And then, somewhere along that first year on the show, Chris started dating Lorne's assistant, this girl named Erin Maroney. Erin was great, just a lot of fun. And I thought it was the start of a whole new thing for Chris, a really good direction. It was the first time I'd seen him in a real relationship, you know, ever.

DAVID SPADE:

We'd always be outside Lorne's office waiting for whatever, so we had a lot of interaction with Erin. Chris would hide underneath her desk, and he'd pop out and surprise her when she got back. He flirted with her all the time, and it paid off. They started dating. Erin was very cute, very sweet.

She went back to Wisconsin with him once, and she'd tell hilarious stories about what it was like around that dinner table. She's kind of a preppy East Coast girl and there she is with seven Farleys fighting over chicken and steak, and the mother's passing around a "yuck bag" where they throw all their extra bones and corncobs. I don't think I ever would have put those two together, but I think she saw through all the other stuff to see that he was a good guy and a fun guy, and as history shows sometimes that's enough.

TOM ARNOLD, *friend:*

Chris was in love with Erin. He talked about her all the time. She was very smart. Actually, she had the best line ever. They were all flying back from Los Angeles to New York, and Chris kept coming up and talking to Lorne, sucking up. So, after the third or fourth time he came by sucking up to Lorne, she turned to him and said, "Pace yourself, Tubby. It's a long flight." I think that's why he loved her. A funny woman who's attractive *and* smart, now that's what you want.

TODD GREEN, *friend, Edgewood High School:*

Chris really wanted to end up with an Irish Catholic girl that his family would approve of—and Erin fit the bill. Despite the fame, and despite the access he had to all these beautiful women, he really just longed for, as he would say, "a nice Irish gal." He was in love with the idea of them together.

TIM MEADOWS:

It was the first time I'd ever seen him in a serious relationship. It was surprising. I could see why he was attracted to her. They both had a similar sense of humor. She was also very cute, just had a really sweet personality, and she's really funny. I really liked that time of his life, because it was nice seeing him with someone who cared about him. He had someone who was actually going to make a home for him.

LORNE MICHAELS:

He saw in Erin someone who liked him for who he was. They would go to mass together on Sundays. He took her home to meet his parents, and I know she did the same. Her mother loved Chris. I think they just genuinely liked and cared for each other. But it was always more of a brother-sister thing than a boyfriend-girlfriend thing, from my perspective.

TIM MEADOWS:

Basically, that first year, we only had each other. And we all had one thing in common: We couldn't believe that we were doing this show. The people from *Saturday Night Live*, they were our heroes. It's like if you dreamed of being a Major League Baseball player and you got your chance to do it—only there's really only one baseball team in the country, and they've drafted you.

After the first season wrapped in May, we had this party at the restaurant downstairs at Rockefeller Center. A bunch of us went back up to the office for a little after party. Then, about four in the morning, Farley and I were both leaving at the same time. We were waiting for the elevator, and he said, "Timmy, can you believe this is our life?"

I said, "Chris, I think that every day."

Then he just grabbed me, and hugged me. He couldn't believe where his life was going.

CHAPTER 7

The Place in Alabama

LOVERBOY, *band:*

Everybody's workin' for the weekend.

Everybody wants a new romance.

Everybody's goin' off the deep end.

Everybody needs a second chance, oh.

C hris Farley's life was going in two wildly different directions at once. With "Chippendales," "Super Fans," and a number of solid turns in supporting roles, he had established himself as one of the standouts at *Saturday Night Live*. But his problem with drugs and alcohol had worsened severely. Around the office, Chris was always happy and hardworking, determined and focused. The sloppy, crazy party guy showed up at social functions here and there, but he was no longer a nightly fixture. Chris, knowing what was at stake, had learned how to hide his problem. And safely hidden, it festered.

The summer following his first year on the show, Chris returned to Chicago and dropped by Second City to see his old friends. He had clearly been using and was in no condition to perform. The cast pleaded with him not to go onstage, but during the improv set he burst out from behind the curtain anyway. The audience greeted him with a huge cheer. But as he began to stumble his way through a scene, his inebriation was obvious to everyone. People began to boo. After one scene, an audience member yelled, "Get the drunk off the stage." Even in his failed stand-up comedy routines at Marquette, Chris had at least come off as affable and good-natured. He had never suffered wholesale rejection quite like this. The crowd's reaction cut deep.

On June 16, 1991, worried that the management at *SNL* would hear of the incident, Chris checked himself into the Hazelden recovery facility in Center City, Minnesota. It was the first time he sought treatment for his addiction.

Red Arrow camp counselor Fred Albright once observed, in his unique Wisconsin vernacular, that "Chris was extremely complex, and yet as easy to understand as a ripe watermelon." The doctors and therapists at Hazelden, in somewhat more sophisticated language, came to the same conclusion. Their diagnosis of Chris would come as no surprise to anyone who'd ever spent five minutes with the boy:

> *Chris's inclination is to be compliant. . . . Whenever Chris has been confronted for not meeting unit expectations he has apologized and assured that this will not happen again, [but he] does not appear to be willing to fully accept responsibility for his behavior. . . . Chris allows his fear to dictate the terms of his recovery. . . . Chris has identified that his use of humor serves the function of diverting attention from issues that may be painful. . . . that it's with humor that his family deals with conflict and pain. . . . Chris sees his life and his drinking as a benefit to his work as a comedian, and this may complicate his motivation to get help for these issues. . . . [Aftercare issues include] compulsive overeating, possible obsessive compulsive behavior. . . .*

Diagnosing the problem was easy. But unlocking it and treating it would prove to be a complex proposition indeed. After twenty-eight days, Chris checked out of Hazelden, but the program had accomplished little, and his destructive behaviors quickly resumed.

That fall, Chris returned to New York for the 1991–1992 season, his second, on *Saturday Night Live*. He moved from his apartment near Times Square to a place near Riverside Drive on Manhattan's Upper West Side. Along with Chris Rock, Chris was promoted from featured player to repertory player, and escalators in his contract pushed his salary from $4,500 to $6,500 per show. That year, Adam Sandler, David Spade, and Rob Schneider graduated from the writers' room to join Tim Meadows as full-fledged featured players.

Despite the unusual influx of so many new performers, *Saturday Night Live* still belonged very much to its senior members. Kevin Nealon took over the Weekend Update desk from the departing Dennis Miller; Mike Myers's long-running "Wayne's World" sketch had spawned a hit movie; and Phil Hartman and Dana Carvey would dominate the coming election year with their lauded takes on Arkansas governor Bill Clinton, President George H. W. Bush, and feisty contender Ross Perot.

Chris, always happy to be a team player, continued to do his best in small, supporting parts, such as Todd O'Connor in the "Super Fans" sketches and as Jack Germond in the *McLaughlin Group* parodies. He took on starring roles in now-classic sketches like Robert Smigel's "Schmitt's Gay." And veteran writers Jim Downey and Tom Davis saw a unique side of Chris underneath all of his wild-man antics and brought it brilliantly to life in Chris's signature piece, "The Chris Farley Show."

Through all of this, most of the cast and crew of *Saturday Night Live* failed to see the true nature of Chris's spiraling addiction. But over time, deep cracks began to appear in the wall he had built up between his personal and professional lives. It soon became readily apparent to all that Chris Farley was headed for a serious reckoning.

TOM DAVIS:

Saturday Night Live had really changed. The smell of marijuana no longer hit you when you stepped off the elevator; that sort of thing just wasn't tolerated anymore. However, Fiddler's Green was a bar down on Forty-eighth Street. It was the nearest watering hole to the seventeenth floor. Not literally. There was the Rainbow Room and one other really high-end restaurant that sort of frowned on long-haired, bearded comedy writers dashing in for a quick Rémy Martin. But Fiddler's Green was an Irish bar, like a real Irish bar. A lot of NBC people, mainly the union guys, they'd go there to drink. So it became a convenient place to duck out to. Around ten-thirty at night, when everyone else was eating candy bars and drinking coffee, you'd excuse yourself, grab your copy of *The Gulag Archipelago*, say you had to take a dump, and then sprint up Forty-eighth Street to get booze.

Chris discovered this fairly early on, and so I had the experience, on more than one occasion, of running into him there. I'd see him doing shots of tequila, literally throwing the shots back in a way that made me cringe. I like drinking, but you can't drink like that. He was going for oblivion. On one such night I told him, "Chris, don't go back to the office. Don't let them see you like this."

"Okay," he said.

Twenty minutes later we were both back in the office. He was obviously drunk in front of these younger writers, and it was funny to them. He would entertain them and they would all laugh. But if you were aware of what was going on, it wasn't so funny. He would slap himself so hard that you could see the mark on his face, and that would get a laugh from those writers, but I would see the mark on his face, and I just saw disaster.

DAVID SPADE:

We saw him drinking, but then everyone was drinking, so who cares? I started to notice it was a problem more when I'd leave him at night. I'm a lightweight when it comes to that. I couldn't keep up, and he'd get angry when I'd leave him at the bar. He'd start getting mad that I wouldn't stay and drink with him. Like, really mad.

Then I started noticing that when we would walk down the street, strangers at sidewalk bars and restaurants would recognize us from the show and go, "Hey, Spade and Farley! What's up! Come and have a drink with us."

And Chris would go, "Okay."

I'd be like, "Are you kidding?"

Even the people at the table, who'd been half joking, they were like, "Wait, he's actually coming over?"

And so he would go drink with random people. Then the drugs kicked in and it escalated.

TIM MEADOWS:

In Chicago, everybody socialized and drank at a bar after the show. And that's just part of Chicago; there's a bar on every corner. In New York, he made more money and the drugs got harder. That was the big difference.

CHRIS ROCK:

He got high and we didn't, so he stayed away a lot.

STEVEN KOREN, *writer:*

I had a different perspective than most. I saw things that other people didn't see. I eventually became a writer, but when Chris got to the show I was still a receptionist. I would answer the phones until eight or nine at night and then stay late and write jokes to try and get them onto Weekend Update. Sometimes I was there until four, five in the morning. I'd be hunched over a desk in some dark office and I'd hear the elevator, and Chris would come in with some shady-looking characters, people I'd never seen before. They'd go back into some office, turn on some music, and I wouldn't see or hear from them for a couple of hours. I didn't know what was going on, nor was it my place to say anything.

Then there was one incident where an office got messed up, and I got yelled at the next day. They thought I'd done it because I was the only person there that late. Turned out it was Chris and a bunch of these people. That was really the beginning. That was when I was like, oh, he's doing *other* things, beyond the norm.

KEVIN NEALON:

I remember seeing him being a little more sweaty in sketches. His moods would change more. When he first showed up he was that lovable Chris guy. Then you started to see sides of him that were a little more irritated, more impatient.

TIM MEADOWS:

Tom Davis was the first one at the show to say something.

TOM DAVIS:

And when Tom Davis is the one doing the intervention on you, that's when you know you're in trouble.

TIM MEADOWS:

He got me and Sandler and Spade and we all went over to Chris's dressing room. We sat him down and said, "You're hurting yourself, and you need to stop." We were young. We didn't know much about interventions. We just told him that we loved him and we didn't want to watch him doing this to himself, and that it was time to grow up.

TODD GREEN:

Chris and I had stayed close through college, and I moved to New York about nine months after he did. We tried to do an intervention in New York pretty early on. Me, Tom Farley, and Kevin Cleary all went to lunch at P.J. Clarke's. We tried to say to him that we loved him and we were worried about him, and he just didn't want to hear any of it. It was very confrontational. "Who are you guys to judge me?" That sort of thing. It wasn't easy. Kevin, Mike Cleary's brother, was the other big part of Chris's life in New York. Kevin died on 9/11, but in those days the three of us were always together.

MIKE CLEARY, *friend, Edgewood High School:*

Kevin was Chris's sounding board for the first three years of *SNL*. They were incredibly close. Kevin and I never went a day without talking to each other at least once, and so the few times we did go two, three days without talking, it was always because of Chris. And Kevin would never, ever talk about it. All he'd say was, "I had to deal with something."

TOM FARLEY:

Any time I was called in to bail out Chris, Kevin Cleary was there. I couldn't deal with Chris without Kevin, but I know Kevin bailed Chris out several times without me. He was the guy. He kept the pieces together.

Right before Christmas during Chris's second year on the show, Erin Maroney called me and said I needed to come down to Chris's apartment. He'd trashed the place. Kevin and I went over, and it was a mess. Chris stumbled out and was like, "What's up with you guys?" Trying to play it off like it was nothing.

Erin had also called Al Franken, so he came as well. Franken had a talk with him, but he was still pretty out of it. Franken also said he knew some people at Smithers, a rehab facility in New York, that he could get

Chris in there. But I called my dad, and he said, "Just get him home. Get two tickets and fly him home and we'll deal with it here."

I got him up to my apartment in Westchester. My wife drove us to the airport. This was on a Sunday. I got him on the plane, this little puddle jumper. He immediately said to the stewardess, "Gimme a screwdriver." So I gave him one. That's what they tell you to do. Give them anything they want to keep them pacified until you can get them to the rehab facility, to avoid a confrontation. So he drank the screwdriver and then just crashed out in his seat. There were some mechanical problems, and we sat out on the tarmac for an hour. He was out cold the whole time. Finally, they came on and said the flight wasn't going anywhere any time soon, and we all had to deplane back to the terminal. I woke him up and dragged him down the stairs out onto the tarmac. He looked around and said, "Damn, looks just like Westchester."

"Chris, it is Westchester. We haven't gone anywhere."

"Oh."

We went back in. There was no bar in this tiny airport, so there was nothing to do but sit. Chris started getting loud, like, "What's going on here? Why are we just sitting here?" And I kept trying to keep him quiet. We waited for another hour, and then finally they canceled the flight entirely. I called my wife. She came back to pick us up. After we got home, she took our daughter and said, "Look, I'm going to my sister's while you figure this out."

So she took off, and Chris went inside and just crashed in our bed to sleep it off. It was a long, long night. I called home and told my parents he'd be a day late. I took him back to the airport the next day, but I didn't go with him. I had to go back to work, so I just put him on the plane. I figured by that point he could fly home by himself.

Chris rolled off the plane in Madison, and of course the first thing out of my dad's mouth: "Hey! You look great! That a new blazer?" No acknowledgment of the problem. No discipline. No nothing. Refused to deal with it. It was only at my mother's insistence that he agreed to check him in to the local hospital for a few days, and then, after Christmas, after the incident at the hotel, they sent him back to Hazelden.

KEVIN FARLEY:

Around Christmas, me and my girlfriend were in Chicago, and we went out with Chris and Robert Smigel. They'd just done the halftime show at the Bears game at Soldier Field. We went out to the Chop House, and Chris was getting into it pretty hard. He was just ripping it up. Smigel eventually left, because Chris was too much to handle. I took him back to his room at the Westin Hotel. I said, "Chris, just go to bed. Let's just go to bed and sleep this off." And I left him in his room, assuming that he would stay there.

HOLLY WORTELL:

Chris called me up and said, "Come and meet me at Carly's." So I went and met him. That night he got really drunk really fast. People around us were starting to leave. It wasn't fun anymore. It was trouble. We got out onto Wells Street and I said, "Chris, where are you staying?"

He told me his hotel, which was downtown. Even if I'd told the cab-driver where to go, I doubt Chris could have made it back. So I went with him and got him up to his room. I didn't think I could leave him alone, so I said, "Can you call your brother? Where is he?"

"I don't know."

Then Chris got into the minibar, taking out all the little bottles and just shooting them. I yelled, *"Chris, stop it!"*

"No!"

He downed a few more of them, and then he looked up at me and sort of lunged at me. I stepped aside, but his momentum kept him careening forward. Now, we were about fifteen stories up in this high-rise hotel, and the room had these large picture windows that started about four feet up, went all the way to the ceiling and ran the whole width of the room. Under the window was this waist-high radiator. Chris ran smack into the plate-glass window and smashed right through it. His body was hanging out at a ninety-degree angle, and if not for this radiator that caught him at his waist, he would have crashed right through and fallen to the street below.

He hung there for a few seconds. Then he lurched back in, and I screamed—his arm was sliced open all the way from his shoulder to his wrist.

And at that moment I sort of lost all my emotions. I said, "Chris, we have to go to the hospital right now." I walked over to the phone, I dialed the hotel operator, told them there'd been an accident in one of the rooms and they needed to call an ambulance. I grabbed Chris and said, "Let's go."

"I want to put my jacket on first," he said.

"No, let's go."

"I wanna put my jacket on!"

So I said okay, helped him put his jacket on, we walked out, got in the elevator, went downstairs, and there were three security guys waiting for us. They hadn't called an ambulance, because they said they didn't know exactly what the situation was. I said, "Well, someone's been hurt, and we need one right now! I could sue this whole hotel!"

I walked outside and hailed a cab. We got in, and I said, "Northwestern Hospital. Emergency room. Immediately."

We took off and drove as fast as we could to the hospital. I remember the last block was a one-way going the wrong way. The cabbie stopped and turned and looked at me, and I said, *"Just go."*

He took off going the wrong way on this street, did a U-turn, and got us to the emergency room. I got Chris out, took him in, and did what I could to fill out the paperwork to get him admitted. Someone came up to me and said, "Isn't that the guy from *Saturday Night Live*?"

I said, "Yes. Please keep this quiet and tell the next shift to keep it quiet."

"Absolutely."

I sat there for a while. Then I asked if I could see him. They were calling in a specialist to look at him, but they said I could go in and visit first. I walked into his room, and the curtains were drawn on either side of his bed. I pulled them aside and looked in and he was lying there. His arm was laid out and the muscle was just hanging open. With his other hand he was just lifting up the flap of skin and poking around and looking inside. I told him to stop. He was still inebriated, and obviously in some state of shock.

The doctors came in. I went back to the waiting room and called the family. Then, when they started to arrive, I went home.

KEVIN FARLEY:

Holly called, and I went to see him. He was sitting there, still hammered, with his arm all bandaged up. He had already tried to sneak out of the hospital that morning to go get a bottle of vodka. I looked him in the eye and said, "Chris, you can't do this anymore. You've got to sober up. It's time to sober up."

* * *

After slicing his arm open in Chicago, Chris agreed to go back to rehab, but it was a brief visit. He returned to New York—too soon, in the eyes of many—to get back to work on the rest of the *SNL* season. He joined an outpatient program, but used and manipulated the system beyond the point of any real effectiveness. Chris's near-death experience in the hotel may not have opened his eyes to the full extent of the problem, but it did open plenty of others'. When he returned to New York, his arm tied up in stitches and swathed in bandages, his friends and his family could ignore the problem no longer.

TOM FARLEY:

When I walked into his apartment that Christmas and saw that it was trashed, that was the first time I woke up to the reality of the problem. I was a big drinker, and what had brought my behavior under control was having a wife and settling down; she just wouldn't tolerate it. And here

Chris had this really nice girlfriend. They seemed to have a nice relationship. When I saw that she wasn't doing the same for him, that's when I realized his problem was of a whole different order.

Mom had known for a while. She saw it way before everyone, but after that night, seeing his apartment and putting him on the plane, that's when I started going over to Mom's camp.

JOHN FARLEY:

No one educated the rest of the family for a long time, and we didn't educate ourselves. I've got seven years sober now, but at the time? Recovery? What was that? I didn't know. I was chugging beers right alongside Chris, saying, "Gee, sucks for you." It was like Chris had a net thrown over him, and he was taken away from the party, but the party just kept on going.

KEVIN FARLEY:

The first step is to recognize it and to talk about it, and when Chris almost went out the window we at least started to talk about it. We all acknowledged that Chris had a problem. Except for Dad. He would never even mention the incident. And of course there was no discussion that Dad's drinking might be a problem. Never.

Then, it's one thing to talk about it. It's another thing to do something about it.

CHARNA HALPERN:

I got a phone call from Chris's manager, and he said, "I know that you have some kind of hold on Chris. You gotta talk to him. And you gotta talk to his family, because we don't know what to do anymore."

So I called Mr. Farley and said, "We've really got to help Chris. When he comes home, he can't drink. And you can't drink, either, because it's so much a part of your relationship."

And Mr. Farley said, "I don't have to quit drinking. I'm not the one with the problem. Del Close stopped drinking. If he managed to do it, Chris is gonna have to do it."

"Yes, but he can't," I said. "Maybe we can help him if we all stop drinking."

"I'm not gonna do that."

FR. MATT FOLEY:

You liked Mr. Farley. You really liked the guy, but his world was very black and white. He was very caring, but there was the right way and the wrong way with him. There was no middle ground.

Growing up, we were always told you can be critical inside the home, but don't ever bring it out in the street. That's an Irish Catholic thing, a clan thing. In Chris's case that aversion to dealing with matters openly would be even more multiplied, because if Chris had an eating and a drinking problem, that would mean somebody else in the room had an eating and a drinking problem.

TOM FARLEY:

Chris was sent back to rehab, but it was really more of a quick fix. Get him in, patch him up, and send him back on the road. Nothing was really accomplished by it. But when he went back to the show in January with his arm covered in bandages, it was a wake-up call for everyone else, too. Nobody could hide from the problem anymore.

TOM DAVIS:

The story was that he'd gone through a plate-glass door, not a high-rise hotel window. That story was accepted at the time, because, well, going through a plate-glass door is bad enough on its own.

Chris knew that he had fucked up and that he was going to have to answer questions about what had happened. He was not unintelligent. He was very aware of all these forces swirling around him. Rather than have rumors floating around, he chose to reveal the problem to us, to go on the offensive about it and try and make a joke out of it.

He came into the writers' room and took his shirt off and went "Behold!" doing this shticky, horror-movie kind of thing. We all saw the Frankensteinian stitches up his arm—and nobody laughed. It was horrific. It was maybe the first time that those young guys didn't give Chris a laugh when he wanted it. We were all just like, "Holy shit . . . oh, fuck."

JIM DOWNEY:

Farley always reminded me of the lyrics to that old Irish wake song, "The Parting Glass": "All the harm e'er I've done, alas! it was to none but me." That was Farley. I don't think he knowingly ever hurt another person in his life, and, quite honestly, the drug problems are not remotely the first thing that I think of when it comes to Farley; I think of him being goofy and funny around the office. I didn't notice that it affected his work at all.

MIKE SHOEMAKER:

It was never a problem in the office, and it was never to the point where it was an embarrassment, ever. You knew that he was drinking, but he was always functional. And there were never problems Saturday night when the show went to air.

TIM MEADOWS:

The only time he would drink too much and it would be noticeable and annoying was at the party after the show every week. And he was never an angry drunk, which is kind of an easier drunk to diagnose. That person obviously needs help. But Chris would just get sloppy and tell you how much he loved you, and he wanted to hug you and make you laugh. What I think, and this is just my opinion, is that he would drink when he got home after work every night, after read-through and after rehearsal.

TODD GREEN:

He may not have let on anything up at 30 Rock, but those times in New York, those were rough. He was over at Kevin Cleary's a lot, either trying to hold it together or coming off a binge. I know Erin dealt with a lot of the fallout, too.

KEVIN FARLEY:

Chris wanted to marry Erin. He even bought a ring. And she was just a super person, had a lot of patience. But she couldn't handle the ups and downs. I think she was probably scared to death. Who wouldn't be?

TOM FARLEY:

I couldn't tell you exactly when, but at some point the relationship was just over. She was staying with him a lot, and then she wasn't anymore. He'd gotten that ring, but I don't know if he ever even proposed. Ultimately that was never in the cards.

TODD GREEN:

Erin was so young then. I mean, she was a kid. But she really tried to help him. I remember going up to her parents' place in Westchester—me, Kevin Cleary, and her—and trying to figure out how we could help Chris. We just talked and looked at each other like, "What are we going to do?" Not a whole lot was accomplished.

It's funny. Mrs. Farley would call me and say, "If there's anything you can do to help him . . ." And, naturally, I would do anything, but you're so ill equipped at that age. The gravity of it is enormous and really beyond your understanding. You just think, *I'm* his friend and *I'm* different and *I* can get through to him.

Labor Day after his second year on the show, Chris and I went up to Newport and stayed with his cousin. He was holding it together, but I knew he was using. He cleaned up a bit, and we went into town, where we ate at the Black Pearl, which is the restaurant where his dad and his mom went on their first date. Chris called his parents to tell them he was there, and he was really happy about it. He seemed leveled out, and I was trying to rationalize it in my head. Oh, he's okay. Things are better now. Things like that.

But when we got back to New York, I dropped him off at his apartment on the Upper West Side. As I pulled away, I looked back down the street. I saw him turn away from his front door and hop in a cab going downtown, and I knew where he was going.

TOM ARNOLD:

I'd seen a sketch Chris had done on *Saturday Night Live* where he impersonated me when I was married to Roseanne. It was very funny. I talked to some of the other guys from the show, and they said, "Oh, you have to meet Chris. You guys have a lot in common." So Roseanne and I went on and we hosted the show and I realized that Chris and I had an extra lot in common; I'd been sober since December 10, 1989.

Chris came out and we spent some time together. He worked on my HBO special, and he did stuff on *Roseanne*. As I got to know Chris, Lorne Michaels talked to me about him, saying he was afraid Chris had a problem, was kind of caught up in the Belushi thing.

In September of 1992, Chris was staying with me and Roseanne for a week. I had a show called *The Jackie Thomas Show*, and he came in and played my brother and, you know, I could tell. There were times when he didn't want to be around me at all. He disappeared a couple nights. We shot the show Friday night—he was great on the show, by the way—and after the taping I said, "Hey, why don't you come upstairs to my office real quick before you take off back to New York."

"Sure," he said.

He came up, and me and Rob Lowe and some other guys did an intervention on him. Everybody told him how much they loved him and how they were worried about him and how we wanted him to go to rehab right now. He said, "Well, I'd like to go back to New York first." Which, you know, is a classic addict thing to say. "I just want to go back and get my clothes and stuff." What they mean is: "I want to go see my dealer to get high before I go in."

We said, "Well, you know, when you go into rehab, they give you other drugs that kind of detox you from the drugs you're on now, so it'll get you fucked up."

"Oh, really?" he said. "So you're telling me if I go right now to this place, I can get fucked up?"

"Yeah, pretty much, for a couple days."

"Well, let's go."

So we all drove down there, and he went in.

TOM FARLEY:

After Tom Arnold's intervention, Chris finally seemed to get serious about it. He stayed at a facility out there, came back, and spent time at Hazelden's New York inpatient facility. Then he moved to this halfway house that had just been opened. It was on Sixteenth Street and Second Avenue. It was transitional housing for people trying to regain their footing in society. I wasn't even allowed in there. He might have had a room, but I believe it was just a bunch of cots in the basement, and they had their meetings upstairs. He was living there full-time and going to perform on national TV every week.

TODD GREEN:

Kevin and I met him over there a lot. At the time it was like, "Holy shit. This is where Chris is living?" But Chris liked it. He was glad to have it.

AL FRANKEN:

When he was living at Hazelden, he'd bring guys from the halfway house to see the show. Chris came to me a lot, because I often wrote about twelve-step stuff. I would talk to him about it and encourage him to go to meetings and stay on the program. I understood the ins and outs of the program, because I go to Al-Anon, which is for family members and friends of alcoholics. Chris knew I believed in the program, and he believed in it, too. And that's the aspect of this that people may not know. He *tried*. He really tried.

TODD GREEN:

It was a cycle. There were times when he was in really good shape, but other times there would be so much pressure to drink, and he'd ask me and Kevin to take him home; he was incapable of pulling himself out of a social situation that was bad.

ALEC BALDWIN:

I've done a lot of drug and alcohol rehabilitation work, privately, with friends over the years. Chris knew that, and so he really reached out to me for a brief period of time. I talked to him after a show and said, "Here's my phone number. I want you to call me."

And his persona offstage was exactly like the "Chris Farley Show" sketch. He was like, "Whoa, this is *your* phone number? And it's okay if I *call* it?"

"Yes, Chris. It's okay. Just call me, and we'll talk about whatever you're going through."

That lasted for a couple of months. He'd call and we'd talk. Then he'd go back to his old habits, and we'd stop.

DAVID SPADE:

Everyone wanted to take care of Chris. The hosts would hear about the problem, and they'd say, "Can I take you to lunch?" And I think Chris liked the attention of that more than the actual conversation. I used to do an imitation of Chris going, "Alec Baldwin, are you in recovery? We should go to lunch."

"Okay."

"Tom Hanks, you're in recovery, we should go to lunch."

"No, I'm not."

"Well . . . do you do drugs?"

"No."

"Are you afraid of the dark?"

"No."

"Have you ever seen a scary movie?"

"Yes."

"Me, too! Let's go talk about it."

FR. MATT FOLEY:

He wanted to find a nice woman, go and live in the suburbs, and start a family and be like everybody else. I think he felt if he did that he could escape it. But to stay in the environment he was in, he was never going to. They find you, those people. They always find you.

One time I came to visit New York, and Chris sent a driver to pick me up. The driver didn't know who I was. He's just going off about Chris's women, and how he always hooked Chris up with hot girls. All this wild and crazy stuff. Then halfway through the ride he says, "So what do you do?"

"I'm a priest."

Well, the conversation came to a dead halt after that. I'm not naïve, certainly, but it was a window into the kind of world Chris was in. How do you not find trouble in that world?

ALEC BALDWIN:

Chris's problem was that everywhere he went, people thought he was Falstaff. Chris was going to be the jolly fat man who would hoist a beer with you and snort a line with you. Everywhere he went someone was shoving a mug in his hand.

MICHAEL McKEAN, *cast member:*

While we were filming *Coneheads*, I was talking to Lorne, and one of us mentioned the fact that Chris was keeping clean at the time, and Lorne said, "Yeah, he's being good. That's the deal. We've already done the fat guy in the body bag."

TOM DAVIS:

I said to him once, "Chris, you don't want to die like Belushi, do you?"

And he said, "Oh, yeah, that'd be really cool."

And I actually started crying. I wept for him. He said, "Davis, you're crying."

"Yes, Chris. I'm crying for you."

He said, "Wow. Thanks, man."

I didn't say you're welcome.

TODD GREEN:

I never bought in to the fact that Chris was obsessed with Belushi. The press just seemed to make such a huge thing about it. I watched *Animal House* with Chris. I watched *Saturday Night Live* with Chris. Sure, we all thought Belushi was great, but I can't ever remember Chris being obsessed with the guy.

MIKE SHOEMAKER:

I think he romanticized Belushi's death, but that's not the same thing as having a death wish. Chris also wanted to be what Belushi couldn't be. He wanted to have the Chris Farley story be its own story. So I think he was of two minds on it.

LORNE MICHAELS:

Chris romanticized Belushi's life and his death, to a certain degree, but I told him there was nothing romantic about it. I said, "John missed most of the eighties, all of the nineties, and I don't think that was his intention." I was pretty brutal with Chris. I mean, we buried John.

KEVIN FARLEY:

When Chris finally cleaned up, the difference was that for the first time Lorne looked him in the face and said, "I will fire you. I'm not going through another Belushi, and I will fire you." And he meant it.

STEVEN KOREN:

Chris had really been doing well. He'd been clean for a while. Then we were doing the Glenn Close show just before Christmas. We were in the middle of this read-through, and Chris had written a sketch. I thought it was hilarious, but Chris didn't seem to think it went well. We had a half-hour break in the middle of the meeting, and Chris just didn't come back for the second half.

TOM FARLEY:

Chris left the show and went over to Hell's Kitchen and scored some heroin.

DAVID SPADE:

I found a bunch of bags of coke or heroin in a drawer in our office. I said, "What are these?" I didn't even know.

He said, "Get the fuck out of here!"

And he kicked me out of our office. Adam came in and asked what was going on. I said, "Farley's out of it, and there's some shit in there. I don't know what it is."

Chris was pretty good with Adam, so Adam said, "Let me talk to him."

Adam went in the office.

"Fuck you, Sandler! Get out of here!"

Adam came back out and said, "That didn't work too good."

I said, "Let's talk to Marci and see what she can do."

Marci came in and said, "Where's Chris?"

"Fuck you, Marci!"

She said, "I'm telling Lorne."

JIM DOWNEY:

Lorne said, "I think we have to fire him."

TOM ARNOLD:

Lorne called me. He said, "Chris relapsed. He's in his office, weeping. He's crying out for help so loudly that we can hear him out in the hallway."

LORNE MICHAELS:

It was a very adolescent cri de coeur, an attempt to play on everyone's sympathies. But as soon as I heard it was heroin, I was having none of it. I had been through it with John, and I wasn't doing it again.

MIKE SHOEMAKER:

I don't remember Chris actually being fired. He was suspended. But we never said "Empty your office." Because then what could Chris do but go on a binge? But it was severe, and there was an ultimatum attached. Either you come back clean or you don't come back. We never said, "You're outta here," because the problems always manifested when he was "out of here," because this was the only thing he cared about.

TODD GREEN:

The week he was kicked off, he watched the show with me and Kevin at Kevin's apartment. It killed him not to be on.

JIM DOWNEY:

I just sat there in the meeting with Chris, being somewhat cold about the whole thing. It was easier than being warm, and probably more effective. He would start to shake and cry, and I would just tune it out. It was a manipulation. He was trying to get your sympathy so you'd let it slide. He had plenty of people wanting to play that motherly role, and he needed people to say, "This is real simple: Fix the problem or you're out."

LORNE MICHAELS:

I basically just told him, "This is what it is, and I'm really, really disappointed. And you have to get some help, because this is not a problem that you can solve by yourself."

I don't know where I had heard about the place in Alabama, but I thought it was exactly what he needed. It was a real stripped-down, no-nonsense place. I had also seen enough of the Hollywood version of rehab where nothing actually happens. I wanted a place to get his undivided attention. That and the threat of losing the show were the only things that could do it.

TODD GREEN:

Kevin Cleary and I drove him to the airport. That was really hard. It was right before Christmas, and that was always an important time of year for Chris, to be with his friends and his family. No matter where any of us were, we always made it a point to be together in Madison for Christmas. So it was just heartbreaking knowing he was going away to spend it in Alabama at the kind of place he was going to.

We were driving to LaGuardia and it was really quiet in the car, and the song "Bad" by U2 came on. And while we were sitting there, listening to this song, Chris out of nowhere just asked, "What's this song about?" And it wasn't like Chris to ask something like that. Kevin and I were like, oh shit. We didn't really know what to say, so we just told him. "It's about trying to save a friend who dies from a heroin overdose."

"Oh."

Nobody said anything else. We just sat back and listened to the rest of the song. We got to the airport, and in those days you could still walk with someone all the way to the gate, so we went through security with him and walked through the terminal to meet his plane. After we said good-bye he walked over to the gate, and, right at the entrance to the jetway, he stopped and looked back at us for a moment. He had this deadly serious expression on his face. He gave us a thumbs-up, turned around, and walked onto the plane.

ACT II

CHAPTER 8

A Friendly Visitor

TOM SCHILLER:

He was a kind of secret, angelic being who tore too quickly through life, leaving a wake of laughter behind him. As corny as that sounds, it's the truth.

For the next three years, Chris Farley stayed clean and sober. At Lorne Michaels's behest, he had spent the entire Christmas break at a hard-core, locked-down rehab facility in Alabama. Unlike the celebrity resort and spa recovery units of Southern California, this joint was one step above prison, and it was staffed by, in the words of Tom Arnold, "a bunch of big black guys who didn't take any of Chris's shit." And it worked.

Chris's puppy-dog personality and endearing sense of humor had allowed him to weasel his way out of just about any difficult situation he'd faced in the past. But the people in Alabama weren't having any of it. And, finally, Chris wasn't having any of it, either. He realized he could no longer bullshit everyone, and he knew it was his last chance to stop bullshitting himself. He took the program seriously, took its message to heart, and took a new direction in life when he returned to New York. He moved into an apartment on the Upper East Side in the same building as Dana Carvey. A year later he would move back downtown to a new apartment on Seventeenth Street, a place chosen specifically for its proximity to his old halfway house and its steady availability of meetings and support groups. As the hoary cliché goes, Chris was a changed man. He was calmer, more thoughtful, and more focused.

He was also funnier. Chris missed the first show of 1993, but he was soon back in full swing, and over the following year he would establish himself as the show's new breakout star. That February, the writers resurrected "The Chris Farley Show," this time with one of Chris's childhood idols, former Beatle Paul McCartney. The very next week Chris got to share the stage with returning *SNL* legend Bill Murray. The coming months brought some of Chris's most memorable characters, including the blustery Weekend Update commentator Bennett Brauer, the outlandish man-child Andrew Giuliani, a ravenous Gap Girl, and the titular heroine of Adam Sandler's "Lunchlady Land."

And on the second-to-last show of his third season, with Bob Odenkirk's blessing, Chris dusted off an old script lying around from his Second City days and brought it in to the weekly read-through. It was a hit, both at the table and on the air. That Saturday night, with one unforgettable performance, the phrase "van down by the river" assumed its permanent place in the national lexicon.

STEVEN KOREN:

Chris had been doing the Motivational Speaker character at Second City, but I didn't know what it was. Since Bob Odenkirk had already written it, they just needed a writer to babysit it through production, check the cue cards and all that. It was never anyone's favorite job to get. Little did I know.

So I was sitting there watching the rehearsal, making sure the camera angles were right, and I said to Chris, "You know, you're gonna hurt your voice talking like that. Are you sure you want to do the voice that way?"

He was like, "Don't worry, Steve. I got this one down."

That was a good lesson for a young writer: just trust the actors. When he did it live the place exploded.

DAVID SPADE:

In rehearsal, he'd done the thing with his glasses where he's like, "Is that Bill Shakespeare? I can't see too good." But he'd never done the twisting his belt and hitching up his pants thing. He saved that for the live performance, and so none of us had ever seen it. He knew that would break me. He started hitching up his pants, and I couldn't take it. And whenever the camera was behind him focusing on me, he'd cross his eyes. I was losing it.

Once we started laughing, Chris just turned it on more. And we're not supposed to do that. Lorne doesn't like it at all, but Chris loved to bust us up. Sometimes after the show he'd say, "All I'm trying to do is make you laugh. I don't care about anything else."

NORM MacDONALD, writer/Weekend Update anchor:

Lorne didn't like us cracking up on air. He didn't want it to be like *The Carol Burnett Show*. He hated that. When people crack up on *Saturday Night Live*, it's normally fake, because we've already done the sketches and rehearsed them so much. But it was always Chris's goal when it was live on air to make you laugh, to take you out of your character, and he always succeeded. You could never not laugh.

He would do little asides, especially to Sandler, even if Sandler wasn't in the sketch. One time Chris was in a Japanese game show sketch, and when he went to write down his answer for the game, he just took a big whiff of the Magic Marker and did a look to Sandler off camera. Sandler wasn't even in the sketch, but if you watch the tape you can hear him laughing offscreen.

MICHAEL McKEAN:

It was nice to share the stage with that kind of manic energy. For one thing, you knew the focus was elsewhere. No one was watching me. I could have sat down and eaten a sandwich during some of the sketches we did together.

CHRIS ROCK:

You never really shared the stage with him. It was always his stage, and deservedly so. The weird thing is that nobody got mad about that. There's a lot of competition on that show, but no one was competing with Farley. We'd all get upset if someone else had a sketch on and we didn't, but I can't think of one person who was ever upset about Chris getting a sketch on. No one ever complained.

ALEC BALDWIN:

Whenever I was watching Chris perform I would think, "How do I get where he's at? How do I get to be as funny and as honest and as warm?" There are comics that I've worked with who are the most self-involved bastards you've ever met in your life, and they can't fake the kind of decency Chris had. Chris was someone who was very vulnerable; it was a card he played. It was a tool in his actor's repertoire, and yet it was something totally genuine. Even when he plays Matt Foley, and he's hectoring people in this totally overbearing way, there's a tinge of the character's own neediness. Even underneath that, there's Chris.

KEVIN NEALON:

He was so fallible. People just felt for him. Women felt protective of him, because they could tell he wasn't watching out for himself. And men related to all his anxieties and imperfections.

LORNE MICHAELS:

One time we were in the studio, and Chevy Chase came by. Chris was practicing one of his pratfalls. He showed it to Chevy, and Chevy said, "What are you breaking your fall on?"

Chevy always had something to break his fall; you plan these things out. But Chris had watched Chevy and bought the illusion of it. How do you fall? You just fall on the ground and you don't mind the pain, because that's the price of doing it. So there was an honesty and a straightforwardness in him that people responded to.

NORM MacDONALD:

What I would do with Chris, when it came to writing a sketch, was just listen to him and observe him. There was this one thing he did. He'd tell a story—and I'm not doing this justice—but he'd tell a story like, "Anyways, Norm. Did I tell ya I seen my friend Bill the other day, and I says to him, I says, I look him right in the eye and I says to him, I says, I says to Bill, I says to him, get this, what I says to him is I says, get this, what I says, you won't believe what I says to him, I says . . ."

And of course the joke was that he'd never get to what he'd actually said to the guy. And Chris could keep this going for twenty, twenty-five minutes straight. He'd do it two hundred different ways. It would just get funnier and funnier and funnier. When you can reduce something to four words and be funny for twenty-five minutes without an actual joke or a punch line, that's genius. It's not even really comedy anymore. It's almost like music, like jazz variations.

I always liked comedians who just keep repeating things until nobody's laughing anymore, but then they take it so far that eventually it's funnier than it was in the beginning. There are only a couple of performers on the planet who can do that. Andy Kaufman could do it, and Chris Farley could do it.

So I had him do it on Weekend Update. Lorne had decided that the "I says to the guy" segment would last for thirty seconds, which I knew would never work. At dress, I told Chris to do it for four minutes. So he did, and it was just like I thought. People weren't laughing for a while, but then right as he hit the four-minute mark it was really starting to kill. That's when I realized he should have done it for eight minutes.

But he never got to do it on air, because Lorne went ballistic on me that I'd let Chris go so far over time. I tried to explain to Lorne that it wasn't funny for thirty seconds, but Chris understood it completely.

ALEC BALDWIN:

There are people who are smart in a way that has no applicability to performance, but Chris's brains and his quickness inside of performance were amazing. He knew exactly how to scan a line, exactly what inflection to have, how to time it, what expression to make. A great performer is someone who puts together a half a dozen things in an instant, and Chris was one of the most skilled performers I've ever seen in that respect. And he knew that his opportunity would come. He wasn't sitting there, calculating how he was going to trump you or dominate the scene. He just patiently waited for his moment and then arrived fully in that moment.

STEVE LOOKNER, *writer:*

When it came to performing in your sketches, Chris was never some egotistical guy who was going to take your material and do it however he wanted to. He wanted to make sure he was getting the sketch the way you wanted it.

FRED WOLF, *writer:*

The highlight of my career, still, was the first sketch I got on at *Saturday Night Live*, this thing called "The *Mr. Belvedere* Fan Club." Chris had a big turn in that sketch where he played a crazy person obsessed with *Mr. Belvedere*. He brought down the house. Afterward he came up to me, saying,

"That was funny. Thanks for the good stuff." I couldn't believe that about him. To me, it was the other way around. I should have been thanking him.

DAVID MANDEL, *writer:*

He always went out of his way to make sure people knew what material was yours, that they were your jokes, and he was just the guy who said the lines.

IAN MAXTONE-GRAHAM, *writer:*

I worked on some of the Motivational Speaker sketches, because Bob Odenkirk was gone by then. Matt Foley was very much Chris's character, but Chris was also very loyal. We always had to call Bob up and read it to him over the phone and get his blessing.

SIOBHAN FALLON, *cast member:*

There was always an air of competition at *Saturday Night Live*. At read-through, people would purposefully not laugh at something even though it was funny, because they wanted something else to make it on the show. But Chris would laugh no matter what. If it was funny, he gave it a big, big laugh. He didn't discriminate. He was honest.

NORM MacDONALD:

I don't think Chris knew how to hate. I'd feel bad sometimes, because I'd be complaining and I'd go, "You know who sucks?" And I'd go off about so-and-so, some guy on the show. And Chris would immediately go, "I think he's funny, Norm. Why don't you like him?" So then I'd just feel like a jerk.

DAVID MANDEL:

The show was in a very weird spot at that time. During the election year, everything was Phil Hartman and Dana Carvey doing Clinton and Bush and Perot. Chris was a full cast member, and incredibly popular, but in those sketches he'd just do small, memorable turns as Joe Midwestern Guy. Al Franken and I wrote the sketch where Bill Clinton goes jogging and stops in at McDonald's. In that one Chris played Hank Holdgren from Holdgren Hardware in Fond du Lac, Wisconsin. In a lot of those small supporting roles I think you saw the road not taken for Chris. If he hadn't found comedy, you could totally see him being the friendly hardware-store guy.

TODD GREEN:

When Chris interacted with celebrities, the guest hosts, he would always introduce me by saying, "This is my friend Todd. We met in second grade and grew up together." He was proud that he was my friend, and he wanted to share that. I remember him regaling Glenn Close with stories of Madison, and you could see that she saw the genuineness in him. She just looked at him and said, "You really are an amazing guy."

I'm a huge, huge Beatles fan, and so when Paul McCartney was on the show, that was a really big deal. Ten years earlier, Chris and I had been listening to Beatles albums in our basements. He called me during the week at like two in the afternoon and said, "What're you doing?"

"What am I doing?" I said. "I'm working, like most people."

"You know what I'm doing?"

"What?"

And then he took the phone and held it up, and I could hear Paul McCartney singing "Yesterday."

"I'm just here, hanging with Paul McCartney," he said. Then he giggled and hung up the phone.

The night of the show, he said, "Listen, I want you guys to hang out in my dressing room tonight. I have a surprise for you."

So, Kevin and I wait and watch on the monitor in the dressing room. McCartney comes out and does the first song, and we watch him, wondering, "What's the surprise? Why didn't he come and get us?" Whatever. Didn't matter. It was one of his new songs. Then the second song comes and goes, another new one, and still no Chris. Just before the end of the show, when we're pretty sure Chris has forgotten about us, he barrels into the dressing room and says, "Okay, Greenie, you're on! Follow me!"

We go running down the hallway to the studio. Paul and Linda McCartney come out. Chris introduces me to them. I'm in a state of shock, and the four of us walk out to the stage together. Chris and I stop just short of the cameras, and Paul and Linda go out and he sings "Hey Jude."

And at that moment, Chris wasn't a member of the show anymore. It was just two buddies from Wisconsin who grew up on the Beatles, listening to Paul McCartney. Chris literally forgot that he had to go back onstage for the good-nights.

I think, deep down, all of the guys from Edgewood figured that one day we'd end up back in Madison and it would be just the way it was. I think even Chris believed that. Even ranked against all the fame and money and stardom, he felt the days back at Edgewood were the best days of our lives.

KEVIN FARLEY:

When you come to the conclusion that you're an alcoholic, and you go to these stupid meetings, they're filled with down-and-out people right off the street. I'd go to Madison, and I'd see Chris, who was on *Saturday Night Live*, had money, had fame. He'd go and drink coffee and talk with these regular folk, and he could talk to them more easily than he could talk to Mick Jagger or Paul McCartney. He felt more at ease with the average Joes.

What he loved was the honesty. Nobody is as honest as they are in one of those meetings, when they're admitting their faults, admitting that they're broken human beings. Contrast that with the *Saturday Night Live* after party, where everyone wants you to think they're hot stuff. They're putting on airs, and it's all bullshit because we're all just broken people anyway. To witness people being honest about themselves and with themselves is a life-changing thing, because it's something you so rarely see. That's what's truly amazing about recovery, and amazing about how it changed Chris.

TOM FARLEY:

He was a lot more fun to be around. He was much, much funnier. You could have thoughtful, engaging discussions with him, and he wouldn't get mad or defensive. That was a huge difference from when he was drinking.

For Chris, being in recovery was a little like being at camp. That's how he treated it. Make your bed every morning for inspection, that sort of thing. And that carried over once he got out of rehab, too. As disgusting a slob as he was before, he was that clean and organized once he got sober. He turned into a neat freak.

BOB ODENKIRK:

After all the years of being in and out of rehab, I never thought that Chris could take it seriously. But one time I was at this party out in L.A., and I saw him turn down a beer. He was saying no, and he meant it. I thought, oh my God, *he figured it out.* He knows how dire this is, and he's really taking charge. It wasn't about pleasing everyone else. It was about him and his choice. I was really impressed, and I thought, wow, nothing is going to stop this guy.

TOM FARLEY:

Toward the end of Chris's *Saturday Night Live* run, my son was born, and he had to stay in intensive care for a week. One day I asked Chris to watch the two older girls while my wife and I went to the hospital. We went down to his apartment, and we were ringing the buzzer, waiting for someone to let us in. There was no answer. I was starting to wonder where the new, reliable Chris was. Then, around the corner here he comes with these huge bags of Cheetos and ice cream and these enormous Barney dolls, walking down the street. It was just a great sight. Chris was so happy that we'd asked him to look after the girls, that we trusted him with that responsibility. He was so proud that he could be a better part of their lives.

KEVIN FARLEY:

Chris paved the way for the rest of us. When he went down to Alabama, I started to look at myself. I was doing the same stuff he was—coke, pot, drinking all the time. I saw where I was headed. I never went into rehab. I just walked into a meeting one day. That's when I realized we all are alcoholics, the whole family. My mother stopped drinking then, too, at the same time I did. We would go to meetings a lot together. We realized Dad was an alcoholic, and we saw the patterns very clearly once we'd changed our own. But Tommy, Johnny, and Dad were still drinking. Barb was the exception. She was never a drinker at all.

TOM FARLEY:

When I look back, or when people ask me what regrets I have, what I realize is that I always felt that Chris's problems were his own. I was still drinking, and I didn't take an active role in his recovery. It was his deal, and that was that. Then one day he asked me to come to his second-anniversary meeting, which he was going to lead. I said, "Great, where do you meet?" He gives me the address of this place down on Eleventh Avenue and Forty-something, the real fringe of Hell's Kitchen. You go down there and you think, Jesus, what am I walking into?

But that's where Chris liked to go. He had his choice between meetings on Park Avenue and in Hell's Kitchen, and he wanted to be with the desperate, hard-luck cases to remind himself that his celebrity didn't put him above them in any way. He stood up there in front of them and said, "Look, I woke up the same way you guys did this morning, wondering if I was going to stay sober today. My disease is no different than yours." And it wasn't bullshit. He just seemed so wise and intelligent and in control. I just sat there thinking, this is my *brother*? I looked at him in a whole different light from then on.

NORM MacDONALD:

What's hard for a comedian is that they make a living on their anxieties and their self-doubts, but in real life they try and separate themselves from that. Chris didn't do that. He was absolutely honest in what he was.

CONAN O'BRIEN:

You got the sense with Chris that he wasn't punching a clock. And, obviously, that isn't always a fun way to live. But it was fun for everybody else.

DAVID MANDEL:

Emilio Estevez hosted the show in support of *Mighty Ducks 2*, which we were given a screening of. We saw it in a private screening room. No one really cared about *Mighty Ducks 2*, so only a couple of us were there.

Now, in *Mighty Ducks 2*—which, if you need your memory refreshed—they're training for the Junior Olympics, and they let some street kids from L.A. join the team. So now they have some black kids on the squad, and they do a giant musical montage where they take the rap song "Whoomp! There It Is" and change it to "Quack! There It Is." And of course it was the *actual musicians* who'd sung "Whoomp! There It Is." They'd sold out to Disney and done "Quack! There It Is."

It was so ridiculous that those of us in the room started clapping along and jumping up and down and dancing with the music in the middle of the screening room. The next thing you know, Farley's pants are down around his ankles, and he's standing up on a chair, smacking his ass in time to "Quack! There It Is." I have never seen anything funnier in my life. And yet when you look back sometimes you think, you know, maybe that was a cry for help.

SARAH SILVERMAN, *cast member:*

The cast was on a retreat, sitting around a campfire, and Chris sidled up to Jim Downey. I overheard him say in this little-boy voice, "Hey, Jim? Do you think it would help the show if I got *even fatter*?"

Jim said, in his parental voice, "No, Chris. I think you're fine."

Chris said, "Are you sure? 'Cause I will. For the show."

Chris was fucking around for sure, and seeing the back-and-forth of the conversation was hilarious, but there was an element of truth in it: He would do anything to be funny.

NORM MacDONALD:

I never thought about it as needing attention, because Chris laughed at everybody else, too. He loved Sandler and Spade and me, guys who were much less funny than he was. And he was always more generous in giving you a laugh than in taking one for himself.

His greatest love was just the act of laughter itself. As much as he made other people laugh, to watch Chris do it was the most beautiful thing you'd ever see. Nobody could laugh with as much unbridled glee. He'd just go into these paroxysms of mirth. If Chris laughed at one of your jokes, you felt like the king of the world.

STEVEN KOREN:

Chris was really smart. He knew exactly what he was doing. It's the same with Jim Carrey. He knows the exact degrees to which he's being big or small or clever. When they're that good, they know the difference between being laughed at and laughed with. There's a definite awareness. I guess Chris was a victim of his own desire to make people laugh, but also I think his heart was so big that if he was the butt of the joke it was okay. He wanted to give people laughter so much that it was okay if it hurt him a little bit. It was a conscious decision, I think.

JAY MOHR, *cast member:*

No one was laughing at Chris. Everyone was laughing with him. Show me someone who was laughing at Chris Farley, and I'll show you a real cocksucker.

DAVID SPADE:

I would have to write sketches all week to try and stay alive on the show, and Chris would be written for, so he didn't write a lot, or read. So while I was busting my hump, he'd be bored behind me trying to amuse himself. One night he goes, "Davy, turn around."

"I'm busy," I say.

"Turn around."

"Dude, if this is Fat Guy in a Little Coat again, it's not funny anymore."

"It's not."

"Really?"

"I promise."

So I turn around and he's got my Levi's jacket on, and he goes, "*Fat Guy in a Little Coat . . .* give it a chance."

And the coat rips, and that's how we wound up putting it in *Tommy Boy*.

TIM HERLIHY, *writer:*

When comedians get together . . . I wouldn't call it one-upsmanship, but it is like a game. Who can be the funniest? When I knew Chris, he was surrounded by the elite of comedy. Sandler's a huge, funny star, but you always knew Farley was going to top him. He was the funniest among a group of very funny, talented people. All of us who worked with him are richer for it. We're better writers, better performers.

FRED WOLF:

Comics are a pretty strange breed. Put all of us in a room and we can fight among ourselves and disagree with all our bitterness and neuroses. But when it came to Farley, it was unanimous: He was the best.

NORM MacDONALD:

What astonished me about Chris was that he could make *everyone* laugh. He could make a child laugh. He could make an old person laugh. A dumb person, a smart person. A guy who loved him, a guy who hated him.

IAN MAXTONE-GRAHAM:

He was a very funny, jovial presence in the office. He'd be very, very outgoing, and then he'd have this very cute, shy thing he'd do where he'd sort of retreat into himself. Hugely outgoing and hugely shy. That was the rhythm of his behavior. You can see that in some of his sketches.

BOB ODENKIRK:

Most of my memories are just of hanging out with Chris and him making me laugh *so hard*. But then, if Chris wasn't being silly, if he was just listening to you quietly, that was as funny as when he was worked up. "The Chris Farley Show" on *SNL*, that was Chris behaving himself.

JOHN GOODMAN, *host:*

"The Chris Farley Show," that was Chris.

MIKE SHOEMAKER:

That was Chris.

STEVEN KOREN:

That was him.

JACK HANDEY, *writer:*

He was basically playing himself.

TIM MEADOWS:

That's how he acted whenever he was around someone he admired. Until he got to know you, he really was that guy—shy and asking a lot of dumb questions but not wanting to be too intrusive. It was a very endearing quality.

TOM DAVIS:

I thought of that sketch originally. I thought, what the fuck are we going to do with this guy? He's just over the fucking top all the time. I button-holed Downey and said, "Let's do 'The Chris Farley Show' and just have him talk as he really is so he doesn't go over the top."

JIM DOWNEY:

Farley was such a comedy nerd. He knew all the old shows, better than I did. He'd come up and say, "Do you remember that superheroes sketch on the show where they were having that party?" Then he'd proceed to do the entire sketch for me, his version probably longer than the original. He'd finish that and be like, "You remember that?"

"Yes, Chris," I'd say, thinking this was all leading up to something significant. "What about it?"

"That was awesome."

So we decided to put that in a talk-show format, with some poor sap being trapped on a talk show with Farley asking him retarded questions. We submitted it, actually, as a joke at read-through. I thought it was too inside, and so would never make it on the air. But Lorne liked it immediately, and seemed to have big hopes for it.

At dress, Steve Koren was watching it, grinning ear to ear and laughing. And of course the audience loved it. I don't think it was just Farley being adorable. I guess there was just something universal about it, and I didn't appreciate the resonance it had.

The first one was with Jeff Daniels. Then we did Martin Scorsese. By the time Paul McCartney came around, I actually didn't want to bring it back at all. I just thought, what can you do that's different? If you just do the same thing over again just because people liked it, they might stop liking it. But Lorne insisted on doing it.

LORNE MICHAELS:

Actually, I think Chris was the one who was adamant about doing it with McCartney.

ALEC BALDWIN:

We were just dying. We couldn't believe how perfect it was. How hard is it to make Beatlemania funny again? How hard is it to make gooing over McCartney funny? We didn't know if that would work. But Chris came on, and we were sobbing with laughter it was so funny. It was going along, and then Chris says, "You remember that time you got arrested in Japan for pot?"

And McCartney just suddenly changed his tone. "Oh, those are the things I'd like to forget, Chris."

They played it perfectly.

JOHN GOODMAN:

The funniest bit that I ever saw him do was that McCartney interview. When I first met him he was like this kid who kept staring at me, just like that character did. I don't know why, but he seemed genuinely thrilled to meet me. It wasn't a celebrity type of thing, either; it was just that he couldn't get enough of other people, of their stories. He was endlessly curious.

BOB ODENKIRK:

I said once—and it was misquoted in that fucking *Live from New York* book—that Chris was like a child. How it reads in that book was that I meant Chris was like a little baby, which wasn't what I said at all. The whole quote—which they didn't include, because they're dicks—was, "Look, don't take this the wrong way, but Chris was *like* a child. He was like a child in his reverence and awe of the world around him." And he was. He was so respectful of everyone, like he always had something to learn from you.

JAY MOHR:

I learned from Chris how to have more fun. Nothing is that serious. Acting is really a ridiculous way to make a living. You're playing make-believe, and Chris never got away from that fact. Kids never come home and say, "I was over at Michael's house and we played make-believe. It was awful. We were in a spaceship and I had a helmet on and there were Martians and then we chased them through the woods—and it just wasn't my thing." No kid has ever said that. It's make-believe. You paint as you go. I have a three-year-old son now. I open up his coloring book and say, "What color are these footprints going to be?"

"Green."

Great fucking idea. Green footprints, that was Chris.

MARILYN SUZANNE MILLER:

I would write songs and musical numbers for *SNL*, and when Kelsey Grammar was host I wrote a sketch called "Iron John: The Musical." Chris sang in that one, and he came up to me after the performance and said, "I love those musical things. I just love them. I really want to do more of them."

Musical numbers are very emotional things, and it's a very childlike desire to want to have that kind of honest, sincere outlet. He wanted to share as much of himself with the audience as he could. He was not a great singer, as I recall. During the rehearsals, beads of sweat would literally drip down his forehead as he was trying comically hard to hit all his cues and hit all his notes. He so much wanted to succeed. And when you see a young guy working like that, with sweat running down his forehead, that's kind of a wonderful thing. When the old cast would get laughs, we were practically counting them. We were very calculating. Chris wasn't a calculated performer. He was out there for the love.

IAN MAXTONE-GRAHAM:

They have a meeting with the host every Monday night, and there were always two jokes that we used to do every single week. Let's say Kevin Bacon was the host, and Tom Arnold was set to host the next week. Lorne would announce, "Everyone, this week's host is Kevin Bacon." And everyone would applaud.

Then Al Franken would say, " And next week: Tom Arnold." And everyone would applaud much louder. That was the little icebreaker they'd do to set the host at ease and poke fun at him a bit.

The other thing that would always happen was that at the very end of the meeting, Farley would jump in—kind of like that determined kid on the football team that's never won a game—he'd jump in and say, "C'mon, let's *do it* this time!" It was always very funny and sort of combined his childish eagerness with great comic timing and a great sense of the moment.

ALEC BALDWIN:

When you were on the set with Chris, he'd be giggling and pinching you and saying, "Where you want to go after the show, man?" It was like being in homeroom in high school. There's a quotient of people at *Saturday Night Live* for whom the show is like operating an elevator. We go up. We go down. What's the big deal? Then there were the people like Chris who made it their mission every week to make it the best show possible, and enjoy it.

ROBERT SMIGEL:

Just seeing Chris at the door of my office would put a smile on my face. He radiated this earnestness, and he really *believed* in the work that he did. Chris was also unique among comedians in being so open about his faith and spirituality. Most people in this industry are so caught up in being sarcastic or casually ironic that they're loath to admit that they actually care about anything. Admitting that you believe in God is the same as admitting that you like Bob Seger. Okay, even I'm not crazy about Seger. But I like Springsteen, and even Bruce is just too earnest for lots of comedy writers to give it up for.

CONAN O'BRIEN:

There are a lot of us in comedy who are a lot more Catholic than anybody knows. Our Catholicism is sort of under our skin. People were surprised at the depth of Chris's faith; to me it made perfect sense. A lot of people think that they're mutually exclusive. How can you be dancing in a Chippendales thong and going to mass at the same time? But if you're Catholic you think, *of course* that's how it works.

TOM FARLEY:

Pretty early on, Chris told me he'd found this church, St. Malachy's. "They call it the Actors' Chapel," he said. He totally ate that up. In his mind it was this place where all these old Broadway stars and vaudevillians had come to mass and prayed and found guidance. The first time I went with him, these old ladies who were sort of scattered about the pews would break out with the most beautiful voices during the hymns. They'd really belt it out, and you could picture them singing in their old musicals and operas. It was really special for Chris in that way.

MSGR. MICHAEL CRIMMINS, *priest, St. Malachy's:*

He used to come on Tuesdays and Thursdays to the noon mass. He went to confession regularly. He'd bring his mother and his family to mass whenever they were in town.

Sister Theresa O'Connell was really his mentor and spiritual adviser. She knew him well. Unfortunately, she's passed on, and they kept their relationship very private. But she suggested to him that he volunteer through our Encore Friendly Visitors Program, and he did.

SIOBHAN FALLON:

Chris lived close to me, and we went to the same church, Holy Trinity on the Upper West Side. He'd go to St. Malachy's from work and Holy Trinity on the weekends. As he did everything big and great, he'd be in the back of church, praying intensely, bowed down in this dramatic position, practically kicking himself over whatever he'd done the night before. I'd say, "Hi, Chris."

And he'd say, "Well, God's gonna be mad at me this time!"

I have no doubt that Chris is sitting pretty up in heaven, entertaining everybody. He was a good guy. He's taken care of. You can say that addiction is a selfish disease, but Chris wasn't selfish. He always looked outside of himself. At that stage of someone's career, in your twenties and early thirties, you're so selfish and so self-consumed—especially actors. I think you'd be hard pressed to find anyone at that age who was thinking about anything other than getting themselves ahead. And so for Chris to be doing the work he was doing was amazing.

TIM MEADOWS:

A kid from the Make-A-Wish Foundation came to *SNL* once to meet Farley. I got to see that, but I had no idea that he was a part of this program at St. Malachy's. He never talked about it. I was one of his best friends, and I didn't know about it until after he'd passed away.

NORM MacDONALD:

It was amazing at the funeral to hear people talking. It was like, "My God, this is a person I never knew."

SR. PEGGY McGIRL, *executive assistant, Encore Community Services:*

Whenever he came here he was very regular and without any airs. He had a quiet way about him; he didn't like to have any attention focused on him at all. His main concern was just to be there to help the seniors. We have parties twice a year for people who are homebound, seniors and people with disabilities. One is in the spring and the other is around Halloween. If Chris was in town, he was always there.

KEITH HOCTER, *volunteer, Encore Community Services:*

I met Chris through the parties at St. Malachy's. We worked the door together. He was just extremely friendly, not at all hung up about who he was, and he was pretty famous by that point. He just showed up and did what the rest of us did, which was whatever the sisters told us to do.

For a lot of the seniors, this was their big social event of the year. The party would have about a hundred and fifty people. A lot of them were in wheelchairs and walkers, and back then the church didn't have an elevator. The party was in the basement, and the only way down was this old, narrow set of stairs. It had one of those side-rail lifts, but the thing never worked.

Chris and I and the other volunteers, we'd each grab a corner of the wheelchair, tip them back, and then just talk to them and keep them calm while we took them down. We never dropped anybody; I guess that's the first measure of success. And we never had anyone freak out on us, either. Half of our job was to get them down safely. The other was to make them feel good while we were carrying them down. Then, at the end of the evening, we would stay and, one by one, help carry them all back up to the street again.

JOHN FARLEY:

One time we were in Chicago, coming back from filming this HBO special where Chris had this quick little cameo. As we get out of the limo at Chris's apartment, there's an old woman standing on the corner, begging for a quarter to get on the bus. Two minutes later, she finds herself in the back of a limousine with a hundred dollars in her hand. And Chris tells the limo driver, "Take her anywhere she wants to go."

The next day the same driver comes back to pick Chris up, and he says, "Do you have any idea where that woman wanted me to take her? Please, let's not do that again."

AL FRANKEN:

Tony Hall is a former congressman from Dayton, Ohio. His son Matt had leukemia, and a mutual friend asked me to go and visit him at Sloan-Kettering. The second time I went there I said, "Who's your favorite cast member on *SNL*?" It was Chris. So I asked Chris if he'd come and visit him, and he did.

Matt just loved it. His parents are very Christian, especially his mom, and Chris and I were just swearing up a storm. Matt laughed. His mom didn't know whether to be happy or shocked or what.

After we'd spent a while with Matt and said good-bye, Chris went around and visited every single kid in the cancer ward. He stayed there and entertained every last one of them. Then at the end of the day, as we were walking out of the hospital, Chris just broke down and started sobbing. I think it was all sort of wrapped up with his own issues that he was dealing with at the time. I said to him, "Don't you see how much joy you bring to these people? Don't you see what you just did, how valuable that is?"

Chris went back and visited Matt again. When they had Matt's funeral, I went, and they had made a bulletin board of "Matt's Favorite Stuff." In the middle of it was a photo of him and Chris from that day.

FR. JOE KELLY, S.J., *priest, St. Malachy's:*

He believed that comedy was a ministry of its own. Anything that made people laugh was worthwhile. But at the same time, he wanted a little more than that. He was a bit of a disturbed guy. I'm talking personally, now. A bit of a disturbed guy.

He used to come up to my room here, just to sit and chat and talk about different things, especially about how important the Friendly Visitors Program was to him. He felt that without the program, without the work he did here, his life wouldn't have much meaning. Doing what he did here gave him a purpose outside of some of the trivial work he was doing in entertainment.

Anybody who's constantly making a fool of himself and getting laughs out of those crazy facial gestures and so on, very often they're hiding something they don't want to face themselves. I think that was the case with Chris. He was a much deeper person than he let on. One gift he had was the ability to make people laugh. The other gift he had was himself. Just being the person he was was a gift for others. And I don't think he realized that for quite some time.

SR. PEGGY McGIRL:

We have a residence, a converted hotel, that is now a home for the homeless and the mentally ill, and Chris used to visit a man named Willie. He also spent time with another resident, a woman named Lola, but it was mostly Willie.

Willie was about seventy years old, and he had been homeless before coming to our residence. Chris took Willie out to dinner every week, and to famous restaurants. Chris treated him as an equal, always. He would take him to Broadway shows, take him out to ball games. If Chris was walking down the street on the way to his office, he'd stop in to see how Willie was doing. Whenever he had to go away for work, he'd send Willie postcards, and whenever he came back he always brought Willie a souvenir. They were friends for over five years.

TODD GREEN:

On the one-year anniversary of Chris's death, St. Malachy's was having a memorial mass for him, and I went with Tommy and Kevin Cleary. There was an elderly black guy there with a Chicago Bulls hat on. He was not quite homeless, but clearly one step away from it. He stood up to speak. He said his name was Willie, and he talked about Chris and about all the things he had done for him, all the time Chris had spent with him. Kevin, Tommy, and I, we just looked at each other—we had no idea.

The man spoke for a little while longer. Then he started to break down crying. He said, "This hat, this is the last thing Chris ever gave me, and I really miss him."

SR. PEGGY McGIRL:

After Chris passed, Willie became very quiet. Eventually, some time later, he moved back down south to be with his family, to let his family take care of him. Whatever problems had put him on the street and made him homeless, he overcame them and went back home.

When you receive love, it releases you from the things that trouble you. Just knowing that someone cares about you can give you strength and courage. And I always believed that it was Chris's love for Willie, and the things he did for Willie, that finally set him free.

CHAPTER 9

The Magic Sixty-six

FR. TOM GANNON, S.J., *friend:*

People always ask me what kind of guy Chris Farley was, and I say, "Go and see *Tommy Boy*." That's Chris Farley.

In the summer of 1991, director Penelope Spheeris was working at Paramount Studios, preparing to shoot a feature-film version of "Wayne's World," Mike Myers's popular *Saturday Night Live* sketch about two kids with a cable-access television show. Lorne Michaels approached her about using Chris Farley in the movie. Chris was still a relative unknown. He had only one year of television under his belt, and Spheeris had no idea who he was. But, she says, "Lorne told me we should give him a part because he's going to be the biggest thing ever." On that recommendation she cast him sight unseen as a security guard at the movie's Alice Cooper concert. As film debuts go it was a small one, but Chris carried it off well.

Wayne's World, meanwhile, carried off buckets and buckets of money. The low-budget comedy shattered everyone's expectations, earning

$121 million at the box office. Paramount immediately ordered up *Wayne's World 2*, as well as another *SNL* franchise movie, *Coneheads*.

SNL alum Dan Aykroyd sat down with writer Tom Davis, and the two began drafting the story of Beldar and Prymatt Conehead as a movie. Aykroyd, impressed by what he'd seen in Chris on television, wrote a part for him as Ronnie, the love interest of young Connie Conehead. Over the following year Chris took on other supporting roles, as a roadie in *Wayne's World 2* and as a security guard in Adam Sandler's *Airheads*.

By the end of Chris's fourth year on *Saturday Night Live*, he was hands down a cast favorite, and Lorne Michaels felt that the young star was ready to carry his own feature—an original story, rather than another *SNL* franchise picture. Drawing on personal experience, Michaels laid out the central premise of the plot: a father who dies too soon and a son forced to take on responsibilities for which he is not prepared. *SNL* writers Bonnie and Terry Turner took on screenwriting duties, and Paramount bought the idea immediately, based largely on the casting of Chris Farley and Rob Lowe as brothers.

Very little of the original concept and script made it to the screen. The Turners' draft was largely discarded, and *SNL* writer Fred Wolf wrote the bulk of the final screenplay, receiving no credit for it. Wolf wrote most of the story on the fly while director Peter Segal and producers Bob Weiss and Michael Ewing scrambled at record speed to get the film off the ground.

The story that ultimately emerged was that of young Tommy Callahan, heir to a Midwestern auto-parts manufacturer. When Tommy's father dies, he has to make his dad's annual sales trip to save the company and his hometown. Joining him on the trip is his late father's assistant, Richard Hayden, played by the acerbic David Spade. Lorne Michaels had paired up the two close friends on a hunch that their complementary talents might make them the best comedy duo since John Belushi and Dan Aykroyd hit the screen in *Blues Brothers*, fifteen years earlier. Brian Dennehy took on the role of Big Tom Callahan, with Bo Derek as his bride. *Doc Hollywood*'s Julie Warner was cast as Chris's love interest, Michelle Brock. Aykroyd played the heavy, a competing auto-parts magnate named Ray Zalinsky. And Kevin and John Farley also turned up in small roles as their older brother endeavored to give them a leg up in show business.

Few on set knew it at the time, but they were working with Chris at the single high point of his life. He was confident and self-assured, and it showed in his performance. Thanks in no small part to Chris's commitment, *Tommy Boy* lives on today as a minor classic, a staple of cable-TV comedy, and a brief glimpse of what might have been.

BOB WEISS, *producer:*

I got a call from John Goldwyn at Paramount saying, "We have this picture. Would you come in?"

"Do you have a script?" I asked.

"No."

"Whaddya got?"

"We've got thirty pages and a release date."

"Okay."

So I met with Lorne, and a lunch was set up at the Paramount commissary for me to meet with Chris.

He sat down at lunch, and he was really like an enthusiastic kid. He was just thrilled about being there and wasn't jaded in any way. How refreshing it was to have someone like that inside the Paramount commissary. You told him any piece of what was going on and it was "great." It was "cool." It was "exciting." And that's infectious. You can build on that.

Originally, there was another director involved. I acquainted him with the facts of our shooting schedule, and he left the picture; he was afraid his head would explode. Then Pete Segal agreed to come on board.

MICHAEL EWING, *associate producer:*

Tommy Boy, at that point, was called *Billy the III: A Midwestern.* It was changed because *Billy Madison* was being shot at the same time. Bonnie and Terry Turner had written the first draft. It was a sweet script, but it was a bit of a mess—and it was a famous bit of mess, because now Chris Farley was attached to it and it was going to get made. I walked in to the office the first day, and Pete said, "Well, what do you think of the script?"

I said, "I think we have work to do."

FRED WOLF:

I shared an office at *SNL* with Spade, Sandler, and Rock. Farley was always coming over to our office to hang out. It almost seemed like he was a part of the office, too. I was the quiet guy who observed them, and so it seemed like I might be a good guy to bring a little of their sense of humor to the page.

Jim Downey and I were hired to do a polish of the Turners' script. We were working on it literally as the pages came in. Then Downey had to go back to the show, leaving me to do what amounted to a full rewrite. We all went up to Toronto, and I started commuting back and forth to the show, just like Chris and David did. I got married while the film was being shot, and at one point I was writing pages from my hotel room in Hawaii and faxing them in. It was crazy.

PETER SEGAL, *director:*

Even though there was no script, I really believed in Chris. One night before production started, I was driving him to the Palm in L.A. to meet Brian Dennehy, who was to play his father. This was at a time when *Saturday Night Live* was in its nadir. People were writing all the articles about *"Saturday Night Dead"* and so on. And here we were with a movie with a fixed start date and no finished script. Chris turned to me and said, "Pete, everyone expects us to fail."

"Yeah," I said. "I think you're right."

"Our only victory will be a success."

And at that point I knew we were bonded, because we were both taking a leap of faith in each other, that we were gonna go through this as comrades. Fred Wolf had given us sixty-six pages. I called them the Magic Sixty-six, because that's all we had. We left for Toronto with very little to go on. It was like taking the pin out of a grenade and going jogging.

FRED WOLF:

It was my first movie. I didn't know enough to know that it was abnormal, though obviously it was. Pete and I would write until three or four in the morning, and then he'd have to be on the set by six. Then, while they were shooting what we'd written the night before, I'd be in the hotel room writing the scenes for the next day.

PETER SEGAL:

Fred and I would meet for dinner, or lie out on the floor of the hotel room with note cards, talking about things that'd happened to us. Fred would say, "I once left an oil can in the engine, and the hood flew up in my face."

And I'd say, "Great, put it down on a card. It's in."

Then I told him how I was once backing up at a gas station in Glendale and I hyperextended my car door on the cement post. So that went in. We just started building these stacks of cards.

After that, Fred and I would go to dinner and watch Chris and Dave interact, and we'd literally just start taking notes on things that they would say to each other. One day on the set, Chris came out with a new sport coat, and he said, "Does this coat make me look fat?"

And Spade said, "No, your face does."

I stopped what I was doing and said, "Wait, wait, wait. What was that? Say that again! That's gold! We gotta put that in the movie!"

Unfortunately, we ran into trouble with the start date. We were warned that if we started past a certain day in July we would run into the *Saturday Night Live* season and then we'd be splitting time with the show, which we ended up doing.

ERIC NEWMAN, *production assistant:*

Lorne had Paramount give us a plane that would shuttle Chris and David and me back and forth from Toronto to New York. It was my job to accompany them wherever they went. Mostly Chris. David didn't really need the accompaniment. We went back and forth twice a week. We'd shoot on Tuesday, fly down Wednesday morning, do the read-through, fly back up to Toronto, work for two days, then fly back down on Friday for blocking, do the show, then fly back to Toronto at four in the morning.

MICHAEL EWING:

To have Chris and David flying back and forth was actually lucky for us. We had a chance to write material so we'd have something to shoot when they got back. I would get calls at two in the morning from Pete and Fred. They would call and say, "You gotta call the casting director. We need a police officer for this new scene."

So I'd have to call casting, then wardrobe, then do everything to make sure that actor was ready first thing in the morning. The scene when Chris and David drive the car up to the airport, ditch it, and throw the guy the keys? That's that guy. He was hired at two-thirty in the morning and had to be on the set at sunrise. And that happened on a daily basis.

BOB WEISS:

It was rough, but the beautiful thing in *Tommy Boy* of course is the chemistry between Chris and David Spade. It wasn't like, "Hey, let's invent a comedy team." It's not that easy. There was just a hunch that their personal relationship would really pay off. And it did. A lot of what you see in that movie is who they really were. We started filming, and I was like, "Fuck, this is funny." They just hit home run after home run.

PETER SEGAL:

When *Tommy Boy* came out it was resoundingly dissed by every critic. But a couple of them, and one in the *L.A. Times*, said these guys were the new Laurel and Hardy. I was too young to really appreciate the Hope and Crosby *Road* movies, but there were certain comedy teams that were produced in the eighties, like Eddie Murphy and Nick Nolte, or Gene Wilder and Richard Pryor. It was kind of neat to think, God forbid, that these guys could become like them.

MICHAEL EWING:

We were having a reading of the script up in Canada. The studio had flown in for the occasion, and we knew we didn't have a third act. It was a fucking mess. It didn't go so well. But Chris was being his wonderful, boisterous self, kind of the life of the party, and at one point David Spade turned to him and said, "Chris!" Then he made this hand gesture like he was turning down his hearing aid a little bit. That was the first introduction that I had to them and their relationship.

DAVID SPADE:

We got close just by spending twenty-four/seven together. He trusted me enough to know I was a really great friend. And I was a huge fan—*fan*'s an odd word, but I really thought he was talented, and he knew that I genuinely believed that. During *Tommy Boy*, and even during *SNL*, I was always trying to come up with ways for him to score, to think of jokes for him, and that's a sacrifice you maybe don't see a lot of in show business. When we presented together at the Oscars, I came up with a punch line so I could set him up and he could get the laugh. Over time we just built up a mutual trust and respect.

ERIC NEWMAN:

Chris and David were somewhat competitive, which comes from being on *Saturday Night Live*. They all have that.

David was always looking to get out of work, wondering when he'd get days off. So we're on the plane one week, the three of us, and I get out a schedule. I have a copy, I hand David a copy, I'm taking David through it, and Chris goes "What is that?"

"Oh, David wanted a copy of the schedule," I say.

Chris rips my schedule out of my hand and says, "I get whatever David gets!"

Then he starts looking at it—sideways, because he can't figure it out—flips it upside down, can't figure it out, then drops it and abruptly pretends to fall asleep. It was hilarious. He'd acted out a little bit, and he knew it, so he tried to make it into a joke. He knew there were guys who became movie stars and became dicks, and he didn't want to become that guy.

LORNE MICHAELS:

I always said that while making the movies, Chris would put on thirty pounds and David would lose thirty pounds, but no matter what, the amount of weight in the frame stayed the same. Chris would get bigger, and you'd be saying "Get Spade a banana," because he was wasting away.

ROB LOWE, *costar*:

Chris and David were literally like an old married couple. They could be so petty with each other in ways that were so funny and unbelievable that you were never really sure when it was an act, which it often was, and when it crossed over to become real, which it often did.

The two instances I really remember were when they fought over me, like I was some girl. We were shooting in Toronto, and Spade and I had been at the gym at the same time and we ended up hanging out in the

Jacuzzi. Then, the next day, Chris said to Spade, "Where were you? I called you in your room."

"I was hanging out in the Jacuzzi with Rob."

"You were in the Jacuzzi with Rob?"

"Uh . . . yeah."

"Why didn't you guys call me?"

And it became this whole thing of who was in the Jacuzzi with me, and it just went on from there.

DAVID SPADE:

Then, one night after flying back from New York, Chris goes, "I got the flu, so when I land I'm going right to bed."

"Okay."

We got in to our hotel in Toronto. Chris was being cranky and grumpy, and he went to bed. Rob Lowe called, and I said, "Farley's crashing. You want to grab a drink?" He said sure. So we went down and we had one quick drink and went to bed, because we both had a six A.M. call.

The next day I'm sitting in makeup. Farley's staring at me in the mirror, biting his lip, which means there's a fight coming. He goes, "How's Rob Lowe?"

"He's all right."

"Huh? How's Rob Lowe?" And he kept saying it. "How's Rob Lowe?"

I said, "Uh, I don't get it."

"Where's your precious Rob Lowe?"

"Oh, you mean last night. Yeah, I had a drink with Rob Lowe."

"Oh, yeah. I heard all about it."

We'd just been together too much at that point. So we come to the set, it's twenty-five degrees and I'm huddling on the ground, waiting for the scene to start, trying to eat a tuna fish sandwich with my freezing fingers. Chris walks up and steps on the sandwich and my hand with his boot. I yell, "Ow, you motherfucker!"

And he goes, *"Huh?! How's Rob Lowe?"*

"*What?!*"

I throw my Diet Coke on him and he throws me into a wall and down the stairs and he comes to hit me and they yell, "*Action!*"

We both freeze in the middle of this fight, wait for our cue, and then open the door and walk in. I just stare at the other actors for a moment, and then I say, "Fuck this." And I walk out.

I just leave and go back to my room, and Farley goes, "What's *his* problem?"

Chris was actually jealous of Rob Lowe. He admitted it later. That's probably why I'm not married now; my first experience didn't work out.

MICHAEL EWING:

Best friends are always competitive, and comedians and actors are always competitive in a certain way. That's just part of it, that's part of the one-upmanship. And that carried over into their lives, with women and with friends. When you get people like Chris was, like Dave is, those are complicated relationships.

PETER SEGAL:

David had a boldness about calling out the elephant in the room where nobody else would. It was all playful, but it was the kind of humor that unless you knew Chris you would never go there. There was a lot of honesty in Dave's jokes toward Chris, and I think Chris appreciated the ballsiness of it. The guys from *SNL* all tell me that everyone felt Chris was the funniest guy. So for Dave to be the one to crack Chris up, well, that was like being the one to pluck the thorn from the lion's paw. He had a friend for life.

JULIE WARNER, *costar:*

David doesn't drink or do anything bad. He's very orderly, very much a grown-up at a young age. That stability is part of what attracted Chris to him. But I could see David's frustration. He knew that there was so much danger for Chris. He felt responsible, and it's too much responsibility for any one person. I've been around enough addicts to know that your greatest fear is to be abandoned. Chris knew David was never going to leave him, so there was safety there.

DAVID SPADE:

He trusted me. He also thought I was smart, whether I am or not. He would always ask my advice on a million things, and I would just try and help him in the best way I could. He had his problems, and it was a mounting pile of them as time went on. It was really hard for me. It scared me for myself. I wasn't even half as famous as he was, and I'm having my own weird stuff going on. Is this what it's like, being famous? Because it's getting harder and scarier to watch.

KEVIN FARLEY:

At the time of *Tommy Boy*, Chris was on his second year of sobriety. He already had a year under his belt. He was down to maybe 225 pounds, which was a pretty good weight for him. He could move really well in that movie, and it showed. That was probably the best he ever looked, and his sobriety was probably the best it had ever been. Everything was clicking on all levels.

MICHAEL EWING:

Every night after we'd finish shooting, I'd take him either to a meeting or to church to visit with his priest. Sometimes both. He would call the priest also, sometimes late at night. He was completely straight during that whole shoot. He was dedicated to helping himself, and he was totally serious about it.

PETER SEGAL:

He was very superstitious, and I think it all tied in to habits that he felt would keep him on the straight and narrow. His habit of visiting his priest every day, it was as much for the routine as for the actual counseling.

DAVID SPADE:

He had to pull up his pant leg twice and tap the ground twice before every take, which over the course of an entire movie gets a little annoying, to say the least. So one time while he was tapping the ground like that I said, "You know, Chris, the good thing about the devil is that he won't come to you. You have to summon him like you're doing now."

"What are you talking about?" he said.

"You see, I like God. That's just my own thing. But you like to tap on the roof of hell and invite the devil to join you."

"*Shut the fuck up.* That's not what I'm doing."

"Well, there's no superstition in the Bible, Chris, which you'd know if you ever leafed through it. That's something the devil made up so people would invite him into their lives."

He was fucking stunned. I loved it. He didn't know what to do. Even though I was totally bullshitting him, it sort of sounded like it made sense, and he just stared at me, frozen.

PETER SEGAL:

And there was no joking about that stuff, either. Every time he smoked a cigarette he brought it out backwards to his lips and touched it, and then turned it around and put it in his mouth. If he turned around, did a 360-degree turn to the right, he'd have to unwind and do another 360 to the left, like how you'd spin if you went around the corner and forgot something and came back for it. You'd ask him about it, and he'd say, "I gotta undo. I wound up to the right, and I gotta unwind to the left." There were all these habits. For some reason, I think they were comfort factors to Chris.

JULIE WARNER:

Chris looked everywhere for safety and support, and he felt very safe within the family he'd found on this film. Whatever feeling of acceptance he craved, I think he found it there.

Chris was very silly with me at first. He was like, "I can't believe they cast someone so pretty to be the love interest." He had this kind of goofy thing that he did around girls. It was like, "Oh, Julie, I can't even look at you. You're so pretty. I can't even talk to you."

It was put on, but it was obviously his defense for the fact that he couldn't have a real moment with you. That whole aw-shucks character he did on "The Chris Farley Show," that was all very deliberate. He'd say stuff to me like, "You were really good in *Doc Hollywood*. Especially in the naked part. You remember that time in *Doc Hollywood* when you were naked? You remember that? That was *awesome*."

At the beginning it was funny. Then it went on for weeks, every time I saw him. I even said to David, "Is it always going to be like that?"

He said, "Chris can't talk to girls he thinks are pretty."

To be an actor, you have to make it real, play off the other person, listen and react. And Chris had that. We really connected when we were acting together. Interestingly, when Chris was on camera, it was the only time I could get him to look me directly in the eye.

PETER SEGAL:

We went to a club one night after work. Chris came in a three-piece suit, wearing his black horn-rimmed glasses. There were a lot of pretty women there, and Chris looked really tense. I said, "What's the matter?"

He was looking at these beautiful women at the bar, and he said, "Pete, beauty makes me angry. I can't tell whether I want to take 'em home or club 'em over the head with an empty wine bottle."

I've quoted that line to so many people over the years. It was hilarious, but you could tell that he was tortured by his own insecurities. He was the bravest guy in the room, yet fearful in ways that he would never let on.

MICHAEL EWING:

Chris was very self-deprecating, so self-deprecating. It would leave you always thinking, you know, *ouch*. You could see that there was some wound just below the surface, just a hair below the surface, and sometimes not even that deep. One time on the set, the crew was cracking up after the take, which happened a lot, and Chris walked by and said, "Yep, everybody likes it when fatty falls down." I was like, oh, there's the crux of it.

JULIE WARNER:

It's hard for me not to be able to connect with someone I'm working with. At a certain point during the shoot, Chris was doing his routine, and I stopped him and said, "Can I have lunch with you? Can I just sit and talk to you?"

So we had lunch in his trailer, and he made about forty jokes about "I can't believe you're in my trailer" and all that. But eventually it all just went away. All the shtick, it was just gone. We talked about football, about Madison. I think once he realized I was a safe person he stopped being so sheepish. He had an amazing ability to keep people at arm's length.

We had one kiss at the end of the movie. It was kind of a throwaway moment, but he talked about it all morning. I really wanted to put him at ease about it, make him feel like I was psyched about it. Because I wasn't unpsyched about it or anything, and I actually thought Chris was sexy.

Talent is sexy. Chris was a big guy, but he was cute. I hated that he didn't feel worthy of that. The first time we kissed the crew applauded and ribbed him a little bit. He was really embarrassed, but once he got past it he was fine.

There was something deeply lonely about him. Profoundly and deeply lonely. He was a man. He wanted that kind of companionship, and yet he did not know how to get it.

TOM FARLEY:

Even though our dad was incredibly proud of Chris's career, Chris always suspected that what Dad really wanted was for him to settle down with a wife and kids. It's like, no matter how successful you are, until you show that you can raise a good family you haven't really proved yourself. That was the struggle that Chris always went through, wanting to be a family guy like Dad was and yet wanting the success in his acting life, too. But very few people can make it work on both ends successfully. If Dad had had a choice, he would have been running for Congress or making deals on Wall Street with all his Georgetown buddies. He'd given that up. But Chris could never be content with his professional success, because he was living by Dad's barometer and not his own.

FRED WOLF:

We weren't trying to write a movie about Chris and his dad, but I think a lot of it just subconsciously worked its way in there.

PETER SEGAL:

In writing that movie, we pooled our emotional stories as well as our comedic stories. It was all done out of desperation, and then, ironically, there was serendipity to it. I think Chris brought a lot of his relationship with his dad to that movie; he tapped into those feelings when Big Tom

Callahan died. But it wasn't Chris's story. It wasn't Fred's story. It wasn't my story. It was everyone's story.

BOB WEISS:

When Terry and Bonnie Turner were writing it, Terry would say, "Well, this is like my father's story." And Lorne would say that it was like his father's story. Turns out it was a lot like Chris's father's story. It made me wonder, well, whose father is it? I mean, what's the deal? But that's why the film is so accessible. We all know the dynamic of trying to struggle under this giant paternal shadow. It's universal.

BRIAN DENNEHY, *costar:*

When I got on the set I figured my job was to be like Chris, not for Chris to be like me. I had to create this crazy, Rabelaisian character who would be an older, more settled version of Chris's character. There was never any conversation about it; it's just something Chris and I both understood. When we did the scene outside my office where we did that sumo thing, bumping into each other, that was my idea. I said to Peter, "It should be like two crazy-ass rednecks or sumo wrestlers who meet in a bar and start tussling like wild bears." Because that's what they are, these characters. All that came out of my watching Chris and thinking what it would mean to be his father.

I think that character loved his son and, to a certain extent, spoiled him. I think he also represented the ideal father for all of us. Psychiatrists might not call him the perfect father, but a lot of kids would.

KEVIN FARLEY:

Chris always used to say, "I'm only doing funny stuff to make one guy back in Madison laugh." And if you saw my dad around town, talking about Chris, he'd be gushing. He couldn't have been prouder. But like a lot of dads, he was a little reserved about actually showing that to us. You want to have your dad say you did a good job. And Dad would do that. He'd go, "Good job, son." Really brusque and understated. But most families, especially Irish families, they just don't communicate that well.

BRIAN DENNEHY:

We all grow up with that necessity to be what our fathers want us to be, and probably, ultimately, failing. There's no question about that. My father's been dead now for twenty-five years, and there's not a day that goes by that I don't find myself thinking about it. Our relationship was unusual, my father's and mine. Our family was classically Irish Catholic in the sense that the family was unquestionably the most important aspect of all of our lives, and yet we were not close, if that makes any sense. There is an emotional distance between us that exists today.

Philip Larkin, a British poet whom I love very much, wrote a poem that really says it all: "They fuck you up, your mom and dad / They may not mean to, but they do. / They fill you with the faults they had / And add some extra, just for you." And that's not a criticism of parents, but I think it says that there's something inevitable about it. Your parents want you to know things that they've learned, but they can only do so much. You've pretty much got to learn it yourself.

PETER SEGAL:

Knowing more now about his relationship with his father, I recognize a lot of things in hindsight. Chris was a really good athlete. He idolized his coach, who was also a father figure. And I realized that the best way to work with Chris was not as a director but as a coach.

For example, take the day he shot the scene where he looks at his grades and says, "A D plus! I passed!!!" He wasn't getting it right, and he was so furious with himself. I told him to go out and run around the quad a couple of times and come back in. I said, literally, "Take a lap." There were times when he'd be so amped up with coffee and cigarettes that I'd have him drop and do twenty push-ups. I just needed him to work it off.

He'd go, take the lap, do the push-ups, then he'd come back and he'd look at me like I was about to put him into the game. And that was okay. Every actor is different, and that was how I had to deal with this particular person. In that instance, I was his coach. He would have walked through a brick wall for me if I'd asked him to.

ROB LOWE:

Pete Segal is a comedy mathematician. He really understands the timing and the beats in a way that a lot of other directors don't. And Chris's style was very wild and unstructured and, frankly, lacking in technique. So it was a good mix between the two of them.

JULIE WARNER:

I'm sure Paramount wasn't thrilled about the amount of money that was being spent, but Pete knew there was a gold mine there, and he was determined to get at it. He knew that the movie was only going to work if Chris was free to have fun, and that meant making sure he felt safe and not pressured. He gave Chris the trust and patience that I don't think he found anywhere else. Once Chris felt that safety, he was able to shine.

MICHAEL EWING:

What people responded to in the movie was the comedy, number one, but also this underlying heart that's woven through it. They're dancing at the wedding, and Brian Dennehy suddenly drops dead of a heart attack. I mean, what comedy has one of the main characters drop dead a third of the way through the movie? This is a comedy that people thought was just light and fun, but it also dealt with real things in a real way.

We were just a little movie, and by the end of the shoot Paramount didn't really want to spend any more money on music or anything. They said, "Here's the money to make the movie, and not a penny more."

Then Sherry Lansing saw the first screening. I was sitting across from her, and as the lights came up I could see there were tears running down her face. We went outside; she gave Pete a big hug and gave me a hug and said, "My God, where did all that heart come from? That wasn't in the script."

It was just one of those rare things that happens in movies sometimes. It all came together. Then they approved the extra money to do a real score and everything.

FRED WOLF:

The critics totally missed the point of *Tommy Boy*, and, of course, history has proven them wrong. It's seen as this mini comic gem. A few years ago, *Time* magazine listed the "Top 10 Movies to Watch to Make Yourself Feel Better." It went all the way back to *Adam's Rib* and *Cocoanuts* with the Marx Brothers, and *Tommy Boy* was on that list. That was really great to see. I wanted to fax that to every movie critic in America.

ROB LOWE:

To this day, people stop me on the street and say they love *Tommy Boy*. It's the ultimate movie for fifteen-year-old boys. And if you compare *Tommy Boy* to what they're making today for fifteen-year-old boys, it's the fucking *Magnificent Ambersons*.

DAVID SPADE:

Looking back it feels like it was a big hit, even though it wasn't. It did all right. It just has nice memories about it. It's the most-talked-about movie that I've ever had any part of, certainly, and that's ninety percent because of Chris.

PETER SEGAL:

The premiere was very small. The movie was about to start and everyone had gone to their seats. I was nervous as hell, and I went into the men's room. Chris came in behind me. He said, "Well, this is it." He was nervous as hell, too. We knew we had been through a real war together. On the same side, but still a war. To this day it's the most difficult shoot that I've ever experienced.

We stayed there in the men's room and talked for a little while, knowing that the movie was starting. It was like that moment when you buckle yourself in to a roller coaster and you know that, as afraid as you are of going up that first hill, there's nothing you can do about it. I gave him a hug, and he said—and he was very adamant about it—he said, "Please don't leave me. Let's do this again. Promise me we'll do this again."

MICHAEL EWING:

I have a tradition that I get all of the actors to sign my movie poster for me. So one day I gave Chris the *Tommy Boy* poster. He took it, signed it, and handed it back to me. And what it said just cut straight to my heart, and really surprised me. What he wrote on the poster was: "Dear Michael, Don't give up on me. Chris."

CHAPTER 10

The Lost Boys

MARILYN SUZANNE MILLER, writer:

In the years I was back at *Saturday Night Live*, I so didn't belong there. But then of course, no one belonged there. The cast didn't belong there. The writers didn't belong there. And we didn't belong there with each other. The whole thing was a real marriage of hope.

Just two years earlier, during the run of the 1992 presidential election, *Saturday Night Live* had been at the top of its game, consistently funny and culturally relevant. But in the fall of 1994, as Chris Farley and David Spade flew back and forth from Toronto to film *Tommy Boy*, they returned each week to find the show slipping further and further into confusion and disrepair.

Cast stalwarts Dana Carvey, Jan Hooks, and Phil Hartman had all left. In their place, Lorne Michaels had hired a slew of actors and comedians, both young and old, known and unknown. In all, the cast swelled to seventeen members, more than double the original group of Not Ready for Primetime Players in 1975. But in spite of all the talent in the room (or because of it), very little seemed to work. The cast was not a team. It was an odd collection of ill-fitting parts. There was little chemistry and no love lost among several of those sharing the stage. It was not a happy time.

Off-camera the changes were just as severe, and the process just as broken. The younger writers were coming to the fore, but the writing staff as a whole never gelled, especially with veterans like Al Franken and Marilyn Suzanne Miller feeling pushed out and stymied by the new generation. Caught in the midst of this chaos, and trying to manage it, was head writer Jim Downey. Downey's experience probably encapsulates best what everyone was going through: At the end of the year he was served with divorce papers on the same day he was fired.

With the show in a rut, Chris found himself in one, too. He put in a hilarious turn as a lost contestant on a Japanese game show, and he took on some of the show's political humor with his impression of House Speaker Newt Gingrich—a role that would even take him to the halls of Congress. But as far as memorable performances go, that fifth year added virtually nothing original to Chris's *SNL* legacy. The Motivational Speaker came back again (and again). So did the Gap Girls and the Super Fans. And as *Saturday Night Live* limped to the end of a particularly disappointing season, Chris's attentions drifted elsewhere.

MIKE SHOEMAKER:

It was a terrible year. Everyone was miserable. And once it starts getting bad, it almost has to get worse.

STEVE LOOKNER:

There was definitely a sense at the start of the '94–'95 season that we needed to make the show better. After every taping there was more discussion over what worked and what didn't, more of a conscious effort to pull things together. Nobody wanted to be the cast that brought *Saturday Night Live* to an end.

TIM HERLIHY:

The ratings plunged. It wasn't just a critical reaction; it was a popular one, too.

JIM DOWNEY:

My feeling was that the show had been running on vapors for a while, but the ratings had been crazily spiked by *Wayne's World*. It annoyed me that the network didn't care if the show sucked while the ratings were high. They only cared if the show sucked and the ratings were low.

DAVID MANDEL:

It was just very unclear what the show was supposed to be. When you look at the 1992 year, you had Carvey and Myers and Hartman, Jan Hooks and Kevin Nealon. Those guys were all-stars. Hartman used to put on a bald cap and play ten different characters with ten different voices in ten different sketches. So the beauty of adding a guy like Sandler to that group was that Sandler could go on Update and do his weird, funny thing and kill with it. Same with Chris. He could be a killer supporting part, like in the "Da Bears" sketches, then turn and have his own starring role, like in the "Chippendales" sketch. That was all you really needed of Farley in a given show. It was like a flavor of something. Jim Downey used to say something very interesting, and I will paraphrase it. He used to say that Farley and Sandler were like the special teams on a football team, the great kicker or the great punter, the guy you need to come on, do his thing, and then get off the field.

After the all-stars like Hartman left the show, it never seemed like a working cast so much as "Here's the Sandler sketch. Here's the Farley sketch. Here's the Spade sketch." All of a sudden, we were playing a football game with nothing but these special teams guys out on the field, and that's not a team that's going to play well for a whole four quarters.

JANEANE GAROFALO, *cast member:*

The system was flawed in a way that funneled the cream to the bottom and the mediocrity to the top. When we did the table read-throughs on Wednesdays, there were always funny sketches in there. Rarely did they hit the air. Downey was still there, but he wasn't spiritually there. I think there were some personal things going on in his life that he wasn't fully present, emotionally. He didn't have the reserves needed to manage the room. The system was just broken.

MARK McKINNEY, *cast member:*

People were clinging to the stuff that worked in a time without a lot of focus. It was really, really hard slogging. But I saw Chris as ensconced in a brotherhood of his own making with several of the writers. He was comfortable in a way that I never was.

JANEANE GAROFALO:

Chris had the luxury of not only being talented but also well liked. When he would come onstage, even just to take his mark during a commercial break, people would start cheering. It was clear that he was an audience favorite, and kind of the go-to guy for a laugh.

FRED WOLF:

All the writers wanted to get their stuff on the show, and you learned very quickly that there were guys that you could count on. You could ride their charisma onto the air. We would do that with Chris.

Ian Maxtone-Graham gave me this diagram he'd made of "Fred Wolf's Sketches for Chris Farley." There were three different dials on it. The first one was labeled "Chris is: Dry. Moist. Soaking Wet." And the dial was set on "Soaking Wet." The second one was labeled "Chris is: Quiet. Talking Loud. Screaming at the Top of His Lungs." And the dial was set on

"Screaming at the Top of His Lungs." The third one was labeled "Chris is saying: Gosh! Oh no! Oh, sweet mother of God!" And the dial was set to "Oh, sweet mother of God!"

It seemed like every sketch I wrote for a while had Chris getting soaking wet and screaming, at the top of his lungs, "Oh, sweet mother of God!" But I couldn't resist writing them, because they would always bring down the house.

ROBERT SMIGEL:

When we did the first "Motivational Speaker" sketch, I added something that I thought was really helpful at the time but that I somewhat regretted later. The sketch was pretty much word for word as Bob Odenkirk had written it at Second City, except for the ending. The stage version didn't really have a topper for Chris, other than "You'll have plenty of time to live in a van down by the river when you're . . . living in a van down by the river!" Chris was so powerful onstage that it carried you to the end. But TV flattens stuff out and I thought it needed something more, so I added the part where he's telling David Spade, "Ol' Matt's gonna be your shadow! Here's Matt, here's you! There's Matt, there's you!" And then he falls and smashes through the table.

It worked really well, but it inaugurated this trend of Chris being really clumsy and falling down a lot. There were several more "Motivational Speaker" sketches, and all of those ended with him crashing through something. Then the writers started having him fall through other stuff. He used to joke about it. "Everybody laughs when fatty falls down." Chris and I would laugh about how hacky it had become. I'd say, "Chris, give me a triple boxtop." And he'd do a certain kind of fall for me.

That sort of broad clumsiness was actually the opposite of what Chris's talents as a physical comedian were. What really struck me at Second City was how graceful and nimble and athletic he was, a brilliant physical performer who was also capable of really specific, subtle things. But a lot of that got buried in this succession of sketches with yelling and pratfalls. It was to Chris's detriment, and the show's.

JANEANE GAROFALO:

I think that the writers began to use him as a bit of a crutch, but that's not entirely the writers' fault. There's a natural instinct among a lot of comedians, particularly younger ones, to want to get a laugh. You want desperately to be liked, and sometimes the quickest route is to be loud and broad in your gestures. I think Chris did that in the beginning, and then, unfortunately, it stuck.

DAVID MANDEL:

As much as the writers used him in a certain way, he also liked working in that certain way. It was easy for him to default to the pratfalls and so on. He could power through a sketch just by hiking up his pants and playing with his hair. Those were stock Chris Farley moves. He also hadn't started wearing his glasses when he should, and he couldn't always read the cue cards. You'd write a quiet, subtler sketch, and he'd flub a line 'cause he'd miss the cue card. So maybe you didn't want to take a chance with him on that kind of sketch, and you'd default to something loud and physical.

There was never any sketch where we said, "This sketch isn't working. Let's have Farley walk in to be the joke." It was not a fallback move. But there were definitely a lot of sketches, especially in that last season, that could be reduced to: "Chris yells a lot."

MICHAEL McKEAN:

It paralleled Raymond Chandler's rule: Any time the action starts to slow up, just have a guy come through the door with a gun. That's how they used Chris. He would bring a lot of juice to what could have looked like lazy writing, and he saved a lot of bad sketches. There was this sketch with Deion Sanders—I mean, the comedy stylings of Deion Sanders, first of all—where this flying saucer lands and they keep sending men in to explore, and they all either get killed or anally probed. Then they send Chris in, and he comes out with his clothes in tatters, virtually naked, having been anally violated. That's all there was to the sketch. In fact, I think I've probably embroidered it a little. But even with that, Chris gave it a shot, and he was funny.

JANEANE GAROFALO:

The Deion Sanders alien anal probing sketch, it was so embarrassing.

AL FRANKEN:

The show was always best when there was a balance between the writers and the performers, when both were operating at their peak level and working together. To some extent, Sandler and Spade and Schneider and those guys were not in sync with the writers, at least with my generation of writers. I was not thrilled with what was happening. But maybe it was just time for me to go.

MARILYN SUZANNE MILLER:

There was a quality among those guys, Rob Schneider, Adam, Chris, and Spade, that it was "our show." It was a very David Spade attitude, and it certainly excluded me. Also, I think they knew that, at the bottom line, we weren't loaded with respect for what they were coming up with.

For some reason the phrase "anal probe" found its way into virtually every sketch. Most of those didn't make it to air, but at the read-through table it seemed like "anal probe," "bitch," and "whore" had assumed the same status as "Good morning, how are you?" It was imbecilic and just as offensive as offensive could be.

TOM SCHILLER:

I think that the humor did change, and I didn't get into it that much. And that's because the times changed. But the stuff we were doing in the first five years of *SNL*, I wouldn't say it was necessarily so smart. When they talk about this "dumbing down of comedy," I think comedy just keeps changing with the times, all the time. You can trace the evolution of vaudeville to *Ed Sullivan* to *Your Show of Shows* to *Laugh-In* to *Saturday Night Live*. And it just keeps evolving.

JOHN GOODMAN:

It's similar to what happened to the guys who took over *National Lampoon* after Doug Kenney and Henry Beard left, when it all fell to tits and racial slurs. Michael O'Donoghue used to say that comedy isn't a rapier; it's clubbing a baby seal. But you can only club that baby seal for so long.

TOM DAVIS:

They were taking their cues from *Animal House*, whereas we had taken our cues from Bob and Ray, Sid Caesar, and Johnny Carson. Comedy just takes these turns. But that show has to stay young. It doesn't matter if you like it or agree with it or think it's funny. It has to stay young.

MARILYN SUZANNE MILLER:

Chris was part of this gang, and he identified with this sort of gang spirit that they had. When he and Adam and Spade did those Gap Girls, it was kind of like the gang was getting together to play, only they were doing it on national television. They were like the Little Rascals, or the Lost Boys from Never-Never Land.

I remember being overwhelmed one night at some of the capers that were going on. All these overtly sexual—and, frankly, homoerotic—hi-jinks. Just constantly grabbing each other's asses—and much worse than that. I went into an office with Al Franken, and he explained to me that when a bunch of guys are marooned on an island together, as was the case with that show, you get this kind of behavior. It happens at boys' prep schools, on submarines. There was a sketch Jim Downey wrote on the old show, "The Adventures of Miles Cowperthwaite." It was about this young boy trapped on a ship with all these pirates, and it was all about manly men being manly and doing manly things at sea to prove their manliness—and they all turn out to be gay. Everything these kids were doing was like that.

JIM DOWNEY:

It became more of the atmosphere of the show, because you had this critical mass of young guys. I always went to all-boys schools, so I have to admit it's something that makes me laugh, you know, when it's done right. Chris would burst through the double doors of the writers' room with his pants around his ankles and his privates tucked back between his thighs doing the thing from *Silence of the Lambs.* He'd start rubbing his breasts and saying, "Am I pretty?" It was just so balls out, so to speak. I mean, you had to give it up for that.

MIKE SHOEMAKER:

Comedy people, when we're alone and insulated, just get more and more shocking, and it doesn't play to the rest of the world. It's the same way to this day. I've seen worse before and since. A lot of it was disgusting, but in the context of this place it was always funny. We were just constantly thinking, oh, this is so damn funny, but if anybody saw it we'd all be arrested.

JIM DOWNEY:

It's hard not to laugh even if you think it's encouraging irresponsible behavior. Sometimes, to get Chris to stop doing something, we'd talk among ourselves while he was out of the room and agree not to laugh no matter how funny it got. Chris'd get perplexed, and eventually frustrated, because no one was laughing. Then he would just escalate more.

Farley liked to do this routine where he would jokingly hit on waitresses. He'd say, "Well, little lady, I've got a problem. I'm in from Moline,

Illinois—work with a grain elevator outfit out there—and I'm in town for a couple days on business. And darn it, if I don't use my whole expense account the home office'll be liable to cut me back. So, how's about you and me do this town up right." And so on, using all this weird, Jazz Age lingo. You'd be like, Chris, what the hell are you talking about?

One night we were at this Mexican restaurant in Midtown named Jose's. It was one of those places where you buzzed downstairs and they let you in and the entire restaurant was up on the second floor. One night, Farley was doing his goofy routine with the waitress all night, and she was kind of rolling her eyes, like, "Yeah, yeah, buddy."

The rest of us, I suppose, were not giving him enough attention, so he felt he had to take it up a notch. He jumped up, scooped her up in his arms, and ran down the stairs and out of the restaurant. I turned and looked out the window, and I saw him dashing up Fifty-fourth Street and getting into a cab with her. We all hung back, staying in the restaurant, like, "We're not going to bite. We can't give him the satisfaction." Then I said, "Jesus, we could all be sued." I was acting in loco parentis with these kids, so I ran downstairs after him. But Chris liked to do that, do big put-ons with strangers who didn't know who he was. In most cases people realized it was a joke and were happy to be a part of it.

NORM MacDONALD:

Chris would do things with girls, like a kid would do. He'd always be like, "You shure are purty. Can I touch your leg?" It was all for the comic effect of how you're *not* supposed to approach a girl. It was all harmless, but obviously because he had a lot of money, some extra came on the show and decided this amounted to sexual harassment.

JIM DOWNEY:

The second-to-last show of the '93–'94 season, I had written a piece about Bill Clinton called "Real Stories of the Arkansas Highway Patrol." We had to go upstate and do some outdoor filming. Some women were extras in the piece, and one of them went up in the car with us. It was me and her and Schneider and Farley. It was a limo, with that wide space between the two rows and seats facing each other. Schneider and I were sitting together, and Farley was next to this girl. He was doing his usual "Hey there, little lady!" shtick. And he was poking her and hugging her, but if you knew Chris you knew it was all playful. I finally told him to knock it off—not because I thought it was assaultive behavior but because it was getting annoying.

Well, this girl went to the talent department and complained, hinting at some sort of legal action for what Chris had done. But Chris never did anything wrong. I know because I was sitting there, and as the producer of the show I never would have allowed it. My impression, honestly, was that she was mostly complaining about the size of her part. She thought she had several lines, and it actually wasn't a speaking role. I think we paid her for a speaking part instead of as an extra, and that was the end of it.

MIKE SHOEMAKER:

Nothing ever came of it. It was actually a very minor incident. It became a much bigger story in people's minds because of the prank that followed, more so than because of the incident itself.

JIM DOWNEY:

So the next week it's last show of the season. Farley came in, and we decided to have some fun with him. It was just completely random and totally unplanned. He came by, and I said to him very casually, "Chris, you know about the lawsuit, right?"

"What?" he said.

"You know, the sexual harassment suit. Anyway, you're not going to do any jail time. That's—don't worry about that. I mean, it's not one hundred percent you won't, but it's at least a sixty to seventy percent chance you won't do any jail time."

"Wh-what are you talking about?"

"You know. The girl from the limousine. Anyway, it's too early to tell, but NBC's lawyers are all over it."

He was really starting to shake and sweat. Then the other writers started gathering around. Mind you, I'd seen Farley do plenty of similar put-ons to other people, so in no way did I think this was unfair. And also, I thought that he needed to learn a lesson, that the kind of outlandish behavior he pulled in the limo can have consequences, even if it's harmless and well intentioned.

I said, "Now, Chris, I used to be a process server, so I know how this works. If you're walking down the street, for the next two . . . well, for the next several months, if you're walking down the street and someone approaches you, do not wait to find out who it is—you *run*. You flat out run."

And then Ian Maxtone-Graham chimed in, "Oh yeah, I was a process server for a whole summer. If they even *touch* you with the document, you've been served. If it touches anywhere on your person."

Eventually, everyone's getting in on this, giving Chris advice on how to hide out and things like that. I don't know what happened with Chris in the intervening days, but we went to the prop department and had them make up a subpoena, and I had one of the writers I knew from *Seinfeld* serve Farley with a lawsuit at the end-of-the-season party. He was devastated. A couple of people were coming up to me, saying, "C'mon, that's cruel. He's close to tears."

NORM MacDONALD:

Chris was just ashen, and the even crueler part was that they didn't let him in on the joke until an hour or two later. To make it that much worse, his mother was standing right there beside him when it happened. It was really terrible.

MICHAEL McKEAN:

It was a really shitty thing to do.

JIM DOWNEY:

And I was like, "Now, wait a minute. I've seen Chris put many a waitress through the paces before. He's a big boy." But finally I said, "Okay, let's end it." I went over and talked to him. It took me about a half hour to convince him that it was a put-on. As far as I heard, he was never mad about it, because he liked to put one over on other people, too. I talked to him a few days later and I reminded him, "You're a celebrity now, and people will be on the make. You should keep that fake subpoena as a reminder not to do anything that could be misconstrued."

And he said, "I don't have it. I burned it."

It was like he had to destroy the evidence of the whole thing.

FR. MATT FOLEY, friend:

Chris was very much a man's man. There were girls who were his friends, but anyone who was being honest would say he did some pretty inappropriate things with women. He was often mean to them. It was weird. It was the trust thing: Will you love me for who I am?

Chris used to say that every girl he went out with before he got famous looked like him with a wig on. Not to slam those women, but it's probably true. Then, all of a sudden, he's famous and these hot girls are all over him. So obviously, sexual issues, relationships, were very difficult things for him. I think he trusted God implicitly; I don't think he trusted people. "Why do these women want to go out with me?" He was very confused by that. He didn't trust them. He didn't know who to trust.

TIM MEADOWS:

That was something we talked about quite a bit. He'd always say, "How could any beautiful girl love my fat ass?"

MARILYN SUZANNE MILLER:

One of the real differences between John Belushi and Chris Farley was that John Belushi was married, whereas Chris was sort of the opposite of married. I wouldn't even put him in the category of "single." He wasn't single; he was the opposite of married.

FR. MATT FOLEY:

He went out with this girl named Lorri—her nickname was Kit Kat—this really hot girl. I was in New York one weekend and Chris told me, "I really like this Kit Kat girl." I saw her on the set. She was this five-foot-ten Victoria's Secret model, long legs, just hot. They clearly weren't going to talk about second-century world history together. Chris said, "What should I do? I don't know if she likes Spade or not. I want to ask her out, but I'm so confused."

I said, "Well, Chris, why don't you go to work today and ask David if it's okay if you ask her out?"

He did, David said it was okay and he asked her out. So here we are on a date, Chris, Kit Kat—and me, his priest. The next night we all went to a movie together. It was just bizarre as hell. It was like I was back in eighth grade.

DAVID SPADE:

Lorri lived directly across the street from me. I'd see her at the deli. She was this Victoria's Secret girl, who I eventually realized was one of the Victoria's Secret girls back from when I used to look at Victoria's Secret and found her quite striking. She was very friendly. I invited her to the show, and we started talking. I didn't have a whole lot of friends in New York outside of *SNL*, so it was nice to meet someone to hang out with.

We became friends and started dating. Chris would hang out with us. She thought he was funny, and I didn't mind that he'd come along. This happened a lot, and he'd always paw all over her, going, "You're so purdy," and all that. And I wouldn't get mad, but I was like, "Dude, be a little more respectful, to me and her. C'mon with that shit."

Then sometimes Lorri and I would go do stuff, and I'd say, "You know, Chris isn't doing anything this weekend. Can he come with us?"

LORRI BAGLEY, *girlfriend:*

Chris and I met because we were both best friends with David Spade. David and I had met, and we just clicked. We'd meet for breakfast, hang out after work. We even wound up living across the street from each other. Before Chris and I met, David would always say, "You're just like Chris. The two of you are the same person."

"I want to meet him," I'd say.

"No, if you do, you'll fall in love with him."

Men being men, I think David would have liked to date me, but for me it was just never like that. He asked me to go to the movies one night, and I said no, because I didn't want to be alone in a movie theater with him. So he said, "I'll bring Chris."

For a year, the three of us were just friends. We were like this fun-loving threesome that hung out together all the time. It was the most fun time of my life in New York. This was all about a year before *Tommy Boy*. I was a model, and I was doing Victoria's Secret shoots, and Fred Wolf said, "We have to have a pretty girl in the movie. It should be you." So I did the scene as the girl in the pool at the motel.

After *Tommy Boy*, we all kept hanging out just like before. Chris and I had never really been alone. We were always with David or a group. But Chris would always do these little things, like pulling my chair closer to his at the dinner table—little things that said, "She's mine." One night after my acting class, we were all at the Bowery Bar, just dancing and having fun. Sandler was there. It got late, people were going home, and Chris wanted to go out some more. Sandler looked at us and was like, "You guys are *baaaaad* . . ." He saw the connection. So Chris and I went out alone. That was the first night he kissed me. He was a very good kisser.

When it all first came up, Chris came to my apartment and said, "I have to work with David. Until I finish *Saturday Night Live*, we can't see each other, because I can't go to work every day and have that kind of stress."

I said I understood, and we stayed apart for like three days. We just couldn't do it. David lived right across the street from me, on West Seventy-ninth, so that didn't make it easy. One night there was an after party for the show. Chris didn't go so he could come and see me, but it turned out David didn't go, either. He came home and saw Chris in the car out front waiting for me to come down.

I was getting ready to head out when David called me. "Is that Chris waiting for you downstairs?" he said.

"Um . . . yeah."

"You fucking bitch."

And he hung up the phone.

NORM MacDONALD:

It drove a wedge between them. Chris wasn't a ladies' man like Spade was. Chris wanted to fall in love and be married. Spade's the opposite. He's a real playboy. Chris decided that Spade had a million girlfriends, so he could have just this one.

TIM MEADOWS:

Spade dates nothing but hot girls, still to this day. But for Farley she was a coup.

DAVID SPADE:

And that was the part that ultimately kind of pissed me off. I had brought him into the mix. I should have just kept it the two of us, but I always made sure Chris was involved, because he didn't have anyone.

Enjoying the early days at *SNL*, (from left) Chris, Erin Maroney, the late Kevin Cleary, and Todd Green

Chris's breakout role at *Saturday Night Live*: the much-adored, and much-maligned, Chippendales sketch, with host Patrick Swayze

As Matt Foley, the thrice-divorced motivational speaker, berating cast mate David Spade (left) and host Christina Applegate

The eponymous heroine of "Lunchlady Land," a rousing high school cafeteria anthem by Adam Sandler (right center)

"Awesome!" Basking in the glow of former Beatle Paul McCartney in an episode of "The Chris Farley Show"
© 1993 EDIE BASKIN

Goofing around during rehearsal as the Blind Melon "Bee Girl," with Second City and *SNL* cast mate Tim Meadows
© 2007 COURTESY OF THE FARLEY FAMILY ARCHIVES

Riding high on the success of the "Super Fans" at Chicago's Soldier Field, with *SNL* writer Robert Smigel
© 2007 COURTESY OF THE FARLEY FAMILY ARCHIVES

Preparing for the big wedding scene in *Tommy Boy*, (from left) John Farley, Chris, Bo Derek, David Spade, and Kevin Farley

"Interestingly, when Chris was on camera, it was the only time I could get him to look me directly in the eye." —*Tommy Boy* costar Julie Warner

"Holy Schnike!" With Big Tom Callahan (Brian Dennehy) on the set of *Tommy Boy*
© 1995 PARAMOUNT

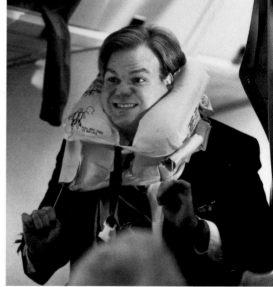

Tommy Callahan fumbling his way to Chicago as
a phony airline attendant
© 1995 PARAMOUNT

Being coached by director Peter Segal
on the set of *Tommy Boy*
© 1995 PARAMOUNT

Chris playing with his dinghy on the set of *Tommy Boy*
© 2007 COURTESY OF THE FARLEY FAMILY ARCHIVES

Escorting his mother (left) to the *Tommy Boy* premiere on the Paramount lot
© 2007 COURTESY OF THE FARLEY FAMILY ARCHIVES

With Lorri "Kit Kat" Bagley

A prop photo used in the filming of *Black Sheep*, with Chris in character as kids' rec center counselor Mike Donnelly

BS - TW - AD - 91   BS - TW - AD - 92   BS - TW - AD - 93

BS - TW - AD - 94   BS - TW - AD - 95   BS - TW - AD - 9(

Performing for the cameras—a contact sheet from a *Black Sheep* publicity photo shoot
© 1996 TIMOTHY WHITE

Rough times on the *Black Sheep* set for Chris and David
© 1996 PARAMOUNT

On the set of *Beverly Hills Ninja*, (from left) Ted Dondanville, John Farley, Kevin Farley, Chris, director Dennis Dugan, and Chris Rock
© 2007 COURTESY OF THE FARLEY FAMILY ARCHIVES

Dear Mom and Dad 12/19/95
I am so sorry to have
put you through so much worry.
I can't explain what happened.
I think the stress of my —
upcomming movie pluse the
problems I'm having with Ninja
got to me. I Wanted to escape.
I Now know more than ever,
Booze is never the answer. I
Can't tell you how awful I felt
The guilt, The shame, The hard work
to get those three yrs gone with
a sip of that Booze. This is a
wonderful place and I'm getting
stronger than ever. One good
thing I know I will never let
anything take away my sobriety
again. Not work, not relationships
nothing. I will have a stronger
sobriety because of this, because
I know how wonderful it is. And so
I'm here getting stronger, I'm only sorry
I'll have to miss you at Christmas.
I'll miss you so much. please think of
me because you can bet I'll be thinking
of you. I love you Both with all my Hart.
Chris

A letter from Chris to his parents, written from rehab on the heels of his first relapse in three years

© 2007 COURTESY OF THE FARLEY FAMILY ARCHIVES

A moment of reflection while filming *Edwards & Hunt* (*Almost Heroes*)
© 2007 COURTESY OF THE FARLEY FAMILY ARCHIVES

With friend and Chicago radio
personality Erich "Mancow" Muller
COURTESY OF PHILBIN FLASH

With Jillian Seely at Tim Meadows's wedding in the fall of 1997
COURTESY OF JILLIAN SEELY

With Adam Sandler, Chris Rock, and *SNL* writer Tim Herlihy, also at Meadows's wedding
COURTESY OF JILLIAN SEELY

US REPORT
BY ERIK HEDEGAARD

LIKE HIS GOOFBALL CHARACTERS, HE IS SWEET, LIKABLE AND OUT OF CONTROL. HE SAYS HE WANTS TO CHANGE – HE DOESN'T WANT TO END UP LIKE HIS IDOL JOHN BELUSHI. IS HE KIDDING HIMSELF? Photograph by Dan Winters

Chris Farley:
ON THE EDGE OF DISASTER

IT'S A SHIMMERY CALIFORNIA DAY, QUITE WARM, PERFECT FOR TRUE-LOVE romance or maybe a quick bonk, and Chris Farley, the comic and really big guy, is cruising up La Cienega Boulevard in a red Mustang convertible. The massive expanse of his forehead and the bristling parabola of his Fu Manchu are dewy with sweat. He's got that hair that shoots out, giving him a zonked, horned look. He's wearing a black linen suit, a shirt the color of flaming napalm and, over his eyes, a pair of highly electric, blue-tinted shades.

At a traffic light, a car pulls up next to his. Farley dips his head, peers inside and sees two "hot tamales," as he likes to call them. Dimly, an idea formulates. It boils down to this: If he plays his cards right, who knows what might develop?

"Hi, gals!" he booms, waving. "How ya doing, gals! Excuse me, gals! It's Rex Flexal here! Hey, do you know how to get to the Beverly Center?"

The girls look him over. It's an odd, suspended moment. They seem to recognize the big guy — this is Hollywood, after all, where just about anybody could be somebody — but they aren't sure. They ponder him, his hefty size, his bright happy cheeks, his otherworldly outfit, trying to make up their mind about what he is, what he stands for, where he could possibly have come from and what his prospects might be.

"What's your problem?" one of them says finally.

"You're a f---ing a--hole," the other one says.

Then they are off, at full speed, leaving Farley — who sometimes calls himself Rex Flexal — far behind.

I turn his way, expecting to see at least mild embarrassment. Instead, Farley wears a comical, stunned-carp look, like he can't believe what just happened. "Do you think they're lesbians?" he bellows in my direction. I find myself nodding vigorously. Then Farley scratches his head and lights a cigarette.

"All I wanted to do was strike up a conversation," he says. "What if I was in need of direction? I mean, what if I was really in need of direction?"

The question hangs in the air. It lingers. And then its specifics fade, leaving behind only the general idea of direction and whether Farley — this fellow in the blue-tinted shades and the flaming-napalm shirt, the man of so many unseemly rumors, mostly having to do with drugs, and drinking, and binge eating, and one or two sexual matters, not to mention the occasional spat with pal and frequent movie-making partner David Spade — could perhaps use a tad more of it, that thing, direction.

AT LEAST PROFESSIONALLY, FARLEY NOW FINDS HIMSELF IN THE MOOD for change. The first time we meet, in Room 905 of the ultraswank Beverly Hills Four Seasons hotel, the first thing Farley says is, "David Mamet just wrote a script for me on the life and times of Roscoe Arbuckle. You know the man, the 1920s comic, Fatty Arbuckle? It's a tragic story. He was a huge star, bigger than Chaplin, but he was brought to his knees through this incident with this girl. She died. He was acquitted. It's a complicated story. It will be a departure from what I've previously done."

The details of the Fatty plot line aren't entirely clear to me, though I have heard the name before. But I do get Farley's point. In the trio of movies that made him a star — *Tommy Boy* and *Black Sheep*, both co-starring David Spade, and *Beverly Hills Ninja* — as well as during

Chris's problems go public four and a half months before his death
US LAYOUT: COURTESY OF WENNER MEDIA

Trying to unwind during one of too many trips to rehab

Fumbling his way through the opening sketch of his catastrophic *Saturday Night Live* hosting appearance, with Tim Meadows (left) and Lorne Michaels

Tom Arnold (right) arriving for Chris's funeral at Our Lady Queen of Peace Church in Madison, Wisconsin

Holly Wortell, Bob Odenkirk, Bonnie Hunt (turned away), George Wendt, and Robert Smigel outside Our Lady Queen of Peace

Lorne Michaels leaving the funeral service

FRED WOLF:

I loved Lorri Bagley. She was great. It's really fun to walk around with celebrities and see everyone's reactions. But when we walked around and Lorri Bagley was part of it, she definitely did not detract from the excitement factor. She just had a stunning quality about her.

TODD GREEN:

She was so beautiful. Chris would just look at Kevin and me and shrug his shoulders like, "Can you *fucking* believe that I'm with this woman?"

We were playing golf down in Hilton Head. Chris was down there at some diet clinic and a bunch of us went down every year to play golf. Chris was actually not a bad golfer, but he wasn't having a good game. He was just getting frustrated. All day he kept muffing his drives and missing putts and getting more and more angry. Finally I said to him, "Farls, why are you so upset? You're dating Kitty Kat."

He just howled. He did that really deep, guttural laugh he had. And for the rest of the entire round, every time he missed a shot he'd just shrug and say, "Hey, I'm dating Kitty Kat."

She was flighty, but she really cared for Chris, and she genuinely loved him.

LORRI BAGLEY:

Chris would tell me stories about his life before he was sober, and I just couldn't picture it. He liked that. He liked that I couldn't even imagine that side of him. He was so organized, and so hardworking. He'd wake up every morning and make his bed, go to his meeting. He had the neatest, cleanest apartment.

And he was so romantic, always a gentleman. He would always walk on the street side of the sidewalk, always stand up when you left the table, and always stand up for you when you came back to sit down. He was very elegant that way, chivalrous, like someone from a different time.

Once we were meeting for dinner in New York. We were supposed to meet at a certain time, and I got there forty-five minutes late. He had been outside waiting for me the whole time, just so he could be there to open the door and make sure he could pay for the taxi. I mean, who does that? That's so much better than flowers.

Although when he did buy me flowers, that was always special, too. I was in this phase where I was always changing my hair color, and whatever my hair color was, he'd match the roses to it. I always loved that. He never got just red. One time the florist messed up and sent me plain red roses. He was so upset he called and bitched them out. He just hated to be typical. He wanted there to be thought behind everything he did.

Another time I was in Los Angeles, and we'd gotten into this huge fight. I said, "Okay, come out to L.A. and we'll work things out." I was staying at the Four Seasons. Every hour on the hour he sent something new. One hour it was flowers. The next hour it was a bottle of champagne. It went on for ten hours.

And the first night I spent with him, he got up to go downstairs to get water. I was lying there without any clothes on. He went to his closet and got out his robe and came and wrapped it around me, just so I would feel safe. He was a beautiful man.

* * *

While things were going well for Chris privately, *Saturday Night Live* had continued to suffer, and it was clear that major structural changes were needed. Early in the year, reporters had begun to take aim at the show's shortcomings, and by season's end the media had launched a full-fledged assault. Particularly derogatory was a *New York* magazine article by a reporter who had lived in and among the cast for several weeks. While the criticisms in the piece were not wholly without merit, its perspective was rather myopic, and its tone was unrelentingly foul. The magazine's cover featured Chris wearing a television on his head—the poster boy for the death of *Saturday Night Live*. And the headline of the piece, "Comedy Isn't Funny," wasn't exactly what Chris thought his legacy at the show would be.

TIM HERLIHY:

The stuff with the press that year was heartbreaking. Not only were they saying bad things, but Phil Hartman was saying things to *TV Guide*, and a lot of us were being misquoted here and there. The show was just being eviscerated.

FRED WOLF:

The worst hit piece was the *New York* magazine article. The guy who wrote that was living in our midst for at least half a season. He was around all the time. Then all this stuff came out and he just tore the show apart.

NORM MacDONALD:

The guy was really down on Chris in the article, but when Chris was telling stories in the writers' room, this reporter was on the floor. He was laughing like crazy. But the guy had the agenda to write this hit piece, and he was going to write it regardless. Even when he came there and found out that Chris was funny, it didn't matter to him. And then to have Chris go to a photo shoot where they put a TV on his head and to put him on the cover—to put a guy through all that, completely unknowing of what you're going to write about him, it was just low.

Later, when Chris filmed *Dirty Work* with me, he was saying he felt bad that he and Sandler had "ruined the show."

I said, "No, Chris. That's insane. They said that at the time, but you guys have all come out as the biggest comedy stars in the world."

MIKE SHOEMAKER:

The irony is that Farley and Sandler were the poster boys for the show's problems that year, and yet every week we'd do a show and they were the only ones getting laughs.

JIM DOWNEY:

What I didn't like was the opportunism of the press. It was a lot of late hits and piling on after the whistle. Basically, to be honest, I just wanted out.

MIKE SHOEMAKER:

At the end of the season, everything was in limbo. Nobody knew who or what was coming back, management included. Nobody thought the show would be canceled, but we thought we might be. There was never a time when Chris and those guys were officially fired. Everyone just kind of instinctively knew it was time to move on. All the writers just left, every single one of them.

DAVID MANDEL:

I'd love to say it was an ax coming down, a real housecleaning, which is what *SNL* needed. But it was more that we were all just exhausted, working like dogs, and people began drifting away. If there was an ax, it was a very passive-aggressive ax, which is *Saturday Night Live* in a nutshell.

KEVIN FARLEY:

I don't even know what word you would use to describe what happened at the end of that year. Weird? Crazy? The whole place runs on rumors and innuendo. But Chris had a lot of meetings with his managers, who told him he'd be fine stepping right into movies. I don't think Chris was fired, and he didn't exactly quit. He just never went back.

LORNE MICHAELS:

Chris's head had been turned by the exposure he'd gotten from the movies. Starting back when he was in the first *Wayne's World*, Chris was only on the screen for a minute, but the audience clearly knew him and liked him and was invested in him. Gurvitz and Brillstein were pressuring him to get out there. There was a Chris Farley business now.

MIKE SHOEMAKER:

There's a sketch at the very end of Chris's last show, written by Fred Wolf. It's Chris and Adam and Jay Mohr and all those guys, playing themselves. They're at the zoo and they're screwing around, daring each other to jump into this polar bear pit. "I bet I can swim across the moat and back before the polar bear gets me." That sort of thing. It was the last sketch that those guys ever did on *Saturday Night Live*, and I always remember it as sort of being a metaphor for their leaving the show. Everybody leaps into the polar bear pit, and, one by one, they all get mauled and eaten alive.

CHAPTER 11

The Polar Bear Pit

NORM MacDONALD:

When Chris left *Saturday Night Live*, it seemed like he wasn't ready for Hollywood. There was the *Cable Guy* thing, the *Beverly Hills Ninja* thing. Hollywood was just ready to use a naïve guy in any way they could to make money. And Chris was naïve, but he certainly wasn't stupid. He saw what was happening, and it hurt him a lot. Perhaps because of his faith, Chris had great confidence in human beings and their capacity for being good. And they're not, really. Especially not in this town.

Paramount Studios released *Tommy Boy* on March 31, 1995. Despite a lukewarm critical reception, it opened number one at the box office and went on to gross a respectable $32 million. Suddenly there was a lot of growth potential in the Chris Farley business.

Paramount immediately ordered up, in essence, *Tommy Boy II*. No sequel ideas followed naturally out of Tommy Callahan's story, but that was no obstacle. The movie's basic formula was lifted, reupholstered, and set down in vaguely different circumstances—and *Black Sheep* was born. This time, instead of playing the screw-up son of a successful father, Chris played the screw-up brother of a successful politician. David Spade no longer played an uptight assistant helping Chris not ruin a sales trip; he played an uptight assistant helping Chris not ruin a gubernatorial campaign.

Chris had signed a two-picture deal with Paramount, and the studio's interpretation of his contract prevented him from taking on any other films so long as they presented him with a "viable" project by a certain date. Fred Wolf was hired to write the screenplay, and on that certain date, under the threat of a lawsuit, he was compelled to turn in whatever script he had. Then, literally at the eleventh hour, *Wayne's World* director Penelope Spheeris was attached to direct.

Chris was a valuable commodity coming out of *Tommy Boy*, and had many options from which to choose. Paramount shut them all down, including a part in the Farrelly brothers' *Kingpin* and the lead in *The Cable Guy* (a project that would involve Chris in a wholly separate legal imbroglio).

And so Chris was shoehorned into the thankless role of Mike Donnelly, a warmhearted but hapless counselor at a community recreation center who's such a political nightmare he's got to be put under wraps during his brother's bid for the governor's mansion. Ever the optimist, Chris was determined to make the best of it. He hired old Red Arrow friend Ted Dondanville to be his personal assistant and constant companion, and then turned his attention to trying to improve the film, bringing in several writers to punch up the script. He also sought out Tim Matheson and Bruce McGill. Matheson and McGill had starred as Otter and D-Day, respectively, in *National Lampoon's Animal House*. Hoping their comedy talents would improve the film's prospects, Chris used his newfound clout to bring them in for supporting roles.

But no matter how hard Chris tried, *Black Sheep* was not going to be *Tommy Boy*. Despite the similarities, the film didn't have the same director or the same producers. Nor for that matter did it have the same stars.

The personal and professional chemistry of Chris Farley and David Spade had inspired *Tommy Boy* and come off beautifully on film. But the fabric of that relationship had begun to fray. Chris was receiving more attention, and more money, which would sow seeds of discontent in any partnership. And then there was the thing with the girl.

LORNE MICHAELS:

Black Sheep was an act of desperation by Paramount. Sherry Lansing felt that they missed it on *Tommy Boy*. They didn't know what they had; they hadn't marketed it well. Then after its release it got reevaluated. If nothing else, Sherry Lansing's son Jack said *Tommy Boy* was his favorite movie ever. Suddenly they wanted another. I kept saying, "We don't have one."

ERIC NEWMAN:

When Lorne was making *Wayne's World 2*, Mike Myers had written a script that the studio, for legal reasons, couldn't proceed with. So Mike, as is his style, dug his heels in and said he wasn't doing it. The reaction from Paramount was severe. They threatened litigation, and Mike found himself with no choice but to make the movie. That's probably why *Wayne's World 2* turned out the way that it did.

When there was a question about Chris doing *Black Sheep*, all the same people were involved, and it got really ugly again. Paramount was making threats. Chris's people were really angry, and they should have been.

DOUG ROBINSON, *agent:*

Our interpretation of the contract was that Chris owed Paramount one of his next two movies. Their interpretation was quite different, and they were really firm about Chris not doing *Cable Guy*, or *Kingpin*, which was another possible project we had lined up for him. Chris was being considered to play the Amish kid, the part eventually taken by Randy Quaid. We really wanted him to do that. But Paramount was putting a lot of pressure on Chris, and he ultimately didn't want to fight it.

FRED WOLF:

I got a call from an executive at Paramount saying that I had to deliver a finished script by midnight on Sunday, the last day Chris was contractually allowed to get out of the movie. If I didn't have a finished script—any finished script—they were going to sue me. I sat down and wrote forty-five pages that weekend. Eric Newman met me at Paramount at around eleven forty-five. We made copies and distributed them to the people at Paramount. They had their script, and they forced Chris to do it.

DAVID SPADE:

Now, we're getting close to summer, and that's the only time *SNL* cast members can shoot movies. I ended up going back in the fall, and Chris didn't know at that point if he was going back or not.

But that summer Chris was also offered $3 million to do *Cable Guy*, and the Paramount deal was for way, way less, probably under a million. The thing was, I didn't owe Paramount anything. I didn't have a two-picture deal. I could say no.

So Chris comes to me at Au Bon Pain under 30 Rock on the way in to work. He sits me down and says, "Listen, I know they want you to do *Black Sheep*, and I owe them a movie and you don't. So when you read the script, if you don't like it then I'm free to go do *Cable Guy*."

"Right," I say.

"But if you say you want to do it, I have to do it, too."

"Okay."

"I read it. I wasn't crazy about it. You read it, and you decide."

And so I'm in a tough spot. If I say yes, Fred Wolf gets paid and gets a movie made, and so do I. If I say no, Fred and I don't have work, but Chris gets to go and do the other one.

I say, "Look, I'll read it, and I'll decide based on no reason other than whether or not I like it. And if I like it, I have to say yes."

"Fair enough."

I read it, and I thought it was actually pretty good. Coming off *Tommy Boy*, I thought Chris, Fred, and I could pull it off.

ERIC NEWMAN:

And so *Black Sheep* was concocted to preempt *Cable Guy*, but, unfortunately, at the same time, the *Cable Guy* deal was falling apart on its own due to the Jim Carrey thing.

BERNIE BRILLSTEIN, *manager/founder, Brillstein-Grey Entertainment:*

It was the worst. Endeavor sent me the script for *The Cable Guy*. You can't even imagine how different that script was from what got made. It was a simple, fun story. Gurvitz and I took it over to Columbia, to Mark Canton. They bought it with Chris attached. We were then going through all the preproduction, and Brad Grey and I got a call from Canton. "Please be over here at six o'clock. It's very important that we see you."

Now, when someone calls you for an important six o'clock meeting, it's never good news, and it's never to give you money, ever. We went over to Columbia and Canton said, "Somehow, the *Cable Guy* script made it to Jim Carrey."

"Somehow?" I said. "Did it fly over there or did you send it by cab?"

That started the meeting out on a bit of a hostile front.

"Jim Carrey wants to do it," he said, "and we want to make it our summer tent-pole movie."

Brad and I had brought Columbia this script, and, without our knowing, they had brought on Ben Stiller, Judd Apatow, and Jim Carrey, who wanted to turn it into a dark, black comedy. They were going to pay Carrey $20 million, and it was the first time anyone had broken the $20 million ceiling. I was very blunt. I said, "You just lost twenty million."

So now Canton says, "Here's what we'll do. We'll pay off Chris. You two can stay with the picture as producers, and we'll pay you."

It was a tough decision. It was a lot of money. It was our script, so I didn't feel bad about taking the money, honest to God. And they weren't going to budge off of Jim Carrey, so as long as Chris got paid, that was the best we could hope for, for him.

PENELOPE SPHEERIS, *director:*

One Sunday afternoon, I got a call from John Goldwyn at Paramount. He put Sherry Lansing on the phone, and they said, "Chris Farley wants to do this movie called *The Cable Guy*, and if we don't exercise our option on him by tomorrow morning, we lose our rights to hold him to another movie." They asked me if I would direct it.

I said, "Well, where's the script?"

"We don't have one," they said, "but we have a great idea."

They pitched me the idea. It didn't seem something I really wanted to do. Then they told me what they were going to pay me—and it was obscene. It was about two and a half or three million dollars. They needed to get the picture done that badly. So, I hate to sound crass, but I did it for the money. Plus, after doing *Wayne's World* I really did love Chris and really did want to work with him. Between those two things, I went for it.

DAVID SPADE:

And that's when the trouble started. I believe up until that point we would have had another *Tommy Boy* on our hands. But Penelope got paid more than all of us put together, because she'd done *Wayne's World*. So all the power went to her. The problem is, you have to give a lot of credit on *Wayne's World* to Mike and Dana. I'm sure she did something right, but as far as the funny is concerned, that's Mike and Dana, in my opinion.

So Penelope says, "I know how to make you guys funny." Which is the first red flag. Chris, Fred, and I knew what we needed to do. We just needed someone to shoot us, but she ripped forty pages out of the script

THE CHRIS FARLEY SHOW

and said, "I'm going to work on this with my friend." All our complaints fell on deaf ears, and Fred got fired.

PENELOPE SPHEERIS:

There was one point in a meeting when we were discussing the script with the studio people. Fred came up with some stupid-ass idea, and I said, "I'm not going to do that."

Then everybody looked at Lorne, and Lorne said, "Well, Fred *is* the writer on the show." Parentheses: The writer is king on *Saturday Night Live*.

So I said, "Okay, you guys can take your two and a half million and shove it up your ass."

And I walked out. I couldn't believe I'd done it, but I was walking across the parking lot and I heard the click-click-click of Karen Rosenfeld's high heels, and she came up to me going, "Penelope, don't leave. Please, please."

They didn't care about me, mind you. They just didn't want to lose the director, any director, for fear of derailing the project and losing Chris.

ERIC NEWMAN:

A movie's like a train, a five-hundred-ton train, and once it leaves the station there's not a whole lot you can do about it. If you're Jerry Bruckheimer it's pretty easy to stand on principle and say, "This movie's not ready." (Not that he ever has.) But if you're not at that level, you work with what you have. Everyone thinks, okay, it'll all come out in the wash. The process will right the ship. And it never does. And so, despite the best efforts of Chris, David, Lorne, and Fred, *Black Sheep* is an entirely forgettable movie. It's a terrible movie. It's a really bad movie.

TED DONDANVILLE, *friend:*

Johnny Farley had moved to Chicago and started performing at Improv-
Olympic, and he and I were drinking buddies. He told me Chris was
looking for an assistant. So I just called Chris up and asked him for the
job, and I got it. I wasn't hired for my secretarial efficiency but because
that concrete wall seals off after you become famous. You can only trust
the people on one side of it, and I was on that side. And of course I'd
taken care of him when he was the poor, starving actor at Second City.

We flew out to Los Angeles on the Fourth of July of 1995, and I was
his personal assistant from that day on. When we got there we moved into
the Park Hyatt hotel. He had a nice suite, with a big living room area. He
lived there for all of *Black Sheep*, and then for all the time we weren't on
location for *Beverly Hills Ninja* and *Edwards & Hunt*. That was his home
in L.A. Filming started about a week after we got to town.

Chris, because of his clout, got them to hire writers to work on
punching up the script three or four nights a week. The guys who wrote
Edwards & Hunt, which became *Almost Heroes*, they came in. Those guys
would come over to Chris's hotel suite, we'd order food, and they'd sit
around for hours going over the upcoming scenes, trying to make it better. Those sessions were a great time, a lot of fun to watch, these intellectual writers setting Chris up and giving him stuff to work on. He'd act it
out a little and tweak it with them.

The process was more enjoyable than the actual product. Not a lot of
that material got worked in, ultimately, because it was all last-second
stuff. So Chris knew it was a piece of crap, but he was going to go down
swinging.

TIM MATHESON, *costar:*

Chris was very positive. Always prepared. You could tell that all the principal performers were just doing it by rote, to fill an obligation, except for
Chris. I didn't much believe in the movie. I just figured it had to be at least
half as good as *Tommy Boy*, and that would be okay. But they just kept

adding and changing crap all the time, and never to make it better. It just got dumber.

FRED WOLF:

If you're going to do something in a slapdash manner, you need the captain of the ship to make sure it comes off right. I think we were all missing that.

On *Tommy Boy*, Pete Segal would call me in my room and say, "We're out here with Chris and Rob Lowe. He's washing him off after the cow-tipping scene. Do you have anything?"

And I knew that any time you had Chris dancing you had comedy gold. So I'd say, "Why not have him singing 'Maniac' from *Flashdance*?"

Then they were able to knock it out on the spot. On *Black Sheep*, the director wasn't speaking to me, and I was banned from the set. Penelope Spheeris fired me a total of three times. Chris rehired me twice, and Lorne Michaels a third time. I missed Pete Segal.

TED DONDANVILLE:

Chris liked the way that Penelope was very open about hearing his ideas. On the other hand, he didn't really trust her comedy chops. He had a fear of her not knowing what was funny and what wasn't, and he was worried about the lack of strong direction. Personally, though, they got along great. He liked the freedom she gave him.

PENELOPE SPHEERIS:

It was actually Chris's idea to get Tim Matheson and Bruce McGill for their parts, specifically because of *Animal House*. For me, I trusted him on it, and then I met the guys and they were just great. My first impulse was, "Who's going to believe Chris Farley and Tim Matheson as brothers?" But they really felt like brothers.

TIM MATHESON:

I went in for the audition, and to my surprise Chris was there. He was the star, and I was just coming in for this supporting part, but he was so gracious and so deferential and so flattering that you honestly would have thought it was *his* audition. But I got the feeling that he was responsible for my being there. I was very grateful for that, and I wanted to deliver.

He wanted to hear anything and everything I could remember about *Animal House*. He wanted to get my take on the whole experience and what it was like working with Belushi. I liked to make him laugh, so I told him as many stories as I could.

Chris had an innocence about him, a golly-shucks-gee kind of thing. John felt like an older brother. Chris felt like a younger brother. John had big designs, was always in charge. He grabbed that ball and ran with it. Chris was always "Golly-gee, what do you think?" Belushi was also a sweet guy, but Belushi was very aware of who he was, the impact he had on people, and the clout that it gave him, both in the industry and just over average people. John was very savvy. You got the feeling that Chris wasn't. Or, if he was, he chose to ignore it. He had a very salt-of-the-earth quality about him. When he introduced me to his brother, it was all about how great his brother was.

BRUCE McGILL, *costar:*

Toward the end of the movie, we all played in a golf tournament, so we spent about six hours out there together. You usually try and keep humiliating experiences down to ten, fifteen minutes, right? But a game of golf is just hours and hours of ego-bruising degradation, which breaks people down and opens them up. If you want to know something about a guy, go play golf with him.

And while we were out there we had a very protracted, involved three-way conversation about what had happened to John, and how he should avoid that for himself. It was fascinating to see how interested he was in Belushi and Belushi's demise—and how adamant he was that he would not go down that road. Cut to two years later and he went exactly the same way. If there was ever a moth to a flame, whether it was conscious, unconscious, I don't know.

LORRI BAGLEY:

When Chris left *SNL*, he told me that the only goal he'd ever had in life was to be on that show, that his father had loved John Belushi on that show, and if he could make it there, he'd make his father happy. That's where the Belushi thing came from—his father.

BRUCE McGILL:

If Belushi made Chris's father laugh, well, there you go. It's positively Greek.

PENELOPE SPHEERIS:

My problem with *Black Sheep* was that then and to this day I find Chris Farley absolutely, brilliantly, hilariously funny. I don't think I've ever even smiled at anything David Spade's ever done. Chris was lovable and positive, and David was so bitter and negative. You take your pick.

I still have a recording of a message David left on my answering machine. He said, "You've spent this whole movie trying to cut my comedy balls off."

DAVID SPADE:

The main problem was that Penelope separated us. She had Chris go off and do one thing and me go off and do another. We kept saying, "Look, our characters just need to be together. We need to fight and bicker and do all that shit."

And Chris wasn't helping much, because he thought he should be doing more dramatic stuff, that the movie should be more about his character and Tim Matheson's character and less about me. He even hinted that "would I mind" if I got paid not to be in it so they could make it more of a dramedy. And I don't think he meant it to be offensive to me. He just wanted to act and didn't want to keep doing fatty falls down. Personally, I thought it was too early; we needed more experience before we tried to do those things.

So they added a few scenes for Chris and Tim to be a little more serious, and they had another writer come in to work on the ending. And I was kind of on my own. I didn't have anyone to play off of. I didn't have Chris, and my humor is funny when I have someone to play off of.

ERIC NEWMAN:

Actors need rules, and those rules need to come from the director. Penelope clearly didn't get David, and she really allowed him to meander. Chris Farley alone is the comedy team of Costello and Costello. You needed the sharp-tongued straight man. You can pretend that you're just making a Chris Farley movie, but you're not. It's a Chris Farley/David Spade movie.

TIM MATHESON:

I sensed that there was something wrong with Chris and David, but I thought it was David not wanting to be the second banana.

PENELOPE SPHEERIS:

You could feel the tension between them, believe me.

LORRI BAGLEY:

I was staying with Chris in his hotel room, and at the end of the shoot he would come back and see me and vent out all of his tension. "You're the reason me and my best friend aren't talking." That sort of thing. It was hard.

TED DONDANVILLE:

It was about the girl, basically, and some underlying jealousy, too, which Spade actually handled very well. Spade was pissed off about how things went down with Kit Kat. I think it was one of those things where Spade thought she was his girl, but they weren't really dating to begin with.

DAVID SPADE:

Dating, not dating, whatever. I don't know what you want to call it. We were certainly hanging out a lot. I wasn't her boyfriend, but we were very close. And I didn't find out from them. It was an accident. For some reason, I wasn't supposed to know. So if she and I weren't dating, then why was I being kept in the dark? And whatever. The problems with Lorri were that I felt somewhat betrayed on both sides. I felt like, here's my friend. I always made sure he got to hang out with us because he said he had no one else to be with, and to have that bite me in the ass later didn't sit right.

TED DONDANVILLE:

I talked to Lorri about it a lot, and according to her, Chris was guilt-ridden over it. She says that she and David were never more than friends, but who knows how women revisit stuff.

LORRI BAGLEY:

Chris and I were just emotional, crazy people. Our relationship was always rocky. Up and down, like being on a ship at sea. David always used to say, "You two are going to kill each other." The thing with Chris, the thing we had problems with, was intimacy. Any time you got close to him, if he let down his guard and really let you in, then he'd push you back out. As close as you got the night before, you'd be pushed that much further away the next morning.

TED DONDANVILLE:

Whenever Lorri would visit L.A., there was a standard pattern to it. They'd start talking on the phone a lot, then she'd come out and he'd send me away. For a couple of days it'd be full-time, lovey-dovey, baby-talk heaven. Then for a couple of days they'd begin to resemble a calmer, everyday, normal couple. I'd be invited back in—the third wheel added to their little bicycle—and we'd all hang out together. Then it'd start to disintegrate into some crazy-ass fight. I'd get a call from Chris in his hotel suite: "Come up. Come through the bedroom." I'd go up and she'd be on the other side of his bedroom door, out in the suite, yelling and screaming, and Chris would be like, "Get her her own fucking room tonight and fly her back tomorrow."

She'd fly back to New York, they'd ignore each other for a month or so, then the phone calls would start and the whole thing would crank up again.

LORRI BAGLEY:

In every part of his life Chris had a role to play. His relationships with people were always predicated on "What do *you* want?" And then he would be that for them. I actually tried to break all those different roles down. We'd fight about it, but then in the end he'd feel better that he didn't have to play some part. I always felt that he could only really be himself with me.

People would never believe that we were together. They didn't understand it, or questioned the reasons behind it. That was until they saw us together. They'd look back and forth between the two of us and say, "God, they're like the same person." One time he was going to do an interview. We were with his publicist in the car. She was like, "Chris, you're so calm." Then she looked over at me.

"Kitten makes me calm," he said. He always said to me, "You're the only girl I feel comfortable with. I've always been nervous and anxious around women, but not with you."

TED DONDANVILLE:

I wouldn't say Lorri *wasn't* attracted to the fame and success, but she and Chris were genuinely close. She will tell you that they had this famous romance for the ages. Fact of the matter is, Chris had other girlfriends here and there. But I will give Lorri credit for being the most important woman in his life. That is certainly true. Unfortunately, of all the girls I saw Chris go out with, I didn't think she was the healthiest or most stable.

DAVID SPADE:

Those two together, with Chris in a free fall, it was like nitroglycerine. I don't know if Chris was in love with her. I know he spent tons of time with her, and she was okay with the other women, or whatever his famous life brought him, because they were "soul mates." I was like, "Shit, is that how it works? I need me a soul mate. That's awesome."

LORRI BAGLEY:

Chris attracted control freaks. He made them feel wanted. And David is a control freak. If he's not in control of a situation, he'll just get out of it. It got ugly, and it was horrible for the two of them.

ERIC NEWMAN:

Every partnership has its problems. Costarring in a movie is hard. I think Chris and David really cared about each other, and they saw that they were good together. But I don't think the quality of that movie was in any way affected by the deterioration of their relationship. While their problems may have impaired the process a little bit, that movie, in its DNA, was a turd.

FRED WOLF:

I grew up in New York City but then later moved to Pennsylvania, to the town where they filmed *Deer Hunter*, so you know how dreary that was. I would take the bus into Pittsburgh to watch the Marx Brothers movies. My dream had always been to work with a comedy team, and here I was. I thought *Black Sheep* could have been a repeat of *Tommy Boy*, but the missing ingredient remained missing. The movie isn't atrocious. It opened bigger than *Tommy Boy*. Both of them were number one in the country, but the drop-off was a lot quicker because, ultimately, it wasn't the same kind of movie.

* * *

Black Sheep wrapped in late summer, and Chris moved back to Chicago, taking up residence at his new apartment in the John Hancock Center, which he had bought after leaving *Saturday Night Live*. Also located in the Hancock Center was the radio studio of Erich "Mancow" Muller, a popular Chicago morning deejay. Chris frequently popped in at the show on his way in or out of the building. Along with regular drop-ins at Second City and ImprovOlympic, the show gave Chris a stage whenever he needed one.

That fall, a small group of people coalesced around Chris, forming a sometime entourage and de facto inner circle. Ted Dondanville stayed on as his personal assistant. Kevin and Johnny Farley had both moved to Chicago to take classes and perform at Second City. The brothers had never been very long apart, but now they found themselves all living in close proximity for the first time since high school. Chris also met a young woman, Jillian Seely. Seely herself had quit drinking several years before, and she was a great help to Chris. They attended recovery meetings together and became fast friends.

And naturally, any decent Chris Farley entourage needed to include a Roman Catholic priest. Sadly, Chris's longtime confidant Father Matt Foley had left Chicago to do four years of missionary work in the small town of Quechultenango, Mexico. The two friends spoke by telephone often, but Chris needed spiritual guidance closer to home. In the months between filming *Tommy Boy* and *Black Sheep*, he had gone to Bellarmine, a Jesuit retreat house in Barrington, Illinois, just outside of Chicago proper. There he met Father Tom Gannon, who would meet with him and talk to him on the phone regularly over the next two years.

Meanwhile, preproduction work was already under way on Chris's next film, *Beverly Hills Ninja*. He worked with the writers and producers on finalizing the script and took daily martial arts lessons from a teacher named Master Guo. For month after happy month, everything seemed fine.

JOHN FARLEY:

When I graduated from college, the family was driving back to Wisconsin from Colorado. I was the young sapling, had no clue what direction to take in life. I had Tommy on one side of me and Chris on the other. Tommy was saying, "Go into business." And Chris was going, "Go into comedy." They were kidding around, tugging back and forth on me.

I went back to Red Arrow Camp to be a counselor, basically piloted a ski boat all summer. Then I tried to get a job driving a Frito-Lay truck. They turned me down. Maybe it was my DUI. Maybe I was overqualified? But I doubt that. So then my mother was buying a new car, and I went with her. I thought, I like cars. Maybe I'll sell cars. I asked about it. One of the salesmen took me aside and said, very seriously, "Son, this isn't a job. This is a career. You're makin' a *career* move here."

"Wow. Thanks."

And I never went back. I figured, comedy, what the hell? I went to Chicago and did exactly what Chris did, started working at the Mercantile Exchange and started taking improv classes at night. Kevin got out of the asphalt business a year or two later when he saw how easily I'd gotten out of it.

KEVIN FARLEY:

I had worked with Dad for six years. In September of 1994, I packed my bags and moved down to Chicago. I lived on Johnny's couch, got a running job at the Chicago Board of Trade, took classes at Second City, and worked as a host there, seating people and doing dishes.

Second City has a business theater, which is upstairs and is pretty lucrative; you can hire players from Second City to perform at your corporate events and write material for you. Eventually, they thought I had a little talent, and they sent me out on these corporate gigs. I got to make a living doing that.

JOHN FARLEY:

I did the corporate thing a bit, too, because it paid well, but mostly I was in the touring company.

KEVIN FARLEY:

Everyone in our family is funny. Mom's hysterical. When you have a large family you want to have your own identity, so we all developed different senses of humor. We're very similar in our mannerisms, but all unique. Johnny is out there. His mind works in a really dark but funny way. I'm a little more goofy and silly. Chris was just outlandish, in your face and raucous. Tom is very cerebral, and dry. Only he never got up onstage with it.

JOHN FARLEY:

If you had to break down the Farley brothers, I'm Chevy Chase, Kevin is Dan Aykroyd, and Chris is John Belushi. And Tommy is Garrett Morris.

TED DONDANVILLE:

I'll be honest: Johnny and Kevin are often funnier than Chris in real life, in more normal ways anyway. Kevin Farley is the funniest guy in the world at a cocktail party. He tells stories, is very engaging. Tom and Johnny, too. The difference is when you put a spotlight on someone, there's a very different kind of funny you need to deliver, and that's where Chris was like Michael Jordan: He would always make the shot. But at the same time, a lot of people who'd meet Chris socially just didn't get him.

JILLIAN SEELY, *friend:*

I met Chris buying a cup of coffee. I really didn't know who he was. I remember he had an Elmer Fudd hat on, and he was wearing those electrician glasses he had. He looked like he was mentally retarded. He'd just finished *Black Sheep* and had moved into his apartment at the Hancock. I worked at a hair salon in the Bloomingdale's building at 900 North Michigan Avenue, and he was there in the building with Johnny. I was looking at Chris and he was looking at me, and we both started smiling and laughing. He asked me if I would marry him, and then he introduced himself. "Hi, I'm Chris Farley."

He asked me if I'd join him that night at a restaurant down the street. It was for John's birthday, I think. I showed up, brought some friends, and we all hung out and had a great time. We ended up going to a restaurant that was open really late and just laughing and talking all night. The next day he called me at work at around nine in the morning and said, "Hey, I noticed last night that you don't drink."

"Yeah, I quit a long time ago," I said.

"Me, too."

He told me a little bit about his problems, and then he asked if I would go to a meeting with him later that night. I said sure. We went to the meeting and then went out to dinner, and we just clicked. From that day on we just started hanging out all the time. We laughed our asses off together.

The thing that was great about being with Chris was that he started all of his conversations with "How was *your* day? What did *you* do?" Nobody does that anymore. That's why Chris was so different from most people. He was not selfish at all when it came to being a friend. We would stay up until three, four in the morning, opening ourselves up to each other, even when we were complete strangers to each other. To this day I don't know why. I've had friends who made me laugh and friends I could have really serious talks with, but I'd never had all of that in the same person like I did with Chris.

KEVIN FARLEY:

We always thought Jillian was super nice. They did hit it off right away.

JOHN FARLEY:

At the time we were busy setting up his apartment at the Hancock building. It was crazy, because the Hancock building is literally a retirement community. That and the studio for Jerry Springer. Chris was the only young person in the building. "Dad says it's the best place in town," Chris said. And maybe it was, back in the sixties, but the people who were hip when they moved in were the only ones still there.

KEVIN FARLEY:

Whenever Chris was in Chicago we would meet and go out to dinner at the Cheesecake Factory, or the Chop House, or Gibson's. Things were clicking with his career. It was a really good time. Nobody was worried about him.

TED DONDANVILLE:

At that point, sobriety was just part of his routine. It wasn't a chore or a burden. It was a balanced part of his life. We weren't hanging out at raging keggers or anything, but we'd go out to things where there was liquor served. People would buy him shots and he'd accept them graciously. Then he'd hand them to me and say, "Here, Ted. You do it."

Even when he was enraged or in a foul mood, he'd just go to a meeting, get himself together, and come back calmer. In the Second City days, drunk or sober, he was always a comedian without a stage, always fucking around. Now he was very much in control of himself. He didn't need to prove something to somebody all the time. He could turn on the comedian when he needed to be there.

JOHN FARLEY:

Chris and Ted, honest to God, were like Felix and Oscar. They were the Odd Couple. Just to watch them interact was hysterical. Chris lived to give him hell, and Ted was like, "Whatever."

Chris would hide things and then demand them from Ted, just for fun. They'd walk out the front door and Chris would go, "Where's the little, you know, my recording thing I need?"

"I didn't see it," Ted would say

"You didn't see it? Well, let's go back and look for it then!"

Then Chris would go back in and wait while Ted looked for the thing and say, "Look! Here it is under the couch!"

"Uh, okay."

"You idiot! Let's go!"

It was fun for Chris to beat up on him like you would a little brother, but Ted could ride out all of Chris's mood swings without even a blip in his pulse rate. He just didn't care. If you put Chris in real terms, he was a company making millions and millions of dollars, and Teddy was in charge. It was like, Holy Lord, this ship is headed for the rocks and nobody's at the wheel.

KEVIN FARLEY:

To be an assistant to a star like that, you've got a lot of people calling you all the time—agents, heads of studios. It's not an easy job. Chris would get frustrated with Ted, because oftentimes Ted wasn't as thorough as he needed to be. But they were friends, so that's why there was never really any employer-employee etiquette to be observed.

TED DONDANVILLE:

Chris was such a people pleaser that he'd give everyone what they wanted, always be so deferential. But he had just as much ego and just as much of a temper as anyone. All of that negative energy had to get channeled somewhere, and it got channeled to Kevin, Johnny, and me. He'd never let anyone else see that side of him, and so we'd take the brunt of it. But we also understood it for what it was, blowing off steam. Any outburst was immediately followed by a shower of apologies.

JOHN FARLEY:

Teddy was a good companion, and honest. He comes from more money than Chris or any of us had ever seen, so he didn't give two shits about Chris's money or his fame. He was just doing it for fun. He was probably the most trustworthy guy Chris could have had by his side. And we all had fun together. We'd go to Second City, work out at the gym. Chris was really into his martial arts training for *Beverly Hills Ninja*.

TED DONDANVILLE:

Master Guo had been a karate champion in Communist China and had defected. He didn't speak very good English, and he only weighed about a hundred and ten pounds, but he was an amazing teacher. He and Chris used to do this thing where they'd stand shoulder width apart, clasp one hand, and then push and pull, and the first one to have a foot pulled off the ground would lose. Chris outweighed his teacher more than two to one, but the guy got Chris off his feet every time, without even trying. He was the real deal. But he was very impressed with Chris for what a fast learner he was. This was the football player in him coming back.

Thinking back on it, the martial arts training was something Chris lacked later on, namely a hobby, something to keep him occupied. It was a noteworthy time in that there was nothing too noteworthy about it. He was sober and happy and having a good time. It was never that way again.

JOHN FARLEY:

None of us saw it coming.

TED DONDANVILLE:

Chris was going to have a Christmas party at the Hancock, but first he had to go to New York to attend a screening of *Black Sheep*. For whatever reason, in the days before he left for New York, he started getting angry. He always had a temper, but this was a little more consistent, and more fierce. It was a gathering storm.

Then a rewrite of *Ninja* came back, and it really sucked. Following right on that, I was filming some of his training to send in to the screenwriters to come up with jokes, but the battery died on the camcorder halfway through the training session. Afterward, we went to look at it and it was all fucked up. Chris went into a rage, yelling and screaming and ranting about this goddamned script. He left Chicago really pissed off.

LORRI BAGLEY:

I picked him up in New York. The car came and got me, and I went to the airport to meet him. We were going to stop by the hotel and then go and have dinner. He got into the limousine, and as we drove off we started talking about work. And while we were talking it was like a black cloud came over him. I saw the Chris I knew literally disappear, just vanish into this distant world. I said, "What's going on?" But he had checked out.

We went by the hotel and then got back in the car to go and have dinner. Chris was quiet for a moment. Then he turned to me and said, "Kitten, I'm drinking tonight."

ACT III

ACT III

CHAPTER 12

Raising the White Flag

TED DONDANVILLE:

That first relapse, that was the big one. The rest were just dominoes.

C hris Farley had been sober for three years. At a time when his commitment had never seemed stronger, he gave it all up with one drink on the flight from Chicago to New York. As news of the relapse spread, Chris's friends and family all asked the same question: why? Some felt it was the gathering stress and anxiety over his career. Others felt that Chris had never successfully dealt with every aspect of his compulsive and addictive behaviors, most notably with regard to food. Still others felt that Chris's sobriety had always relied too much on external motivators, like the threat of losing his job at *Saturday Night Live*. Whatever precipitated the relapse, it happened. And it was devastating.

LORRI BAGLEY:

I started crying. "No, you're not," I said. "You're not going to do that, and you're not going to do it with me."

"I've already started. That wasn't water I was drinking in the hotel. It was vodka," he told me.

We went to dinner, and he started drinking martinis. After that, we went to the Rainbow Room. Steve Martin was there. Chris was acting like a madman. I thought I could get him through the night, call Ted the next morning and find his sponsor, and see where to take him.

I got him back to the hotel room. He was drinking and crying. Then he said he was going to this spot in Hell's Kitchen to get drugs. I said, "If you want to go there, I'm going with you, and then you need to take me home because I'm not going to play with that."

We got in the limo, went to this place, and he went inside while I waited outside. After a minute I got nervous and went in after him. He looked at me and said, "Get me out of here."

So he left without doing anything, and I took him back to the hotel. He just kept drinking and crying and talking about the voices in his head. He kept saying, "How do you turn off the voices in your head? They're in my head. How do I get them out?"

I finally fell asleep as the sun was rising. When I woke up I called his name, and he wasn't there. I waited and waited, not knowing what to do. About an hour and a half later, I started getting ready to go, and he came in with sunglasses on. I could tell he hadn't been to sleep, and he was way too calm and mellowed out from what he'd been the night before. He was on something.

I told him, "I thought that I could handle being around you if you started using again. I thought I'd never leave you no matter what, but I can't be around this. It's just too much." And I left and went home.

TOM FARLEY:

Chris called me and said, "Tommy, you want to go and see a sneak preview of *Black Sheep* in New Jersey?" I said sure. He was staying at the Four Seasons, so I stopped up there. He looked fine to me. The limo was going to pick us up any second, and Chris was getting into the minibar, filling his pockets with the little bottles. I said, "Chris, what are you doing?"

"Oh, I'm just getting a couple of these for the limo driver," he said. "They like that."

And after three years of sobriety, I actually let myself think that was okay. I just didn't for the life of me think he could be lying. We got in the limo and drove out to Jersey.

We were up in the screening room, waiting for everyone to filter into the theater. At one point he said, "I gotta go to the bathroom." I did, too, so I went with him. We got to the men's room, and it was this small, janitor's closet kind of thing. I followed him in anyway. He was like, "What are you doing?"

"I gotta go to the bathroom," I said.

We're brothers, for God's sake. I'd been in the bathroom with him hundreds of times. But all of a sudden he's like, "Get out. I can't . . . I gotta go by myself."

I thought that was very strange, but I left him to it. Then we watched the movie, and we were driving somewhere else, and, same thing, "I gotta go to the bathroom." So we pull over and he goes in someplace to use the bathroom. And, of course, what he was doing was drinking. I certainly didn't see him give away any of his little bottles. I didn't put two and two together until the next day when I got a call from Dad, saying, "What the hell happened?"

"What do you mean?"

"Chris trashed his hotel room at the Four Seasons and did three thousand dollars' worth of damage."

And then it was back to rehab.

KEVIN FARLEY:

When I got the call in Chicago that he had relapsed, it was devastating; devastating to me, devastating to him, and devastating to everyone in the family. He took so much pride in his sobriety, more than any of the movies or work he'd ever done, more than any other success in his life. Those three years were his crowning achievement.

JILLIAN SEELY:

Chris and I had been hanging out every day, and then right around Christmas he disappeared off the face of the earth. He called me early in the morning on New Year's Eve. He said, "Hey, it's Chris."

"Hey," I said, "why haven't you called me?" I was pissed.

"I relapsed."

"You're lying," I said. "I don't believe you."

We had talked so much about his sobriety, and I was so confident in him that I really couldn't imagine it.

He said, "I really want to see you. Will you come and meet me at a meeting?"

There was a meeting that morning. I went with him. He told me about the relapse and the screening. He said that he'd fucking hated *Black Sheep*, that it was just *Tommy Boy II*, only worse.

TED DONDANVILLE:

That screening didn't help. He saw one shitty movie that he'd made, and then he really started worrying that, with *Ninja*, he was working on a second one.

* * *

Beverly Hills Ninja was a script that had been around, and around. Several stars had turned it down. Chris himself had passed on it a number of times. But negotiations for the film had taken a dramatic turn the previous summer, while filming for *Black Sheep* was still under way. Sensing Chris's impending stardom, *Ninja*'s producers got very aggressive. They offered him an ungodly salary, and that changed the whole equation. Chris was still reluctant, and his managers were vehemently opposed, regardless of the payday. But Chris's dad counseled him otherwise, essentially saying, "You don't turn down that kind of money." Show business is not the asphalt business, but in this as in all things Chris listened to his father. He signed on to play Haru, an infant boy orphaned in Japan and raised to fulfill a prophecy as the Great White Ninja. Through a series of slapstick setups and wacky misadventures, Haru makes his way to California and solves a crime. Shakespeare it wasn't.

Chris had rationalized his taking the film by saying it would make a good kids' movie. Another big factor in the decision was simply his confidence. The story was one big, long pratfall, and Chris's abilities as a physical comedian had never failed to deliver huge laughs. But Chris's other major asset was his Midwestern Everyman appeal. Dressing him in martial arts garb and giving him hokey, Zen-sounding dialogue was not a good fit, and it flopped onscreen.

The project was not without its bright spots. It did turn out to be a successful children's movie. Chris Rock was struggling professionally at the time, and Farley used the movie to lend his *SNL* friend a helping hand. But all things considered, it was a serious detour.

Following his stint in rehab, Chris flew to Hollywood in January of 1996 and started production on the film. He stayed clean throughout the shoot, determined not to let the relapse derail his three years of hard-fought sobriety. But the change in him was obvious to everyone on the set. His anxiety was rapidly eclipsing his boisterous amiability, and the strength and serenity he'd possessed just a few weeks before had all but vanished.

ROB LOWE, *costar,* Tommy Boy:

At that point, Chris could have done almost anything, career-wise, and for him to do a movie where he offered himself up as "the fat guy" I felt was a recipe for psychic disaster. I don't want to sound overly dramatic by saying that that movie killed him, but the decision to do it was Chris surrendering a creative part of himself. He was raising the white flag to easy Hollywood mediocrity. I know that he hated himself for saying yes.

BRAD JENKEL, *producer:*

I used to work at a company called Motion Picture Corporation of America. We'd had some success with the Farrelly brothers. We did *Dumb & Dumber* and *Kingpin*. We did *Bio-Dome* with Pauly Shore. Then we got ahold of *Beverly Hills Ninja*. If I recall properly, Dana Carvey had been attached to it at one point, and Chris held Dana in such high regard that he was open to looking at the script. Chris really was the first guy that we went to. We offered him a ton of money.

TED DONDANVILLE:

One day while we were filming *Black Sheep*, Chris's agents showed up. Agents always stand out because they're the only ones in L.A. who wear dark suits. They were really happy, really up. They came rushing in and met Chris in the trailer. *Beverly Hills Ninja* was a movie that he had rejected a number of times. "No, thanks. Pass." But this time the script came in with an offer for $6 million, which at the time was like a three hundred percent increase in what Chris was making. All of a sudden it was like, "Eh, maybe the script isn't so bad after all. . . ."

BERNIE BRILLSTEIN:

Marc Gurvitz and I, we told him not to do *Ninja*. It was about a fat guy in tights. Let's face it, who wants to see Chris like that? It was an embarrassing film. But the offer was $6 million, which even then was a lot of money. Chris called up and said, "I have to do it. My dad says I can't turn down that kind of money."

DOUG ROBINSON:

After his father weighed in, there wasn't much of a conversation. I remember sitting with Chris in his trailer at Paramount, telling him that there would be other big paydays down the road. It was one of those situations where you want to advise your client not to do it. But you could see that as soon as you told him the amount of money involved, the ship had sailed.

LORNE MICHAELS:

It was a bad decision in that no one was telling the truth and people had all kinds of different agendas. There are so many rationalizations: "It'll get your price up." "It's important to keep working." "Not every movie's a masterpiece." But Chris was an incredibly sensitive kid. No matter what he did, he always had some kind of hope for pride in his work, and so for Chris to do something that empty just didn't feel right.

LORRI BAGLEY:

It was fear. He took that movie out of fear. Chris's only goal in life was to be on *Saturday Night Live*, and after that was over he would always say, "I never imagined myself being a film actor." And I'd think, oh shit, he's out of his comfort zone. Movies and Hollywood and all that are out of his comfort zone, and things are going to get difficult.

KEVIN FARLEY:

Chris loved football, and he loved being part of a team. *Saturday Night Live*, Second City, those are team sports. Chris was competitive. He wanted to win, but he wanted the whole team to win. Winning doesn't mean anything if you can't share it with someone.

When you're a movie star, all the pressure is on you as an individual. But if you put too much pressure on one player, you're not going to win ball games. On a film, clearly one guy is making the most money, and they're banking on him, win or lose. His career is on the line. In Hollywood, you're kind of alone.

TED DONDANVILLE:

The crew used to joke that when the *Beverly Hills Ninja* action figures came out, the Haru figure would come with its own Ted figure. Unlike most personal assistants, I was never out running errands and taking care of other things. Chris always wanted me to delegate that stuff to other people so I could stay, literally, right next to him all the time. We'd work all day and he'd be like, "No, c'mon. I'm taking you to dinner."

On that movie he was hung out to dry. That was a Chris Farley movie from start to finish. Except for those few Chris Rock scenes, every scene hinged on him.

BRAD JENKEL:

Farley wanted Chris Rock in the movie. He was very adamant about that. It was almost to the point where he wouldn't do the film if Rock wasn't involved. I think it was a bit of a life raft for him. I distinctly remember that Chris's best days on the set were the days that Rock was there.

Whatever reservations Chris may have had, to me he was just so appreciative, and grateful, and he really felt a personal responsibility that came with taking that much money. I had never experienced that with an actor before. He was so excited that we were hiring him, let along paying him so much, that during shooting he'd often say to me, "God, I hope I'm doing okay. Are you guys happy?"

And that kind of raised the bar for us. After he'd say those things to me, I'd walk away going, "Oh jeez, I hope *I'm* gonna deliver for *him*."

Chris also helped develop the script. When we went into *Ninja*, we wanted it to be a really broad, adult movie, and, to his credit, Chris really took it more in the direction of being a movie for kids and families. That's what he wanted. And thank God he did. It wasn't a huge success, but kids loved it. They really turned out, and that's where the movie made its money.

JASON DAVIS, *costar:*

The producer of *Beverly Hills Ninja* had done a movie that I was in, and I got cut out of that one. But he said I'd be perfect for this. I remember going to audition for it. I had to run into a wall and fall down. That was the audition. When they said I had the part, I got real excited. I got to play Chris Farley as a little kid. At the time, what could have been better? He was one of my heroes.

For my big scene, I was supposed to flip a stick around and accidentally hit this kid on the head. The director said, "You can hit him as hard as you want, because he has padding."

So we do the scene. We're twirling the sticks around, and I smack him on the head, only not on the part where he has padding. The kid goes down for the count. I just remember turning my head over to the right, looking at the director and seeing Chris going "*Oh, fuck*" and laughing his head off. He had this expression like, yup, he's just like me.

TED DONDANVILLE:

The role of the young Chris Farley is supposed to be this shitty little ninja, right? Well, Jason Davis literally was a shitty ninja. He was such a bad athlete and such a spastic little kid that it was funny to see him play this idiot. Chris saw this kid who was just a mess, and that amused him.

KEVIN FARLEY:

Chris liked that kid a lot. He always used to say, "That kid reminds me of me when I was little." Jason was kind of an out-of-control little guy. He'd go up and talk to anybody. Since Jason looked up to Chris so much, Chris kind of took him under his wing whenever he was around.

JASON DAVIS:

For the three days I got to work on the movie, I got to hang out with Chris a lot. Then, about a week later, he called me and said, "Hey, we should go out to lunch."

I thought, wow, that's really awesome. So we went out to lunch, and from then on we just really clicked. We'd hang out. We'd go and do stuff together.

What I loved about Chris was that he was the only person who ever understood me. For a period of time, if I needed to count on anyone, it was Chris. I was like eleven or twelve, and my mom wanted to send me away to fat camp. I was trying every which way to get out of it. I was praying for Chris to kidnap me and hold me for ransom so I wouldn't have to go. But Chris would talk to me about being a kid with a weight problem, and he really helped me a lot. I could call him and say, "My mom's being a bitch. I'm pissed off. I want to run away. I hate it here. What should I do?"

And he'd be like, "Relax. You're obviously going through denial. Your mother loves you. Don't run away. Besides, you'd have to stop at McDonald's every other block just to survive."

NANCY DAVIS, *Jason Davis's mother:*

Jason saw a side of Chris that maybe a lot of other people didn't see. Chris understood what he was going through, and touched Jason in this amazing way. He really did. When Jason was filming *Beverly Hills Ninja* with Chris, he was going through a hard time in his life. His father and I were getting divorced, and Jason had some similar issues with Chris, some weight issues, really deep father issues, and maybe Chris saw that in Jason. It was like he could just sense it, and he really made a point of helping him to deal with it. People are so afraid to talk about what's bothering them, and Chris really got him to open up about it. Jason's always been quirky and different, and Chris gave him the strength to think that was okay.

TED DONDANVILLE:

When I first started working for Chris, he'd been sober for about two and a half years. He was doing really well. He was very comfortable in his sobriety, and very strong. After that first relapse, he was very different. It changed him. He was still sober most of the time, but it was not the same strength and confidence you saw before. He'd be on edge about it. He used to never care if I drank around him. Now, if he found out I'd been out drinking, he'd get angry. So after that first relapse, there was a change. After the second, third, and fourth, they were all kind of the same.

BRAD JENKEL:

It was no secret that he was battling addiction. In preproduction he had it down. He didn't talk about it. He didn't need to talk about it. But then, during filming, he would struggle at times. And by struggle I mean that his actions were a little more overt. He would talk about his need to stay sober. There were a few more mood swings, but his commitment stayed the same. You could tell he was just trying to buckle down and get through it. I appreciated that he was open about it, and we all tried to support him.

TED DONDANVILLE:

The whole time we were shooting *Ninja*, there were no problems whatsoever. He had the first relapse before shooting, and then the second relapse came after—idle time.

BRAD JENKEL:

When he came back for reshoots, he was a different person. I wasn't there that day, but I got calls about all the problems. They couldn't make the film match. He'd put on weight, and he looked horrible. He wasn't the same old Chris. They kind of had to shoot around him different ways.

When we wrapped shooting, I could sense that he was starting to feel that the movie wouldn't turn out how he'd hoped. Chris went into it thinking he was making a good, earnest film for kids, but in the end he wasn't proud of it the way he was about other movies.

BERNIE BRILLSTEIN:

After the first screening of *Ninja*, I took Chris into the bathroom and he just cried on my shoulder. Cried and cried. It was one of the saddest things I've ever been through.

BRAD JANKEL:

I was disappointed, too. It didn't turn out as I had hoped. Thank God it played with the kids, because it missed with the older crowd. Not everything turns out the way you want; some things fail. I mean, you're talking to the guy who produced *Bio-Dome*.

There's a reason they give the Best Picture Oscar to the producer, because it's a collaborative effort and the producer is responsible for bringing all those collaborators together. But Chris felt like the whole thing was *his* failure, and it wasn't.

* * *

Principal photography on *Beverly Hills Ninja* wrapped in March of 1996. Without the incentive to stay clean for work, Chris relapsed a second time and returned to Hazelden in Minnesota. Other than the reshoots on *Ninja*, he spent the spring and early summer in Chicago, passing time with friends and family and working his twelve-step program. It was a frustrating time. Chris would maintain his sobriety for six weeks, two months at a stretch, then head angrily back to the starting line and begin again. It was not easy, but no one could say that Chris was not trying in earnest.

In May, he returned to Marquette to receive the speech department's Distinguished Young Alumnus Award, an honor of which he was exceedingly proud. Then, in June, he joined David Spade at the MTV Movie Awards to accept the Best On-screen Duo award for *Tommy Boy*.

Chris went back to work that August, taking the lead role in *Edwards & Hunt*, a satirical spoof of Lewis and Clark's historic journey to find an overland route to the Pacific Ocean. Before the film's eventual release, the studio's marketing team found cause to change its name, and it has gone down in history as *Almost Heroes*.

Chris had been cast in the role of Bartholomew Hunt, master tracker and woodsman. *Spinal Tap* veteran Christopher Guest signed on to direct. The producers set about assembling a comedy ensemble to flesh out the exploring party, including Eugene Levy and Bokeem Woodbine. Several actors were considered for the lead role opposite Chris, and the part ultimately went to *Friends* star Matthew Perry.

Beverly Hills Ninja had been a bad choice, and *Black Sheep* was no choice at all, but at the time *Edwards & Hunt* was a good bet. On paper, the script recalled the absurdity of classic Mel Brooks, and it was widely thought to be one of the funniest unproduced scripts in Hollywood. As the cast and crew began shooting in the forests and small towns of northern California, everyone believed, somewhat prematurely, they had a bona fide hit in the works.

MARK NUTTER, *screenwriter:*

Tom Wolfe and I were working on a sitcom with our third partner, Boyd Hale. One Sunday, we decided to skip a trip to Anaheim to watch the L.A. Rams—it was raining—and had some beers at a bar in Venice instead. Boyd came up with the original concept of a Lewis and Clark comedy; the ideas flowed freely from there, and we wrote the script in a couple months. Our agent Rob Carlson also represented Steve Oedekerk, who had written for Jim Carrey, and with Steve's help the script made the rounds.

TOM WOLFE, *screenwriter:*

Steve was so hot at the time, because of his stuff with Jim Carrey, that *Edwards & Hunt* became a hot script. Turner Pictures ended up buying it. I don't remember exactly when Farley came on board, but I know he was first. For the other lead, we wanted Hugh Laurie, who's now the star of *House* but at the time was not well known. Turner wanted someone far more famous. I remember one of the executives saying, "Yeah, we could get a bunch of great actors and make a great little movie . . . but then what?"

And of course, from her way of looking at it, she was right. It would be much harder to market a "little" film with "unknown" actors. For a time Hugh Grant was interested, but he bowed out. I remember when Denise Di Novi brought up Matthew Perry for the first time. Being the self-loathing TV writers we were, we weren't that thrilled with a TV actor being the costar. But we were the writers, and this was our first film. The caterer had more power than we did.

DENISE DI NOVI, *producer:*

The script was brilliant. We even hired Christopher Guest to direct it. I've thought so many times about what went wrong. I always like to say I have the distinction of making the only unsuccessful Christopher Guest movie.

You never know with movies. It's kind of like alchemy; the chemistry just didn't work. It had all the right actors. It had a great director, a great script. But I think the tone of the comedy was very odd. It almost read better than it played. It wanted to be a quirky, British, *Black Adder* type of comedy, and here we had Chris Farley and Matthew Perry. It was just a weird combination.

TOM WOLFE:

We thought Chris Guest would bring the right sensibility to the script, but then the notes about changes came from the studio. They saw it from the beginning as a buddy comedy between Edwards and Hunt, and less like the ensemble comedy we saw it as. In one meeting, someone from Turner called *Lethal Weapon* "the greatest buddy film ever made," and I thought, oh shit, this is not a good sign.

TED DONDANVILLE:

They had to trim fat, and so they trimmed a lot of the funny stuff going on around Chris, which, ironically, would have helped Chris's performance. The movie would have been funnier with all the things the peripheral characters had to do, but of course those are the first to go; you have to build a movie around "the star." They cut the ensemble scenes first, Matthew Perry's second, and Chris's never.

BOKEEM WOODBINE, *costar:*

It was one of those things where they should have left well enough alone. Stuff was getting cut, and it was kind of bizarre. We shot the ending one way, and it was a pretty cool ending. Then they totally reshot the ending without my character there. That kind of shit happens sometimes. You don't get your feelings hurt, but the thing is, it affected the film, because it wasn't linear. At one point we're all together, fighting as this band against these conquistador bastards, and then in the next scene they all meet up and regroup—except for me, and it's like, "What happened to the brother?"

TED DONDANVILLE:

The movie came out after Chris died and when Matthew Perry had gone into rehab, and so a lot of the speculation was that drugs were to blame for the movie's failure, but that wasn't true.

The first weekend of filming, we were shooting in Redding, California, and he was drinking then. Denise Di Novi and the other producers, they found out about it, realized it was a major problem, and even threatened to shut down production. Chris thought he'd really blown it, that this time the personal shit had hit the professional fan.

So Chris had a sobriety bodyguard for the rest of the film, somebody who stayed with him the whole time. With that, Chris stayed pretty much okay for the rest of the shoot. As always, it was the work that kept him going.

DENISE DI NOVI:

That was the only incident. We traveled around a lot on this shoot, and whatever city we were in I would try and find a sponsor and a meeting for him to go to. I have to say it made me gain a lot of respect for people in recovery. No matter what teeny-tiny town we were in, within a couple of hours somebody would show up.

He also went to church every Sunday. No matter where we were on the road, he would find a church nearby and go. He got upset one week when we had to shoot on a Sunday. So instead of going to mass, he had a priest come from his church in Santa Monica and say mass for him on the set.

He was great with my kids. I remember I was sitting on the set one day with my son, who was about four and a half. We were playing a game for about a half an hour, and Chris was just watching us, staring. He said, "Boy, your son is so lucky to have you. I bet he's going to grow up to be a really great person."

And there was just such a sadness in that moment. He had a really big heart, but there was a melancholy there. I never really understood where it came from.

TED DONDANVILLE:

During *Edwards & Hunt*, this girl from the Make-A-Wish Foundation who was dying of AIDS wanted to meet Matthew Perry. She showed up on the set, and everyone doted on her. But Chris noticed she had a brother off to the side, whom everyone was ignoring, and who had probably been ignored for a while, what with his sister taking up all the attention. Chris went and brought the brother into his trailer and goofed around with him and just gave him the greatest day of his life. And it was Chris who instigated it. It wasn't the kid coming over and asking to meet him. The boy ended up having a better Make-A-Wish day than his sister did, and he hadn't even made a wish.

LORRI BAGLEY:

If you even mentioned that, say, your friend's mother had died, tears would start to well up in Chris's eyes. He had such a big heart, and when you have a heart that big, you have to find ways to protect yourself. People who didn't know Chris that well just thought he was the most naïve little kid—and he was—but he knew that he was, and he knew how to use it. He knew exactly how to push your buttons, how to hurt your feelings, how to get you to feel sorry for him. Chris even said to me, "I know how to play people's games." And he did. He was always a hundred percent aware of what was going on and what he was doing.

ERIC NEWMAN:

He'd play dumb with people, but then later he'd recount something from their conversations that let you know he knew exactly what was going on. "The Chris Farley Show" character, the guy who asks the dumb questions, that was the guy he could become when he wanted to. It was a defense mechanism. It protected him, and it made people feel better. I remember we were sitting once in Toronto with Jim Carrey. Carrey's father had just died, and Chris sat down with him and kind of took on this obsequious role. At the time I didn't really think much of it, but looking back, he did it to put Jim Carrey at ease, and Carrey is, by all accounts, a pretty uncomfortable guy out in the world.

TED DONDANVILLE:

He had a very high psychological intelligence. Anything that had to be learned in a book he probably shied away from, but he understood people very, very well.

Bob Timmons was a professional sobriety guy. He's the guy who would send out bodyguards to sit with Chris on the movie set. These "sober companions" got paid good money to essentially sit around the set and do nothing. They certainly got paid more than I did. Chris resented that, and he went through those guys like nothing. He would break them down, mentally. It was like the movie *Jeremiah Johnson*, where they only send out one guy at a time to try and kill Robert Redford, until he kills so many of them that they have to have respect for him.

On *Edwards & Hunt* there was a thief on the set who'd made off with some production equipment, and the producers were trying to figure out who'd done it. Gary was Chris's new sobriety watcher, and the producers came around after the theft, asking Chris, "How well do you know Gary?"

"Hmm," Chris shrugged, "not *very*."

Things got a little uncomfortable for Gary after that. People stopped talking to him. Then a couple weeks later he left, never really knowing why. Then they sent out another guy. That's basically how it went. Chris would treat these guys like a new best friend, and then a few weeks later— either passively, aggressively, or passive-aggressively—they'd be gone, not really understanding why it didn't work out.

I don't know that those people helped so much. Ultimately, all those professional celebrity recovery people have their own issues and their own agendas.

ERIC NEWMAN:

Maybe it's a recovery thing, but Chris attracted loonies.

JILLIAN SEELY:

There are some real wackos out in L.A., a lot of really disgusting people. There was one guy who wanted to be Chris's sponsor, but he charged $125 an hour, and this was back in 1996. I'd never heard of anything like that. You're someone's sponsor, but you charge them by the hour? What the fuck?

KEVIN FARLEY:

There's this whole community of recovery "professionals" who charge you money to watch you. They'll escort you to Hazelden and charge you three grand just for riding on a plane. And that really breaks with tradition. You're not supposed to take money for anything you do to help someone in recovery, and, if you do, it's only because those folks have that money to give.

If you go back to the way it all started, with Bill W. and Dr. Bob, they would go and visit hospitals and they would just find drunks, bring them to meetings and start talking to them. They never charged them money for it. You can make the argument that it costs $13,000 to spend a few weeks at such-and-such facility because they've got staff costs and real estate to keep up. But the whole idea of recovery is that it's free. I don't think it does any of these stars any good to try and deal with the problem inside that bubble. The whole idea is to break yourself down and destroy this illusion you have that you can handle the booze again. You go to a Chicago meeting, or a Madison meeting, and you get humbled pretty quickly.

JOHN FARLEY:

Chris needed a psychologist, not a guy punching a clock to sit around with him. I don't know how much Chris spent on them, but those guys charge exorbitant amounts of money. Jillian, Tim O'Malley, those guys didn't charge him anything, and they were the ones who were really helping him. But I think also the studios were stipulating that those guys be around; otherwise Chris couldn't get insured.

BOKEEM WOODBINE:

I saw those bodyguards hanging around Chris, but they were so cool about their shit that I didn't see them for what they were for the longest time. I didn't realize that Chris was going through the struggles he was having.

I remember one Friday we had wrapped for the week, and we were in somebody's trailer. I had a six-pack of Corona, and I was ready for the weekend. Chris had this trick where he knew how to open up a bottle with a cigarette lighter. I held up a beer and said, "Hey, Chris, could you open this for me?"

Everyone just stared at me. Chris said sure. He went to open it, and his hand was shaking. I thought he was making a joke, you know, being Chris. So I just started laughing, saying, "Look at this guy. He's hilarious." And everyone was looking at me like, what the fuck is wrong with you? And I wasn't getting it. It all went right over my head.

Well, about the third beer, Chris obliged me and opened it, but his hands were still shaking terribly. Then he left to go take a walk, smoke a cigarette or something, and Matthew Perry was like, "Bokeem, what the hell's wrong with you?"

"What do you mean?" I said.

"Chris is an alcoholic. He's having a hard time right now, and you're giving him fucking beer to open?"

"Shit, nobody sent me the memo. I didn't know."

Of course, if I had known, I never would have even brought the beer around. But I was impressed by his dedication. I got the definite vibe that he was serious about not screwing up, and it seemed like his mental attitude was getting progressively healthier throughout the shoot. He was more and more upbeat every day we were working.

TED DONDANVILLE:

After *Edwards & Hunt*, when we weren't working, Chris would deliberately do things like going to health resorts or weight-loss clinics, places where he'd be safe and preoccupied with staying in shape. That year was definitely more up than down, and the downs were not so terrible. The relapses were smaller. He'd have a couple drinks, kick himself over it, talk it out, and be right back at a meeting the next day.

KEVIN FARLEY:

Chris was fighting it like crazy. He'd put together two, three months, and you'd think, okay, he's sober again. Then something would trigger it.

TODD GREEN:

Chris had been in L.A. full-time, so that Christmas I hadn't seen him in probably six or seven months. We all got together at some restaurant in Madison. At one point we kind of broke away and had our own little conversation, and Chris said, "Greenie, man, we're almost thirty-three years old and we're not married. God, that's weird." He just seemed really anxious.

I said, "Chris, what's wrong?"

"I just . . . I don't know. I'm playing these parts where I'm just the funny guy, and I'd like to do some more serious stuff."

I told him, "Why don't you come back to New York and do something onstage, Broadway or off Broadway?"

He really liked the idea. He seemed to take it seriously. Then we agreed that if the Packers went to the Super Bowl we would get together there, since we'd both be going anyway. He was doing great, and we were all so proud of him. I walked away from that conversation thinking, Chris is back. We've got him back for good.

TIM O'MALLEY, *cast member, Second City:*

When Chris was at a weight-loss camp that November, he started to put together some time again. I met up with him again sometime that winter. I had about a year sober by that point. After Chris had left Second City, I'd stayed in Chicago, and my addiction just got worse. Eventually, when my brothers wouldn't come and bail me out of jail anymore, I cleaned up. Chris called me, and we started to go to meetings.

On January 20, 1997, we hooked up at a party at the Hancock for a recovery club that's here in Chicago. He had ninety-nine days. He was so happy, happiest I'd ever seen him. I watched him do backflips. He was doing actual backflips in the room. He was jumping and flipping and yelling, "I did it, Tim! Ninety-nine days! I did it! I did it!"

I was so thrilled for him that day. I was so fucking happy that I was crying.

He said, "I'm going to be here in Chicago for a while. If I keep checking in with you, will you help me?"

I took it as a request for sponsorship. He didn't specifically ask me to sponsor him or spell it out like that, but I could tell he wanted help. So for a few weeks he'd call me, I'd pick him up and take him to meetings. He started to get it again. He was happy and it was fun and we could crack jokes and make fun of each other just like we used to.

And then he stopped calling.

CHAPTER 13

The Devil in the Closet

JOHN FARLEY:

Chris said to me once, "You know what my dream is, Johnny?"

"What?" I said, thinking this was going to be some odd, Alice in Wonderland, through-the-rabbit-hole kind of thing. "What's your dream?"

"Here's what it is," he said. "It's me and Dad. We're both really skinny, and we're the coolest guys at the party, doing backflips all over the place and dancing up a storm to 'Twisting the Night Away.' That would be really cool."

On January 11, 1997, *Beverly Hills Ninja* opened in theaters nationwide. Despite a unanimous critical thumping, it earned over $12 million on its first outing, topping the weekly box office. Following *Tommy Boy* and *Black Sheep*, it was Chris's third-straight number-one film.

That January also marked Chris's third-straight month of sobriety. After staying clean during the principal photography of *Edwards & Hunt*, he'd relapsed again in September and, with varying degrees of failure, cycled through three separate rehab facilities over the next two months. Then, in late October, Chris showed definite signs of improvement. When he celebrated his ninety-ninth day of sobriety in Chicago with Tim O'Malley, there was cause for hope.

But Chris's confidence was on the wane. In New Orleans, Todd Green was expecting to meet Chris at the Super Bowl to watch the Green Bay Packers take on the New England Patriots. When Chris didn't show, Todd called the Farley home in Madison, only to be told that the Super Bowl "wouldn't be good for Chris right now." Chris knew all too well what New Orleans's French Quarter would look like after a Packers win (or, for that matter, a Packers loss). He had chosen to watch the game at the home of a friend instead.

Despite making money, *Beverly Hills Ninja* was largely an embarrassment. It bombed with critics and disappointed even hard-core fans. Chris found himself at a professional crossroads. Hollywood had typecast him as the clown, and he had been fully complicit in that, playing the part whenever he was called upon to do so. But fatty could only fall down so many times. Fortunately, a project had arrived with the potential to take Chris in a new direction. Earlier that year, Bernie Brillstein had brought Chris together with screenwriter and playwright David Mamet, and together they'd agreed to collaborate on Chris's first dramatic film: a biopic of Fatty Arbuckle.

Roscoe "Fatty" Arbuckle was a silent-film star bigger in his day than Charlie Chaplin. He was on the receiving end of Hollywood's first-ever million-dollar contract. He was also on the losing end of Hollywood's first-ever sex scandal, being wrongly accused of sexually assaulting and fatally wounding a young woman. Arbuckle watched his career implode even as his innocence was proven in court. Brillstein was drawn to the story for its showbiz history and intrigue. Chris was drawn to it for the man himself. Arbuckle was a brilliant physical comedian who loathed his extra girth and outsized persona, despite having made it his professional stock-in-trade. After years of being made to play the crazy fat guy, Chris was being asked to play the guy behind the crazy fat guy. He was being asked to play himself, a role he rarely performed for anyone. Much like

Jackie Gleason's turn as Minnesota Fats in *The Hustler*, this was the role that would have fundamentally altered the course of Chris's career.

With the Arbuckle biopic ahead of him and ninety-nine days behind him, Chris was in good spirits. On the first weekend in March, the U.S. Comedy Arts Festival in Aspen, Colorado, was hosting a reunion of *Saturday Night Live* cast members, hosts, and writers. Several dozen stars from the show's history attended, from founding fathers Chevy Chase and Steve Martin to freshmen Molly Shannon and Cheri Oteri. For Chris to share that stage was an honor beyond anything he could have imagined growing up. It should have been one of the highlights of his career. It wasn't.

JOHN FARLEY:

I don't know what the hell happened. I remember everything had been fine in Chicago, but on the flight to Aspen he was acting strange. He may have relapsed that morning, or the night before. I just remember sitting on the plane, thinking, oh no.

CONAN O'BRIEN, *writer,* SNL:

When we were in Aspen, you could tell that the trolley was barely making it around the curves.

KEVIN FARLEY:

When I arrived he was already well into it, drinking and doing coke. From there it was just a total disaster. Spade really looked after him that weekend.

DAVID SPADE:

I went to meet him in his room to go to dinner with Lorne, and when I got to him he was already so messed up. We walked into the restaurant, and it wasn't just Lorne. It was Lorne, Steve Martin, Dan Aykroyd, Chevy Chase, and Bernie Brillstein, all these people that Chris looked up to at this really nice, formal dinner. I said, real quick, "Hey, Chris, come over to the bathroom. I gotta tell you something." And I took him into the kitchen, out the back door into the alley, and I said, "We're getting the fuck out of here. You can't sit with these people in this condition."

These strangers showed up, and he started drinking with them. I tried to stay with him, but eventually I just had to go to bed. I was at lunch the next day, and he walked in. He was with the same people and obviously hadn't gone to bed. They were all wired, and Chris's eyes were rolling back. He said, "Davy. Davy, please stay with me. Don't leave me with these people."

JOHN FARLEY:

One day we had lunch at the restaurant on the top of the mountain. While we were eating, Chris started crying, saying, "I can't stop. I just can't stop." He was crying his eyes out right in the restaurant. Chris wore his heart on his sleeve; he didn't care one bit if he was crying in public, but people were starting to recognize him. We were like, okay, we've got to get Chris Farley off this mountain right now.

BERNIE BRILLSTEIN:

During the reunion, Chris was out onstage with about forty people from *SNL*. They were just telling stories, but Chris was crazed. I thought he was going to have a heart attack onstage. Finally, Dana Carvey quietly took him off.

CHEVY CHASE, *original cast member,* Saturday Night Live:

I read him the riot act that weekend. Everybody did. Chris was drunk and stoned and, on top of that, way overweight. I sat with him and I said, "Look, you're not John Belushi. And when you overdose or kill yourself, you will not have the same acclaim that John did. You don't have the record of accomplishment that he had. You don't have the background that he had. And you don't have the same cultural status that he had. You haven't had the chance to get that far, and you're already screwing yourself up."

He kept saying, "I'm just trying to level out."

That's what he said he was doing with the drinking and the cocaine. It's so silly. It means if you took nothing you'd be level already. Why take all this shit that's killing you? And I told him that. I said, "I've experienced this. I've seen who dies. I've seen how far you think you can go, what you can take and what you can't. You're just going to end up being an overweight guy who could fall on his stomach and had one or two funny things in his career, but nothing that's ever really stood out. You'll be a blip in the *New York Times* obituaries page, and that'll be it. Is that what you want?"

BOB ODENKIRK, *cast member, Second City:*

I was at a party for *Mr. Show.* Somebody came in and said, "Chris is out back. He wants to talk to you."

There was this skanky deejay guy, the kind of guy who hangs out in these party vacation towns. He'd tried to pass David Cross some cocaine earlier, so I knew who he was. I go out back, and there's a limo. I go to the door and knock and the window rolls down. There's Chris, and he's packed in there with girls and hangers-on and this fucking scumbag who was pushing coke around. Chris is bloated and red-faced; he hasn't shaved. We talk for a few minutes, but there's really nothing to say at those times.

I'd seen Chris fucked up before, but this time he looked as bad as anyone has ever looked. It was a horrible thing to watch. It's one thing to shake your finger at a friend and say, "You're gonna kill yourself." It's another thing to look at him and know he's going to do it.

TOM FARLEY:

After Aspen, his managers said, "He's going to rehab, and we're serious this time. He's going away for thirteen weeks and he's not coming back—except to present at the Oscars."

KEVIN FARLEY:

Brillstein-Grey sent him back to the lock-up down south, but they thought it would be okay for him to go to the Oscars, under supervision, and present an award.

TOM FARLEY:

This woman who ran the facility said the only way they'd let Chris go was if he was there with someone from treatment. The next thing you know, *she's* the one who's going with him, and she made him pay her extra for her time, buy her first-class airfare, buy her a dress, and do the same for her daughter to accompany her. I don't think that helped. It just made him feel used.

KEVIN FARLEY:

I thought she was really unprofessional about the whole thing. It was her opportunity to go to the Oscars; she basked in the limelight for a little while. We were in the hotel, and she started rummaging through Chris's gift basket, looking at all the high-end cosmetics they put in there. And Chris was like, "What the fuck are you doing? Put that shit down. Don't you think I might want to give that to my mom?"

This woman just got way into it. "Ooh look, there's George Clooney!" Who gives a fuck? Why don't you do your job?

TOM FARLEY:

I didn't get it. Chris's managers were the ones busting him the hardest for fucking up at Aspen, and then two weeks later they were the same ones lobbying for him to come back and present at the Oscars. It was a money thing. The Oscars are exposure, and exposure means money. I guess they thought Chris needed it to help his career.

TOM ARNOLD:

Chris had a fear that his movies were starting to suck, and, you know, I know what that fear is like. But there's always options if you're talented.

BERNIE BRILLSTEIN:

A few months earlier, I'd taken him to New York to meet with David Mamet about the Fatty Arbuckle story. That story has always fascinated me, only because Arbuckle was innocent. Chris came to the meeting at a little restaurant down in the Village, and he was the good Chris, the well-behaved Chris, because he couldn't believe that David Mamet even wanted to meet him. Mamet loved him. It was a great meeting. He said yes before we got up from the table, and he wrote it for Chris. To this day I know that it would have changed his career.

TOM FARLEY:

As soon as he heard little bits and pieces about Arbuckle's life, he said, "This is me." It was the whole idea that nobody understands the real person underneath. "I'm going to tell them about the real Fatty Arbuckle, and maybe they'll understand the real Chris Farley."

ERICH "MANCOW" MULLER, *friend:*

Chris had all these pictures of clowns in his hallway. He said that they frightened and fascinated him, and that he found them sad. When he was drinking he would always talk like Burl Ives and sing old Burl Ives songs. He'd go, "A little, bitty tear let me down, spoiled my act as a clown." He'd sing that over and over and over.

FR. TOM GANNON, S.J., *friend:*

He felt his career was in trouble, and not just because of the drugs. The fatty-falls-down humor was beginning to take a toll. Sometime that year, he told me, "I can't keep this up. I can't keep falling down and walking into walls." But people wanted him to keep doing the same thing, because it assured them financial success.

BOB WEISS, *producer,* Tommy Boy:

Chris had an idea of reinventing himself in a certain way that didn't take into account very real forces in this industry, forces that can be tidal in nature.

FRED WOLF:

By that point, people were coming at Chris from every angle. They were trying to hire me in the hopes that they might make a deal with him. We went to dinner one night in New York, and he was telling me that he wanted to do movies like *Nothing in Common*, the Tom Hanks/Jackie Gleason movie. I was absolutely convinced that that was what he could do. We started throwing around some ideas, and we kept getting interrupted by fans coming up and saying, "Chris, I love you! You're so funny."

And then as they would walk away, Chris would sigh and say, "But that's all they want."

So we kept trying to have this very serious conversation about his career, but the fans just kept coming and coming and asking for lines from *SNL* or bits from *Tommy Boy*. They wouldn't leave him alone.

FR. TOM GANNON:

One night we were at Gibson's. People pretty much left him alone that night. But one couple came up and thanked him for his work and told him how much they loved him. Then they walked away and he turned to me and said, "They don't really love me. If they knew me, they wouldn't love me at all."

I said, "That's not true, Chris. People do love you. They don't love you the same way I do, or your family does, but they're sincere. You bring a lot of happiness into their lives."

He got a lot of that kind of attention, but he didn't get any nourishment from it, and so he felt he needed more of it all the time.

LORRI BAGLEY:

Chris would go to premieres and goof off on the red carpet, but then he'd complain that the business wouldn't take him seriously. I told him, "Chris, when you stop playing the clown, they'll stop treating you like the clown. They'll take you seriously when you take yourself seriously."

PETER SEGAL, *director,* Tommy Boy:

There were bidding wars for Chris on multiple projects, but most of them were not that good. He'd come to me with these scripts, and I'd turn them down. I kept saying, "No, Chris. That's not a good one for you or for me."

So there was a tension between us, because he thought I didn't want to work with him anymore. There was a long time when he wouldn't return my phone calls, and so I sat down and wrote him a long letter. I told him the reason I was turning these projects down was because I believed his potential was so much greater. And I think he realized it, too. He eventually called me back to thank me for the letter.

But I really meant what I'd said. I thought he could win an Oscar one day. I know people might think I'm crazy saying that, looking at his brief career, but I really believed in his talent. It was way beyond what he was showing.

BRIAN DENNEHY, *costar,* Tommy Boy:

Myself, I never understood why you'd want to be the twentieth-best dramatic actor in the movie business when you were already the best comedian in the movie business. But there is this impulse that comedians have to do serious work.

Interestingly enough, I think with the right part and the right director Chris could have done it. There was a sadness and a vulnerability and a fear that existed in his face and in his eyes. Jackie Gleason had it, a sense that "the world can never take away the pain that I feel, pain that I know that I have, but that I don't fully understand." You can see a little bit of it in *Tommy Boy*, but he hadn't even really begun to explore it.

There are two ways to act, and some people are good enough to do both. One is to erect this very complicated, layered character around you in order to hide behind it, in order to disguise and protect yourself. It's a kind of architecture. You're creating a building. It may be a very impressive building, but it's still a fucking building.

The other way to act is to absolutely strip away everything that keeps you and your soul and your mind from the audience. You rip it away and say, "How much more of myself can I expose to help the audience understand this character?" It's more difficult, and it's more profound, because, ultimately, the real challenge of art is to understand more about yourself. And I think Chris could have done it. I think he would have done it, had he lived. But most comedians, in fact most actors, are not capable of that.

* * *

With *Tommy Boy, Black Sheep*, and *Beverly Hills Ninja*, Chris had joined the ranks of elite Hollywood stars who could "open" a film—a certain core audience could be counted on to turn out for any Chris Farley movie. Even if Chris wasn't thrilled with the reigning definition of "a Chris Farley movie," it was an enviable place to be, and a strong place from which to make a bold, smart career move.

But that spring, Chris's dance card was strangely empty. As a rule, studios take out short-term insurance policies on their lead actors to cover any possible interruptions in the production process. Many of those insurers were refusing to underwrite Chris's films until he could once again prove his dependability. And so, while the Arbuckle project plodded along at the glacial pace of most Hollywood development deals, Chris was having trouble getting even a typical Chris Farley movie off the ground.

In this troubled time one good project did come his way, a voice-over gig for a little animated movie called *Shrek*. In 1997, computer-animated movies were still in their infancy—Pixar's trendsetting *Toy Story* had opened only eighteen months before—and so there was little reason to believe that this fun sideline project would go on to spawn one of the most popular, highest-grossing film franchises of all time. Chris took it on almost as a lark.

Shrek was a popular children's book by William Steig about an ornery yet good-hearted ogre who lives alone in the woods, cast out from the world. Jeffrey Katzenberg, head of DreamWorks Animation, had procured the film rights. Chris was his first choice to play the title role. According to everyone involved, Chris Farley's Shrek was one of the funniest, most heartfelt performances he ever gave. Tragically, no one has ever heard it.

TERRY ROSSIO, *screenwriter:*

Chris was the number-one choice, and everyone was thrilled that he agreed to the project. For an animated feature his voice was perfect, very distinctive. Also, you know, Shrek kind of looked like Farley, or Farley looked like Shrek.

The recording sessions were essentially everybody in the booth rolling off our chairs onto the floor, laughing our asses off. I brought my daughter, who was twelve years old at the time, to one of the sessions at the Capitol Records building. It was her first time ever coming in with me to work, and she concluded I had the best job in the world, listening to funny people be funny.

ANDREW ADAMSON, *director:*

The character of Shrek is to some degree rebelling against his own vulnerabilities. And I think that's probably a reason Katzenberg went to Chris, because there was an aspect of that in him, covering vulnerability in humor and keeping people at arm's length. Within minutes of meeting Chris you saw his vulnerability. Sometimes he would switch on this very gruff persona, and you realized it was because he felt like he was exposing too much.

It didn't make the final film, but at one stage there was a moment in the script where Shrek was walking along, singing "Feeling Groovy," Simon and Garfunkel's "Fifty-ninth Street Bridge" song. Chris was just so into it. When we were recording, I kind of got the impression that he wasn't sure whether he was supposed to be doing a comedic take on the song or a sincere, heartfelt one. He was singing and putting himself out there in a way that was very touching. It made me see the longing in him to do something more genuine with his career. It made me feel bad, because we were in fact asking for a "funny" version. But that he was willing to give it to us, even though he felt so vulnerable about it, made it a very sad and touching moment.

TERRY ROSSIO:

We spoke about the essence or wellspring of Chris's humor; much of it was the humor of discomfort. He would occupy a space of discomfort until it became funny. Shrek, in the Chris Farley version of the story, was unhappy at his place in the world, unhappy to be cast as the villain. So for me,

Chris's comedic persona was key to the creation of the Shrek character—a guy who rejected the world because the world rejected him.

ANDREW ADAMSON:

After Chris died, we all had personal thoughts about whether we could use his voice track and find someone to impersonate him to finish the film. We definitely thought about whether that was the appropriate thing to do, but ultimately we felt that we weren't far enough along in developing the story and the character. The animation process depends a lot on the actor. His death was quite devastating, both personally and to the process of creating the film. We spent almost a year banging our heads against the wall until Mike Myers was able to come on board. Chris's Shrek and Mike's Shrek are really two completely different characters, as much as Chris and Mike are two completely different people.

TERRY ROSSIO:

They're both great in their own way. Mike created a very interesting character, a Shrek who has a sense of humor that's not that good, but it makes him happy. Chris's Shrek was born of frustration and self-doubt, an internal struggle between the certainty of a good heart and the insecurity of not understanding things.

ANDREW ADAMSON:

I always found Chris a very fun person to be around. Containing him in a recording booth was a great challenge, but he was a very down-to-earth guy on a certain level. We had an enjoyable relationship. The drug problem didn't impact his work at all, and to be honest, I had no idea it was happening. Everything I'd seen indicated that he had overcome those demons. He was going through rehab at the time and was very disciplined about it. Any other impressions I had were thirdhand and after the fact. I really felt like he was on an upward spiral.

* * *

And Chris was—that week. But the next week he was back on a down-ward one, and who could say where he was going the week after that? By the time he finished voicing *Shrek* in early May, Chris's ability to maintain his sobriety had all but vanished. His relapses started coming randomly, suddenly, and with alarming frequency.

One of Chris's counselors described him as having the most severe addictive personality he'd ever seen—this in several decades of helping patients. As Chris surrendered his hold on sobriety, his compulsive over-eating ran rampant as well. Chris had fought a constant battle with his weight since childhood. Those who knew him well knew it was the bane of his existence. Given the severe health risks of obesity, Chris was doing almost as much damage to himself with food as he was with drugs and alcohol.

After presenting at the Oscars on March 24, Chris had returned to rehab in Alabama, emerging sober to work on *Shrek* in April and early May. Following yet another relapse, he returned to the outpatient pro-gram at Hazelden Chicago on May 19. It accomplished little. June and July were spent in and mostly out of rehab, and by August the situation was catastrophic.

Chris's relationship with Lorri Bagley, rocky and unstable in the best of times, was severely broken. It never ended, but the blowouts got bigger and more explosive, and the separations grew longer and longer. Friends who were active in Chris's recovery, like Jillian Seely and Tim O'Malley, did their best to keep him on the straight and narrow, but their efforts were increasingly frustrated. Chris would either insulate himself from his friends in order to use, or insulate himself in order not to use. He had so removed himself from his usual social networks that many assumed he was simply off somewhere else, stone sober and hard at work. Chris had never let the trappings of fame and success put any distance between him and his loved ones. But addiction finally succeeded where fame could not.

ROBERT BARRY, *friend, Edgewood High School:*

Toward the end Chris would go hang out with these Board of Trade guys in Chicago. They had tons of money and wanted to hang with celebrities. When he was in Chicago, Chris didn't call up Dan Healy or me or the Edgewood guys anymore. He'd call up those people. I never even visited his place in the Hancock.

FR. MATT FOLEY, friend:

For the last three years I had been living in Mexico, doing missionary work. I talked to Chris and his parents on a regular basis, but then Chris stopped returning my calls. One of the last times I saw him was on a trip to Chicago. We went to work out at a health club there by the John Hancock building. After that we were supposed to hang out all day, but he basically wanted to get rid of me. He didn't want me around because I would have told him he was full of shit.

JOEL MURRAY, *cast member, Second City:*

The people who loved him didn't want him to drink, so he couldn't be with us anymore. I'd invite him over to barbecues and stuff out in L.A., and I could tell that he had a whole other thing going on. It wasn't a celebrity, big-shot kind of thing; it was an "I gotta go do this stuff that I don't want to tell you about" kind of thing. He was the worst liar in the world, so he'd just kind of be evasive. Next thing you know he's hanging out with nefarious types who just want to wind up the comedy toy, and that's never good.

DAVID SPADE:

There's no shortage of those sorts of people. I've talked to Aykroyd about Belushi, and it's the same experience. Friends you've known for three days aren't friends I want to hang with.

I was working in TV, he was off doing his movies, and we'd just slowed down a little bit. It wasn't Lorri. That was done with, but we'd been a little bit on the outs, and because of that I got a lot of shit toward the end about "Why weren't you there for him?" But being that close, I dealt with it all the time. And in that situation, before the guy's dead, he's just kind of an asshole. Truth is, you get a junkie who's wasted all the time and moody and angry and trying to knock you around, you say, "Okay, you go do that, and I'll be over here." I think that's understandable.

TED DONDANVILLE:

Chris never had any animosity toward Spade at all; he had just respected Spade's decision to walk away for a while. But after being all alone on *Ninja* and *Edwards & Hunt*, Chris started to realize how much he needed his friend. It was like Mick Jagger after those first two solo albums—maybe it was good to have Keith Richards around.

TOM FARLEY:

I always told Chris, "You love humor, but look around at the people you're with when you're doing these drugs. These people have no humor in their lives. You keep this up and you will end up surrounded by people who are not your friends." And that's exactly what happened.

NORM MacDONALD:

Sometimes you'd see him with prostitutes. That was mostly at the very end, like when he hosted *SNL*. The amazing thing was how well he treated them. He really fell for them. He'd take them to dinner and treat them so sweetly. He'd treat them equal to any other person at the table. He'd introduce them to you as his girlfriend.

TIM O'MALLEY:

Escorts and strippers are just part of the deal when you're lonely and lost. It's like phone sex, trying to reach out and talk to somebody. Every phone book has a hundred phone numbers in it; you can always dig up someone to spend time with you.

I went into his apartment one night, and he said, "Yeah, I relapsed last night. I had a pizza, and I figured since I'd relapsed on my OA program I'd have a bottle of scotch, and then I went to the Crazy Horse and I spent eleven grand."

"Jesus, you were giving the girls five hundred a dance?"

"Yeah, how'd you know?"

"Because I know how it goes. You were trying to get some girl to come home with you by overtipping her, and those girls don't want anything but more money. First of all," I told him, "separate your food program from your alcohol problem. Food's not going to kill you tonight."

I hated the Overeaters Anonymous program for that, because if he relapsed on that he'd just go ahead and go the distance.

KEVIN FARLEY:

For Chris, by that point, every relapse meant going all the way. Some addicts will put a toe back in the water, but Chris would always dive back into the deep end. And that's what happened when he went to Hawaii.

DAVID SPADE:

I was at the Mondrian in L.A., and Chris was there. He was doing an interview, and he had one of his sobriety bodyguards with him. It was kind of sad, because I hadn't seen him in a while. He came over to my table—the bodyguard let him come over alone for a bit—he came over and he said, "Nobody cares about anything but *Tommy Boy*. Can we do another one? Can we do . . . something?"

"Of course. There's always scripts they want us to do. I didn't know if you wanted to do anything anymore."

"We gotta do it, because that's the only one that matters."

"Okay," I said. "Let's find something."

Then these two cute girls came over. They said, "Hey, come party with us. We're in town with Spanish *Playboy*." Or something ridiculous like that.

Chris said, "I can't."

"Oh, c'mon," they said. "Just come up to our room for a bit."

Chris looked at me. I said, "I'll cover for you. I can buy you about five minutes."

"Thanks, Davy."

He took off, and then the bodyguard came over and said, "Where's Chris?"

"He went to the bathroom."

"Which bathroom?"

"There's one in the hotel."

"You fucked this."

"Sorry."

It was the wrong thing to do, I know. But we'd had a really nice moment together, and I liked that. It proved that we were still close, could still be friends, and I wanted to help him out. But then they couldn't find Chris. He disappeared, and it just turned into chaos.

KEVIN FARLEY:

US magazine was doing a big feature article on him at the time, and Chris was spending his days with this reporter. Chris woke me up in the middle of the night and asked me if I wanted to come down and take a whirlpool with these girls he'd met from *Playboy*. He'd already relapsed and started drinking. I said no and went back to bed. I figured he'd play in the Jacuzzi and then go up to his room and sleep it off. But I got up the next morning and found out he'd relapsed hard, bought these girls plane tickets and gone to Hawaii. When that *US* reporter showed up and there was no Chris, the shit hit the fan. Gurvitz had to put that fire out.

When I talked to Chris about it later, he didn't even remember going to Hawaii. He just woke up there. But when he called Dad from Hawaii, Dad was like, "Hey, you're on vacation!" The level of denial at that point was just crazy.

FR. TOM GANNON:

You cannot understand Chris Farley without grappling with the relationship between him and his father. That was the dominant force in his life. He talked to his father every day on the phone, and was constantly trying to please him. And I think he *did* please him. But the family, which looked so normal on the outside, was terribly dysfunctional.

ERIC NEWMAN:

If you were a shrink, you could retire on that family.

TIM O'MALLEY:

The first people we know as God are our parents. And if you don't get approval from your parents, eventually you can mature and find that from other places. But Chris was never able to do that. He was never able to find it from God or anyone else.

TOM ARNOLD:

Even when he was thirty years old, Chris would literally sit at his dad's feet and tell him stories. I don't think anything made him happier than to sit at the foot of his dad's recliner and tell him stories about show business, or food.

There were a couple other times where I went with Chris to the Taste of Madison, which is this festival in the city square where every three feet there's a booth of a different kind of food. All the conversations Chris had with his dad that weekend were just "Hey, did you have that pork chop on a stick?" "Yeah, that was good. Did you get some of this?" You know, they were surface conversations, the kind I would have with my dad, the kind that don't get really deep. Because if you get deep it's pretty painful.

KEVIN FARLEY:

I think my dad was basically a happy guy, but he had an addiction to food and alcohol. And when you get to be six hundred pounds, you're in such a hole that what are you going to do to get out? And that's what depressed him. He was confused by it. He'd be like, "I don't know how I got this big. I don't know how this happened." I watched my dad's eating habits. Yes, he ate a lot, but was it proportional to the weight he gained? No way. Part of it had to be genetic.

My father was handicapped, and when you have someone in your family with an illness, you want to do what you can to make them feel better. It wasn't just Chris. We all wanted to make Dad happy, because we all knew he was on borrowed time.

JOHN FARLEY:

Then there's the other element to it, not wanting to get skinny or sober because he didn't want Dad to feel bad. Chris said that to me, that he should stay heavy for Dad.

LORRI BAGLEY:

Chris was very protective of his father. One night after I went with Chris to a meeting, he asked me if I wanted to meet his parents for dinner. When we were in the elevator going up to see them, Chris was like, "Look, my dad has this problem. Please don't stare at him."

A year later, the first time I spent the night with Chris, he showed me a picture of his family from when he was a kid, and his father was so thin. I said, "What happened?" But Chris never really told me.

CHARNA HALPERN, *director/teacher, ImprovOlympic:*

I had a very intense night with him alone in my house once. We were listening to a Cat Stevens album, *Tea for the Tillerman,* and the song "Father and Son" came on. Chris started crying. Cried and cried and cried. He said, "I love my dad so much, and I don't want him to die."

I said, "He probably feels the same way about you. You're both in the same situation. You're both alcoholics. You're both overweight. Maybe you can help each other."

"Yeah, but we can't," he said. "It'll never happen."

HOLLY WORTELL, *cast member, Second City:*

His dad was of a different generation. They didn't go to see "headshrinkers." Chris told me that his father finally agreed to go with him to this weight-loss clinic once. They were sitting in a group therapy session, and everyone was going around the circle talking about their issues with food. His dad just stood up and said, "Let's go." They got up and went outside, and his dad said, "We're not like these people. They've got problems. That's not us. We're leaving."

FR. TOM GANNON:

They walked out, checked in to a resort on an island off the coast of Florida, took out a room, and proceeded to go on a binge together. With that kind of enabling, the kid didn't stand a chance. The father was in denial, but in all fairness, I don't think the brothers were straight with the father, either. Dad knew about the drinking but not so much about the drugs. The father never accepted that Chris was a drug addict until the very end, even though the two of them talked every day. So there was a lot of posturing going on.

TOM ARNOLD:

It's not his father's fault, what happened to Chris. It's not. Chris had access to every tool in the world. He went to the best treatment centers, had the best people being of service to him, reaching out to him.

You look at all the pieces of Chris's life, his father, his mother, his brothers, his life growing up, his work—everything. You look at all that and maybe some things are off or a little dysfunctional, but at the end of the day it's his responsibility. It's not like I didn't sit with him a dozen times where he looked me in the eye and knew what he had to do to stay sober. You can't blame your circumstances, and after a certain point you can't even blame your father. You can't blame him; you have to have compassion for him. It all comes down to you, and you've got to be a man about it.

LORRI BAGLEY:

Chris knew that to be himself, to be healthy, he'd have to pull away from the family, and he couldn't do it. He said he couldn't do it. But you have to cut the emotional umbilical cord at some point. Some American Indians have a ritual where you're not allowed to be a part of the tribe until you leave, go out in the wilderness, rename yourself, and come back. Then you're accepted as a man. But we don't have that in our culture. That's why families in the country are falling apart, and why women have to deal with all this Madonna/whore bullshit. It's because men don't grow up, and Chris never grew up.

ERICH "MANCOW" MULLER:

That May, Chris Rock was performing in Chicago. Farley called me and said, "I've broken out of prison. I'm out. I want to go see my boy Chris Rock!" Chris broke out of rehab to go to this show. I met him at his apartment, and I was begging him not to drink. I was sitting there, going, "No. No, Chris. Please."

He said, "Just a little splash." That's how it started off, a Coke with a splash of whiskey—and I mean just a drop. Then an hour later it turned into a glass of whiskey with a splash of Coke. We went to the concert to meet Tim Meadows and his wife, and I spent the whole night fighting him.

TIM MEADOWS:

We went backstage after the show to see Rock, and Farley was drunk, fooling around in front of these girls. We'd been talking about going out for dinner after the show, but Rock and I looked at each other, and I said, "I can't do it. I can't be around him anymore like this."

Rock said, "Yeah, I know what you mean. I'll take care of him tonight."

CHRIS ROCK:

He was so fucking drunk, drunk to the point where he was being rude and grabby with girls. He would go too far and you'd call him on it, and he'd give you his crying apology, the Farley Crying Apology. We probably had about four of those that night.

I remember dropping him off at his apartment. He wanted me to come up and see his place, and I just didn't have it in me. He was so fucked up. I just couldn't go up there. And as I drove away, I knew. It had gotten to that point. I knew that was the last time I'd ever see him alive.

JILLIAN SEELY:

I was waiting for Chris to pick me up for the Chris Rock show, and I got a phone call from him saying there weren't enough tickets and so I couldn't go. That was Sunday. Then Tuesday I got a call at nine o'clock at night from a nurse at the Northwestern psych ward. Hazelden had to send him to the hospital to get sober before they'd let him back into treatment.

Chris got on the phone. "I'm really scared," he said. "I totally relapsed on Sunday and went back to treatment, and they made me come here. Will you come and see me?"

So I went over to Northwestern. I went up to Chris's room, and I heard him go, "Hey, hey, in here."

He was in the bathroom blowing his cigarette smoke into the air vent. I looked down at this stainless-steel paper towel rack, and there were lines of cocaine on it. Chris had gotten one of the hospital staff to bring him coke in the detox ward.

I said, "I'm totally telling on you." I went out into the hallway and started yelling, "Chris is doing cocaine in his room!"

They came in and restrained him. He was screaming at me, "You're a fucking narc! I hate you!" It was like a scene out of a bad movie. It was horrible, really horrible.

KEVIN FARLEY:

The fact that Chris was able to score cocaine *inside* the detox ward was just insane. When you're famous there aren't any rules. That's when I knew things were getting bad. He was in a mental ward. You couldn't get any lower than that.

As a kid, when he watched *The Exorcist*, he was terrified of the idea that something evil could take over your body, possess you, and make you do things you can't control. Here he had this thing that was eating away at him from the inside, and he was powerless to stop it. And that scared the living shit out of him.

FR. TOM GANNON:

On the surface, the Farleys are a wonderful family. They're loving. They're supportive. They're there for one another. I didn't get to know the father. Met him once, maybe. Spoke to him on the phone a couple of times. And I suppose I have to be honest; I didn't care for him that much.

THE DEVIL IN THE CLOSET

Whereas the mother is a lovely person, caught in the same vortex as the rest of them.

And therein lies the key to the problem: They didn't know how to manage Chris. When it's all said and done, I don't know that they were any more or less dysfunctional than any other family, but Chris's personality was so outsized that it sort of took over. It's that old story from his childhood, when the nuns said that Chris didn't know the difference between somebody laughing with him or laughing at him. That played out in the family as well. At what point do you draw a line that this bizarre behavior is too much to handle?

TOM FARLEY:

Nobody ever thought of the problem in terms of Chris's health or the idea that he could die. Mom maybe had some premonitions of disaster but didn't talk about it. No one talked about it—and that was the problem. My parents' reaction was always the same: "Chris is out of control." Or "Dammit, how could he do this? He's going to ruin his career."

And the motivations were always external, like getting fired from *Saturday Night Live*. It was always concern about the symptoms and never the disease, which none of us genuinely understood. But Chris wasn't "out of control"; he was sick. And his sickness was just so deep and so entrenched.

TOM ARNOLD:

It's harder for some people, and I don't know what it would've taken for Chris to really, truly hit bottom. The absolute worst I ever saw him was at a Planet Hollywood opening in Indianapolis that July. It was the bad Chris. I mean, he was just so fucked up. He had his shirt up over his head and people were taking pictures. Kevin was with him. I said to Kevin, "You better get him out of here. I'm gonna fuckin' tackle him, 'cause I have had it."

285

KEVIN FARLEY:

Jillian and I were trying to get him out of the bar, but he didn't want to leave. And at that point I couldn't control him. Either he's going to take a swing at me and we can get into a fight there in front of the cameras, or I can go home. We'd flown in on a private jet that night, so Jillian and I left and took it back together.

JILLIAN SEELY:

We were really quiet on the plane. We were both so sad that Chris had started drinking again. The next day I got a phone call around noon. I thought it would be Chris, calling from Indianapolis, confused and wondering why he'd been left behind and maybe having learned a bit of a lesson. But he was like, "Hey, what's going on? I'm back in Chicago. Want to get lunch?" The plane went right back for him and picked him up. No consequences for his actions at all.

But his behavior at the party made the *Enquirer* and the entertainment TV shows. And then that profile in *US* magazine came out a few weeks later. It was a pretty hard-core article.

TOM FARLEY:

That was the first time there had really been any public exposure of Chris's problems, which is pretty amazing when you look back on it. At that point, he was really staring at the abyss; it looked like he was going to lose it all. Brillstein-Grey went into damage control mode, trying to clean up the press.

They also sent Chris back to Promises in Malibu and made him start seeing this therapist in L.A. The sessions Chris had with this guy weren't really therapy sessions; it was more this guy telling Chris what he had to do, and why, if he wanted to save himself. He really got into Chris's noggin. He hit him in a weak spot, that superstitious thing that he always had. He was telling Chris there was this other side to him, this other being inside him that was bent on destruction. That really played to a lot of Chris's fears, and I don't think it was helpful at all. I think he just confused the boy.

FR. TOM GANNON:

Chris thought of his addiction in terms of good and evil, that drugs were the devil's way of controlling him, and I tried to steer him away from that way of thinking, because it isn't very helpful. Like many Irish Catholics, Chris's spirituality was sort of a mix between religion and superstition.

TOM FARLEY:

He told me that heroin was the devil. "I've seen the devil, Tommy." That's what he told me after he'd tried it.

LORRI BAGLEY:

Chris told me that every time you do heroin, you can feel it take a part of your soul.

KEVIN FARLEY:

Chris would talk about his addiction in those terms, because that was the vocabulary he had for it. A lot of people laugh at that concept, but I think it's as good a framework as any. What is a demon? A demon is something that wants you dead. And whatever was in possession of Chris certainly wanted him dead.

FR. MATT FOLEY:

Chris knew all too well that addiction was a disease. He and I had endless talks about it. He needed to separate himself from the shame that he felt. He needed to learn how to forgive himself and accept forgiveness from others. But I can relate to his thinking. I struggle with temptation every day, as do we all. There is no blessing that comes out of drugs and alcohol, and in that sense they're evil.

TIM O'MALLEY:

They say that you should go back to your faith when you get sober, but it's up to the individual the role that their faith plays. How did I survive? How did I not run myself off the road when I was driving around in my underwear looking for crack? I'd have to say it was God. But a lot of people don't go back, because they feel so burned by the nuns and the priests.

I don't think Chris ever got a chance to really clarify or learn properly some of the ways to sort out your life. So I think he used religion and did the best he could with it, still trying to be a good Catholic boy using the garbage we were taught by the nuns, the angel on one shoulder and the devil on the other. It's a fifth-grader's view of spirituality.

FR. TOM GANNON:

Chris was caught in a transition in Catholicism between an old-church approach to faith and a newer way of thinking. The old view of spirituality was that life was like climbing a mountain. You have to fight onward and upward, climbing with your spiritual crampons until you reach the top—and that's perfection. You pass the trial and you pass the test and you get so many gold stars in your copybook. Then you come before the heavenly throne for judgment, and maybe you've got a couple of indulgences in your back pocket in case your accounting was wrong.

But that kind of faith only gets a person so far. Your spiritual life isn't like climbing a mountain, waiting to find God at the top. It's a journey, full of highs and lows, and God is there with you every step of the way, in the here and now and in the hereafter. The first approach is really a whole lot of smoke and mirrors. It's only the second one that allows a person to grow, but that second view is hard for people to get ahold of unless they get in touch with themselves.

Chris didn't feel that he was worthy of God's love. He felt he had to prove himself. Well, you're never going to get very far in any relationship with that kind of belief. Imagine if you had to prove yourself to your spouse every single day; that's not the way love works. In all of our talks, that was the one thing I really tried to work with him on, adjusting to this different idea of faith, but he never really moved from one to the other. It's hard. It takes a long time to come around to that way of thinking, and Chris just ran out of time.

CHAPTER 14

Fatty Falls Down

CHRIS FARLEY:

The notion of love is something that would be a wonderful thing. I don't think I've ever experienced it, other than the love of my family. At this point it's something beyond my grasp. But I can imagine it, and longing for it makes me sad.

In January of 1997, Chris Farley had the number-one movie in America and a ninety-day sobriety chip of which he could rightly be proud. A mere seven months later, all of that seemed an impossible memory.

On August 1, Chris's relapse at Planet Hollywood triggered a small whirlwind of negative press, capped by the September issue of *US* magazine with its profile, aptly titled "Chris Farley: On the Edge of Disaster." Not only had the reporter been witness to Chris's relapse and subsequent escape to Hawaii, Chris himself, in full heart-on-sleeve mode, had divulged a year's worth of personal therapy in just a few short interviews. Even Chris's friends and manager Marc Gurvitz had given frank assessments of Chris's condition. The piece was a public relations nightmare.

On August 8, Chris checked into Promises, an upscale recovery facility in Malibu, California. He stayed until the end of the month. On September 1, he checked out for a brief opportunity to go back to work, flying to Toronto to film a small cameo in Norm MacDonald's feature film *Dirty Work*, about a guy who goes into the revenge-for-hire business to help raise money for a friend's operation.

Chris stayed clean during his shooting days—he always did—but he would vanish at night, and in general he did not look well. Norm found Chris's behavior unusual; he had never seen his friend under the influence before. He openly questioned Chris as to whether or not it was a good idea for him to continue working, but Chris insisted that he was fine and that, after such a long professional drought, he was grateful for the opportunity. At that point, *Shrek* was an ongoing concern, and the Fatty Arbuckle biopic was still alive somewhere, but Chris's inability to get insured had effectively stalled his career. The only producer willing to give him a shot was Brian Grazer at Universal, who wanted Chris for a film called *The Gelfin*, which would begin filming in January with newly minted star Vince Vaughn.

On September 10, Chris's part in *Dirty Work* wrapped and it was back to Promises in Malibu. By this point he had cycled through a dozen rehab facilities in under twenty-two months, and the routine treatments had reached a point of diminishing returns. He knew the system better than most of the counselors assigned to his case. Institutions that once frightened Chris now merely bored him. The constant physical strain of using and drying out frayed his nerves. And the long, dark nights spent alone in strange beds ate away at what little reserve of humanity he had left.

Chris was convinced—or, more aptly, had convinced himself—that there had to be answers elsewhere. On his tenth day at Promises, fed up with the whole ordeal, he went down to the basement, flipped the master circuit breaker, and cut the power for the entire facility. Once the lights were restored, the security team found Chris lounging in the common room, naked, quietly leafing through old magazines. "You found me!" he proclaimed. The police were called, and he was asked to leave.

A now-familiar pattern played itself out, and by mid-October Chris swore he was ready to recommit himself to sobriety. He rented a house in

Los Angeles and asked Kevin to move in with him. Kevin now had four years sober on his own, and Chris thought his brother would be able to take him to meetings and keep him on track.

In truth, no one could keep Chris on track but Chris, but there was one place where he had managed to stay sober and happy: his old job at *Saturday Night Live*. Marc Gurvitz called *SNL* producer Lorne Michaels. They agreed that having Chris come back to host might help him in some way to deal with his problems. But the week Chris arrived in New York, he wasn't just having problems, he was having a full-blown meltdown. The results, broadcast live on national television for millions to see, were not pretty.

KEVIN FARLEY:

He was gasping for air by that point. I lost him for three days. It was the weekend before he was supposed to host *Saturday Night Live*, and he was just gone. I was staying at the house, and Marc Gurvitz was calling me, saying, "Where's Chris? We've got to get him on a plane. Lorne expects him in New York."

I told him I had no idea where Chris was. For all I knew, Chris could have died that weekend. He was with Leif Garrett, of all people. Leif fucking Garrett, and some other losers. When Chris finally showed up, high on heroin after three days missing, Leif came into the house and was like, "Your brother's so fucking funny, man." I almost took him out right there, but I was so sad and spent with the whole situation that I just didn't have the energy to punch him in the face.

That whole weekend was so sad and out of control. I think Chris planned it that way, to be gone right up until he had to leave, so that there would be no chance of anyone having an intervention and sending him back to rehab. He was planning on carrying the party right on to New York; it rolled right into *SNL*, and the result was a complete disaster.

LORNE MICHAELS:

The decision to have Chris come back and host wasn't made because he was red hot in show business and it would be great for the show. I think it might have been some desire of mine to help him get back in touch with a time in his life when he was happy. When he was at the show, he knew what the rules were, and I felt it might help him to come back.

TOM GIANAS, *writer:*

When he got back, you could tell that things were bad. He was very tense, distracted and, well, fucked up. I don't think Lorne expected that, otherwise he never would have let him host. We sure didn't expect it. I still thought he was sober. We went out to dinner Monday night after the pitch meeting, and we were running interference with waiters all night, trying to keep liquor and booze away from him. And that lasted the whole week.

MOLLY SHANNON, *cast member:*

He was just indulging in everything: girls, Chinese food, drugs, booze, cold syrup. Everything.

MARCI KLEIN, *talent coordinator:*

By Tuesday night, I knew he was out of control. I had heard that he'd been going up to some of the newer cast members and saying, "Hey, let's go out!" And a lot of the new cast, they really looked up to Chris, wanted to go with him and hang out with him. So I called a meeting with everyone. I met with them in the talent office, and I said, "Look, I know Chris, and I know what's going to happen. If he wants you to go out, you're not going. If any of you help him get drinks or liquor or anything, if you encourage him in any way, you are going to be a part of helping him die."

TIM MEADOWS:

That was a fucking rough week. I tried to hang out with him as much as I could whenever he was at the show, because Chris would never do anything in front of me. But he started all that shit, like, "I've got to . . . go to my car for something." He would make excuses to leave, and he'd come back and he'd be happy again. That whole week he had these total strangers hanging around.

TODD GREEN:

When Chris got to New York he shut everybody down. I wasn't able to see him. Kevin Cleary wasn't able to see him. I don't think Tommy could even get to him, and the rumor mill was cranking.

TOM FARLEY:

It was Tuesday night at about five o'clock. I was working up in Greenwich, and I knew he was coming out to New York. I called my wife, and I said, "This is weird. He's been here since Sunday, and he hasn't even called me."

She said, "Just get in your car and go down there."

So I drove down to the Waldorf-Astoria where he was staying, and he had this bodyguard sitting outside the door. I went in, and Chris was like, "What're you doing here?"

"I just wanted to see my brother," I said. "I haven't seen you in a while."

"Okay, great. I'm just about to head over to *Saturday Night Live*. They're writing tonight, and I'm going to go help come up with ideas."

So we hopped in this limo downstairs that was supposed to take us over to 30 Rock. Mike Shoemaker had one of the NBC pages in the car to babysit Chris. Chris got in and said, "We've got to make a stop. I've got to pick up some friends on 110th Street."

One Hundred and Tenth Street? Next thing I knew we pulled up at this place in Harlem. Chris went up and came out of this building with two women, looking exactly like what they were. They got in the car, and Chris said, "Okay, let's go to *SNL*."

This NBC kid looked over at me like, "Are you shitting me?"

I just shrugged. So Chris took these two hookers up to *Saturday Night Live*. It was Marci Klein's birthday that night. They were all going out to the Havana Room later. Chris was hanging out with Tracy Morgan and Jim Breuer, talking to them about skits and stuff. I was stuck out in the lobby with these two girls, trying to make small talk. Then Chris went into Cheri Oteri's room to talk with her for a while. I knew where the evening was going, and I knew we weren't going to end up at Marci's birthday party. I got up and knocked on Cheri's door and said, "Chris, you know what, I'm outta here. I'm gonna get some sleep." And I left.

The next day, I called up Kevin Cleary and told him about Chris, that he was just a mess. Kevin said to come back down to the city, we'd take Chris to lunch and have yet another intervention. So I left work, drove in, Kevin and I went to the Waldorf at around eleven-thirty and called up to the room. Chris answered the phone. I said, "Hey, I'm down in the lobby. It's me and Kevin Cleary."

And as soon as he heard those two names he knew what was up. Kevin Cleary was the one person in the world Chris could never bullshit. Chris said, "Yeah, yeah, I'm just waking up. Give me twenty minutes."

We waited a half hour or so, called back up to his room, and there was a "do not disturb" on his phone line. I called the front desk and asked to be put through, but they said he'd left specific instructions not to be disturbed.

Kevin and I went out and had lunch and talked about what we could do, and that was it. I never saw him alive again.

NORM MacDONALD:

I had a sketch I wanted to do with him. The idea was that I'd play Fast Eddie Felson and he'd play Minnesota Fats and we'd play a really long game of pool, just like in *The Hustler*, only we'd never sink a single ball.

Chris told me to come to his hotel to work on the sketch, which was already kind of odd. Why wouldn't we just write in the office? But I went to the hotel and he had this guy guarding the door, and then I went inside and he had tumblers of vodka and orange juice and there were girls there. He kept going in the other room.

Working on a sketch with Chris was never anything but a great delight, but his mind wasn't working like it used to. There was all this self-doubt. He was very preoccupied.

I remember he said to me, "Sometimes, life seems so cruel." He kept saying that: Life seems so cruel.

I said, "Why do you say that, Chris? You're always laughing."

"I don't know," he said. "I just want to die."

I've heard people say that before, and it's sort of a meaningless phrase. Maybe he meant it; I don't know. I don't know how people talk under the influence.

ROBERT SMIGEL, *writer:*

I wasn't writing for the show full-time then. I was just doing the cartoons and occasionally faxing in a sketch idea. In this case, ESPN had asked me to do a "Super Fans" bit with George Wendt about Ditka becoming coach of the New Orleans Saints. When Chris hosted a few weeks later, I figured we could do something similar on the show, so I'd faxed in a version with Chris in it.

Chris's condition was obvious as soon as he showed up. You can't replace a host after the sketches are written and the sets are built, but that doesn't happen until Thursday. And by Tuesday everyone knew how bad it was. Granted, pulling the host even on a Tuesday would have been a huge crisis, but I thought that's what was needed: dire consequences and an inescapable, public humiliation. I thought Chris should be fired. That was the only thing that would teach him the same lesson that he'd learned when Lorne had suspended him and threatened to fire him four years earlier. I actually thought it was a gift opportunity, a chance to help a drowning friend. But I wasn't a full-timer there, and I wasn't part of making that decision.

NORM MacDONALD:

It was shocking to everybody that Lorne let the show go forward.

LORNE MICHAELS:

I don't remember anybody threatening to resign over it. I don't think that the show should be used as therapy, but there was no way for us, for me anyway, to get through to him in a conversation. That didn't work anymore. If Chris couldn't get it any other way, he could at least watch it on television. The thing he most cared about was the show. I think there was a feeling that the process of doing this, succeeding at it or failing at it, could be brutally honest with him in a way that he was no longer getting in a lecture.

MIKE SHOEMAKER, *producer:*

The truth is you're so busy on that show that you just keep moving, and I think we all hoped that the old Chris would kick in and we'd be fine. I was also just mad at him. More than being worried, I was angry.

ROBERT SMIGEL:

That whole show is like watching a slow death march, but the cold open was just the worst.

TOM FARLEY:

I was in shock when I saw the opening sketch. It was Lorne and Tim Meadows talking about how Chris had kicked his drug problem and he'd be in perfect shape to host. Then Chris bursts in, and he's obviously in terrible shape. They'd made jokes about Chris's drinking before, but that was when he was sober and doing well. This was not funny at all.

TIM MEADOWS:

When that sketch was pitched at read-through, nobody knew that by Saturday it would no longer be a sketch but the real, honest truth. At the time I didn't think it was in such bad taste, because that's what we'd always done. We'd always been able to make fun of ourselves.

ROBERT SMIGEL:

They cut that opening sketch and the monologue out of the syndicated version of the show. When you see the reruns, it starts with the opening credits and goes straight into a sketch. I believe it's the only time in the history of the show that's been done.

NORM MacDONALD:

He blew out his voice in dress, and so the live show was just awful. He was like a marathon runner stumbling to the finish line before it even began.

MARCI KLEIN:

I said to Lorne, "I think he's going to have a heart attack."

TOM GIANAS:

He did this incredibly physical scene with Molly Shannon, a Mary Katherine Gallagher scene, and it was on right before the Motivational Speaker scene, where he played the coach of a spinning class. He was just huffing and puffing his way through the scene with Molly, sweating like crazy.

And then, by the time he got to the Motivational Speaker scene, he was gone. It was really hard to watch.

NORM MacDONALD:

They did overuse him in the sketches, knowing what his condition was. In the heyday of *SNL*, back in the seventies, they'd get hosts who were completely drunk, and so they'd just write them out of the show. And this was a far more severe case than that.

I remember trying to stretch out Weekend Update. Chris had just done the Motivational Speaker, where they'd put him on a goddamned exercise bike just to make it that much worse. Lorne's usually pretty tight on time, but I just tried to draw Update out as much as I could to give Chris a chance to rest.

MOLLY SHANNON:

We didn't rehearse the Mary Katherine Gallagher sketch too much. And that's worrisome if you're doing a live performance that's very physical. I was throwing him into tables and breakaway walls. He was throwing me around. We did this big dance. Physically, I was a little scared, because he was so big and he'd been drinking. But I felt, for both the dress rehearsal and the live show, the second the camera was on he was completely there. I was amazed by his performance under the circumstances. With such little rehearsal, and without paying much attention in rehearsal, we put him in front of the audience, and he pulled it all together.

LORNE MICHAELS:

The last time I spoke with Chris was at the party at the end of the show. It was around four A.M. after that very bumpy week. We talked about the show. We talked about his health. I said all the things I'd said before about the way he was living and about taking care of himself. He listened. He agreed. He beat himself up a little bit for my benefit. And I said in the most severe way I could, "You'll never get away with it."

"I know, I know."

We hugged and said how much we loved each other. Then after we hugged, he looked at me with that look we all know so well, that smiling-boy look, and he said, "I was funny tonight, wasn't I, boss?"

"Yeah, you were."

* * *

Following his week in New York, Chris returned to Los Angeles to find that Kevin had moved out, refusing to enable his brother's addiction any longer. Understanding Kevin's need to protect his own sobriety, Chris let it go without any confrontation. Other than a brief visit at Thanksgiving, the two brothers would never speak to each other again.

On November 1, Chris flew to Naples, Florida, where he checked into the Willows rehab facility. He checked out at the end of the month and left to go home to Madison for Thanksgiving. He drank in his car on the way to the airport.

After spending the holiday with his family, Chris returned to Chicago for a brief stopover. He was on his way to the Jesuit retreat house at Bellarmine, a place he often went to find peace and quiet and spiritual refuge. He never made it.

JOHN FARLEY:

Chris got back to Chicago, and he and Ted and I were in the car. "Let's go up to Bellarmine," Chris said.

I said, "I don't want to go to a Jesuit retreat house, Chris."

I didn't, and most people wouldn't. I mean, it's a nice place, but I wasn't in the mood for three days of silent meditation. But I really thought Chris should go, because then he'd be safe, and no one would have to worry about him. You always worried about him when he was in town. It was always a pit in your stomach. I said, "You go up to Bellarmine. You can relax and everything'll be safe. You won't have these vultures around you."

"Please go," he said.

"I don't want to go."

So I walked away, thinking everything was fine. Then, later that night, I saw him coming around the corner in a bar. I thought, oh shit, he didn't go because I didn't go with him. That one stayed with me for a long time. Maybe if I'd taken him to the retreat everything would have been fine. Maybe maybe maybe.

TED DONDANVILLE:

I was supposed to go to Bellarmine with Chris, but then it was one drink, and then two, and then the trip was off. So now Chris needed to hide out, let people think he'd gone on this retreat so he could keep partying. He got a suite at the Four Seasons, right across the street from his apartment, and the party was on.

JILLIAN SEELY:

My hair salon was right downstairs from the Four Seasons. I went in that weekend, and the girls were like, "Chris just came down here in his pajamas with some random girl."

I went straight up to his room. It was a mess. I said to him, "Chris, what are you doing?"

He had the Big Book in his hands, and he was saying, "Jillian, let's get sober! I've got the book."

I said, "Chris, if you read that right now, you're going to go crazy. You can't be drunk and reading from this."

He got all freaked out and he went and grabbed a towel and threw it over the book to hide it, and then he said, "Come in the bathroom with me!" And he grabbed me and pulled me into the bathroom. He was just out of his mind.

Eventually, he calmed down a bit, and we talked a long time that night, about the rehabs, his father, his career. He told me about another movie he was doing. It was starting in February, with Vince Vaughn, called *The Gelfin*. He said, "Read this inside and out. I'm getting sober for the New Year, and you're coming to L.A. with me to do this movie."

He said to me, "Jillian, why don't you relapse with me and then we can go through treatment together and get better for the New Year?"

I said, "No. I'm not going to start drinking just so that I can go to treatment with you."

TED DONDANVILLE:

By the end he'd started thinking, oh, when I need to be sober I can go to rehab, and when I'm free to party, I can go party. He was picking his rehab spots based on which one was easiest, or which one was most comfortable. "Oh, I'm sick of this place, let's try this place." It was just not proper thinking. It was the thinking of an alcoholic.

LORRI BAGLEY:

I felt like I was supposed to save Chris, even though he told me that I wasn't. He said, "I know what I have to do, and the only way I can do it is with me and with God."

Chris knew what he had to do. He knew what he had to do to stay sober—and he chose not to do it. He told me why. He made me promise that I would never tell anyone why, and I never will. But maybe three months before he died, he was in a rehab in L.A. He called me late one night and told me why he wasn't going to stay sober anymore, and, at that point, we both knew what that meant. The thing is, Chris actually had great willpower, and great strength. Once he decided something, it was done.

JILLIAN SEELY:

Any idea that Chris wanted to die is bullshit. Chris was so full of life, and he had a boundless enthusiasm for everything and everyone. He enjoyed his life and savored it and was full of hope for the future.

When I saw him in those last weeks, he gave me the *Gelfin* script and told me he was getting sober and going back to work. When I picked him up to go to my Christmas party, I caught him practicing his karaoke in the mirror just to make sure he'd do a really good job. When he called his mom that night, he was telling her how happy and excited he was about taking her back to Ireland next year. And when I talked to him on the phone three days later and he said, "I'll call you back in an hour," I don't think he thought that was the last time anyone would ever hear from him.

TED DONDANVILLE:

I don't buy that it was a death wish, that it was a slow suicide. I just don't. You have to discount anything Chris might have said to people, especially to women. How was he trying to manipulate them? How was he trying to play on their sympathies?

The only thing was he said to me once, "Do you ever feel like you're doomed?" But I think that's something we all might say at some time or another. So I don't think you can look at what he was saying. You have to look at what he was doing. What he was doing was playing with fire and the consequences be damned, but he was also making a lot of plans for the future.

The binge that started at the Four Seasons lasted about four days, calling friends and picking up strangers and bringing them along. By the end of it I went up to the suite and there were all these food-service carts everywhere, ashtrays overflowing. After that Chris crashed for a few days, slept it off, and took it easy.

FR. TOM GANNON:

Chris called and asked if we could get together to talk. I said, "Sure, I'll come up to the apartment and we'll have mass together."

"I'd love that," he said.

So I went up, we had a long talk, I gave him confession, and we said a mass. Then we went out to dinner, came back to the apartment, and talked some more. He went on about his addiction and how bad he felt about where he was headed, both personally and professionally, and what he should do with his life. I had to be careful about bringing up his father, because he was always very sensitive when you did. I suggested he dedicate himself to going to daily mass, not because that would help with his addiction but because it might give him a safe, grounded place from which he could rededicate himself to treatment.

We both agreed that the rehab programs were getting him nowhere. I think he went to every rehab program known to man; he must have spent about half a million dollars on them. He had all the lingo down, but he didn't have the reality down. People have to internalize those twelve steps and make them their own, and Chris wasn't doing that.

I left around midnight. As I was driving home I just thought, this kid is going down the tubes. I had a deep foreboding. I came so close to turning the car around, going back, taking him to my place and keeping him there for a couple of days. But you can't do that. He's a grown man with his own free will, and what can you do?

TOM ARNOLD:

There was opportunity to cut Chris's money off at the end. You can commit somebody, legally commit them and cut off all their access to their funds. It came up with the people at Brillstein-Grey. They proposed it, but you have to get the family signed off on it. Ultimately it was his father's decision, and his father wouldn't go along.

TED DONDANVILLE:

Gurvitz wanted to send him away for a year, the most hard-core approach possible. But Chris's dad was like, "Chris is a grown-up. He can make his own decisions." And in a way his dad was right. If it wasn't Chris's decision to go, sending him there wouldn't accomplish anything.

TIM O'MALLEY:

By the time I got to Chris that December, everyone was telling me, "Forget it. We've tried. Just give up."

And I said, "You guys didn't give up on me, why should I give up on him?"

The last ten days of his life he called me every day. It was a slow, horrible thing. He'd call at five, six in the morning and plead with me to meet him at the Pump Room.

I'd say, "No, I am not going to meet you at a fucking bar. I will pick you up and take you to a meeting."

"I don't want to go to a meeting. Everybody recognizes me. I get bothered."

"Fine. I'll take you to a halfway house where people are so bottomed out that they don't care who's sitting next to them."

But he still wouldn't go. And it was the same thing every day. He'd call, we'd pray together. He kept saying, "Please, I need your help. I need your spiritual guidance."

I said, "Chris, all I got is what I got. I can't do anything for you unless you want to go to a meeting. You gotta start over, and you can start today."

"I can't start over."

"Yes, you can."

"No, I can't."

And it was the same conversation every day.

thspage.

JILLIAN SEELY:

That Saturday, he asked me to come over, and we hung out. We made Christmas cookies together, went to a meeting. Then on Sunday he called me and I picked him up and we went to my Christmas party. We sang karaoke. I have a picture of the two of us that night as we walked into the club, and we were both sober. Then, by the end of the night, he had started drinking and someone snapped another picture of us. It's the last picture of the two of us together, and you can see the difference.

At the end of the party, I said, "Chris, it's time to go."

He was with a bunch of girls, and he was like, "No, no, I'm gonna stay here."

My friend and I told him he really needed to leave, and he got defensive, saying "You're not the boss of me," and all that. So we left, and he went out with all these people drinking. That was the last time I saw him.

TIM O'MALLEY:

Monday morning, I stopped by his apartment on my way to a meeting to see if he wanted to go. We got in an argument about this Fatty Arbuckle project. He was obsessed with doing it, but his managers had brought him into a meeting and told him he couldn't do it until he'd been sober for two years, otherwise no one would insure him. He didn't think that was fair. To me, that was the first time he'd been fired in his life, for real, where someone actually said no to him. I said, "Chris, this is good. It's good that you're going to let go of this."

"But it's going to get made without me." He had the script and he showed it to me, and he was like, "I have to do it."

"The Fatty Arbuckle movie is not a reality," I said. "It's just a script on your desk. You've got to learn how to not drink. Nothing else comes before that."

"But it's different for me. I'm famous."

"Bullshit. You're no different from me. You're just an Irish fucker who can't stop drinking. This movie is not real. What's real is your torture. You've got to start from ground zero and fix it."

"I can't do it again."

"Yes, you can. I did it, and I had nothing. I had no career. I had no success. If I can do it, you can do it. You have even more to live for."

"But you're strong, and I'm weak."

"Fuck that. I'm as weak as you are."

"But my dad says . . ."

"Fuck your dad. If it were up to me you wouldn't do any work at all for a year. You stay here and you get sober and you work your steps and just get a grip on how to live."

And that's where I left it. That Fatty Arbuckle movie, that was the line in the sand. Either you get sober or you get dead.

TIM HENRY, *friend:*

On Tuesday, Johnny and Teddy and a bunch of guys from Chicago were meeting for lunch at Gibson's. Chris was late, and everyone was getting annoyed. We all had jobs to get back to. I ended up going to the Hancock to get him. Some mysterious girl was there, a joint burning in the ashtray. I was worried, but even though it's so obvious that the inevitable is next, you still don't believe that it's going to happen.

TED DONDANVILLE:

During lunch, Chris was adamant. "This is it," he said. "No more fucking around. We've got another couple weeks to party over Christmas, and then that's it. We're gonna get sober, rent the house in Beverly Hills, get to work on *The Gelfin*. No more fucking around."

He told me he wanted me to hire a trainer, a personal chef; he was going to get back in shape. And those plans were made. I'd rented the house. I was asking around to find a trainer and a chef. Chris had every intention of going back to work in January.

TIM HENRY:

I drove home that day and called Tommy and said, "Chris says he's cleaning up and getting serious after Christmas, but this is a new low."

"I know," Tommy said. "I get these calls all the time."

TOM FARLEY:

I asked Johnny after the fact, you know, "How could you sit there and drink with him?"

And Johnny was like, "What're you gonna do? Chris was already rolling when he got to the table." That's when Johnny just left. He couldn't take it anymore.

TED DONDANVILLE:

I know Johnny had a lot of guilt about what he could have done, should have done. But Chris knew the deal. And you have to remember, there was a physical fear when it came to standing up to Chris, not just an emotional one. He was bigger than you. Johnny said to him once, "You're sick. You've got to stop this." And Chris almost ripped his head off.

When Chris would relapse, all his friends in recovery would abandon him for the sake of their own sobriety. I understand it on one level, having now quit drinking myself, but in some ways it seems perverse. When he needed them the most, they were gone. Johnny and I were the only two people close to Chris who still drank, so we were the only ones around to look after him when he relapsed.

The problem was that even though Johnny and I were heavy drinkers—we could go eight, nine hours—there was always a point where Chris just wore us out. That night, we'd been drinking since Gibson's. It was around two in the morning, and we were at the Hunt Club. These guys wanted Chris to come and party with them at this place up in Lincoln Park. Of course Chris was up for it, but Johnny and I couldn't take it anymore. We had to get off. I said I was going home, and Chris told me to get a room at the Ritz-Carlton, across the street from the Hancock, said he wanted me nearby. He told me to take care of the bill, and he took off with those people. And that was the last time I ever saw him alive.

JOHN FARLEY:

Chris was going to go all night, and I said, "I'm not doing this with you." I had to get away from it. It was making me ill. Chris and I had been living together at the Hancock, and the vibe had just gotten terrible. He wasn't sleeping at night, and it was a mess. There was stuff everywhere. I was like, eh, I shouldn't be here. That was the other big what if: if only I had stayed. But whatever he was going through, I thought he just needed to be left alone. Plus, I wasn't getting any sleep. So I went with Teddy and checked into the hotel.

TIM O'MALLEY:

Chris called me around five o'clock Wednesday morning. I said, "Chris, I'm sleeping. What is it?"

He said, "I really need your help, please."

I didn't know what to do. He had been calling me every day, and we'd been having the same endless conversation. He wanted me to meet him at the Pump Room, again. He said Joyce Sloane was going to be there. I told him that I wouldn't meet him at a bar. I said, "I'm coming downtown tonight for a meeting at six o'clock. Call me if you want to go." And he never called.

JOYCE SLOANE, *producer, Second City:*

We had a lunch date at the Pump Room, me and Chris and Holly Wortell. I had talked to him the night before to confirm the date, and the last thing he said to me was "I'll see you tomorrow."

HOLLY WORTELL:

Joyce and I met there at noon, and we waited and waited and waited.

JILLIAN SEELY:

I got a call from a friend around ten-thirty. She said, "I saw Chris out last night. He was in really bad shape."

So I called. He picked up on the speakerphone. I could tell he was out of it. I heard somebody laughing in the background. I said, "Who is that?"

"It's nobody. It's nobody," he said.

He asked if he could call me back. I knew he wasn't going to. I said, "Chris, do me a favor and just stay in tonight. Please do not go out."

"Okay, okay, I won't go out."

"Okay."

"I love you."

"I love you, too."

"I'll call you back in an hour."

CHAPTER 15

The Parting Glass

FR. MATT FOLEY:

That night I was in Xochitepec, this small mountain village in Mexico. It had no roads and no electricity, and it was about a seven-hour walk from my parish. I was on a journey with a missionary team. We would walk to a town and spend a day ministering to the people there. Then we'd sleep on the floor of the chapel, wake up the next day, and journey on to the next town.

Sleeping in the chapel that night, I dreamt that I was surrounded by my old Marquette rugby friends. We were all talking about someone we had lost. It was such a vivid dream that it woke me out of a deep sleep. I got up and walked outside. There was this big, full moon, and I just stood there and looked up at the sky for the longest time, trying to figure out what this dream meant.

The next day we celebrated mass and then walked several hours to our truck and drove to a village called Santa Cruz, where there was a phone line. There was a message telling us that we had to come home, immediately. And to be out on a journey like that and to get a message that you had to come home, it could only mean one thing. It meant that someone had died.

After Ted and Johnny went home, Chris stayed out, partying with his newfound companions. As Tuesday night surrendered to Wednesday morning, he left the Hunt Club, hit a few more bars, and eventually wound up at the home of a commodities broker in Chicago's Lincoln Park neighborhood, where the party was in full swing until sunrise and beyond. Chris's host offered to hire a call girl for him. According to tabloid accounts of her story, she arrived at the party around eleven A.M.

In midafternoon, having missed his lunch with Joyce Sloane and Holly Wortell, Chris went with the escort back to her apartment. There he joined her and a friend, smoking crack cocaine and snorting heroin for several hours. Chris called a car service to take them to dinner, but when the car arrived she suggested that he was too worn out to go to a restaurant and that they should just go back to his apartment in the Hancock Center. They did.

Once Chris got home, his brother John called and invited him to dinner with Ted Dondanville and friends at their hotel. Chris declined. He stayed in the apartment, where his binge continued into the night. At that point, Chris had been awake for four days, ever since Jillian Seely's party Sunday night. At ten-thirty Wednesday evening, he took Jillian's phone call, assuring her that everything was fine and that he would call her back.

Chris and the escort began arguing over money. Around three in the morning, she decided to leave, collected her things, and headed for the front door. Chris stood up to follow her and collapsed in the middle of his living room. She turned around, walked back over, and knelt down next to him. He was having trouble breathing. She stole his watch, took pictures of his body, stood up, and walked away. Before passing out, his last words to her were "Don't leave me."

On her way out, believing Chris to be safely unconscious, she stopped by a side table in the foyer. She took out a pen and a piece of paper and left him a short note, saying that he was just so much fun, and she'd had such a lovely time.

TED DONDANVILLE:

Johnny and I woke up on Thursday. I needed something out of Chris's apartment, but I didn't have my keys. Johnny had a set, so we checked out of the hotel and he came with me to the Hancock on his way to Second City.

JOHN FARLEY:

Teddy and I walked in and saw him on the floor. At first, of course, I thought he was joking. Then I realized he wasn't. I dropped to the ground beside him and started giving him CPR. That didn't work. I turned to Ted and told him to call 911. He ran to the phone and called for an ambulance. He told them it was for Chris Farley. That was a mistake.

JILLIAN SEELY:

I was at work and they pulled me aside and told me there were these reports going around. I didn't believe it. I went to the Hancock and tried to get the doorman to let me up, but he wouldn't. I kept calling different phones in the apartment. Eventually Ted picked up. I said, "Are they giving Chris CPR? Is he okay? Is he going to be okay?"

He said, "Jillian, it's not a good time. We'll call you later."

I sat in the lobby. Nobody was telling me what was happening. I started getting hysterical. All these news crews started showing up. The EMS teams were coming through the lobby, but they were coming through really slow, taking their time, like there was no more emergency.

JOHN FARLEY:

The paramedics arrived. They tried to revive him, but they couldn't do anything. When they pronounced Chris dead, Teddy knelt down and put a rosary in his hand.

TED DONDANVILLE:

The media latched onto it: "He died clutching a rosary. It's a sign!" But, no, I put it there. I told Johnny I'd handle everything with the paramedics and the cops, and he should go in the other room and call his parents before the story broke.

JOHN FARLEY:

I went into the back room and called my dad. That was horrible. That was the worst phone call anyone could ever make.

KEVIN FARLEY:

I was in my apartment in L.A. I had just rehearsed Tom Arnold's show that morning. I came home around noon, and there were all these messages on my machine. They all said there was something wrong with Chris, and I needed to call home. I called Dad immediately. He answered the phone, and I said, "What's wrong with Chris?"

There was a very long pause. "We lost him."

The room started spinning, and I hit my knees. I didn't believe it. My mind wouldn't even go there. I was lying there, half crumpled on the floor, when Tom came in the front door and said, "We're gonna help you."

PAT FINN, friend:

It was raining the day he died. It doesn't rain much in L.A., but this was one of those days where it just poured. My wife and I had gone out to lunch with our two little girls and we'd just come home. I was outside with the girls, playing in one of the puddles in the street. My wife came back out of the house and told me I needed to come inside. There were twenty-six messages on the answering machine.

LORRI BAGLEY:

I was at my girlfriend's house, visiting her new baby, and the phone rang. It's funny. People don't react to death like you see in the movies, with all the screaming and hysterics. It's not like that at all. It just doesn't compute, doesn't add up. You sit there, and you can't figure it out.

JOHN FARLEY:

I stayed in the back room, so I didn't see what was going on. Teddy was handling it.

TED DONDANVILLE:

The media reports all said that no illegal drugs were found in Chris's apartment, just a few prescription antidepressants. That's not exactly true. While the cops were sweeping the apartment, any time they came across something illegal, a baggie of cocaine maybe, they'd come over, quietly slip it to me, and say, "Here." Essentially, they got rid of the evidence. They were cops, but they were Chicago cops. Chris was dead. Anything illegal he'd been doing was beside the point. Let him rest in peace.

JOHN FARLEY:

They put him in a body bag and took him out. I went down the back way, where I could get to the garage without going by anybody; there were too many people in the front. I got in the car, pulled out of the garage, and then slipped right by them while they were waiting for me to come out the front door. It was pretty bad. It was a madhouse. They'd blocked off the whole street.

DAVID SPADE:

I was at a read-through for my show, *Just Shoot Me*, and Gurvitz called. He said, "I'm giving you about a twenty-minute head start on this, just so you know before the whole world does." I went back to the read-through and I fell apart. They took me in the other room, and I just couldn't stop bawling.

TOM FARLEY:

I was at a meeting at a friend's, talking about some business ventures. In his office, he had a TV with CNN on in the background, muted. I looked over and I saw Chris and David Spade in a clip from the movies. I said, "Oh, there's Chris. Turn it up." He turned the volume on, and just as he did they switched to this scene in front of the Hancock. My friend stood up, handed me his phone, and said, "Take as long as you need."

JIM DOWNEY, head writer/producer:

I was playing in the basement with my son, and my wife said, "There's a phone call for you." So we went upstairs, and as she handed me the phone I looked over and saw the TV, which was muted, and it was a montage of Farley. My son, who was about four years old, started laughing hysterically at what Chris was doing on the television; I put the phone to my ear, and Mike Shoemaker told me Chris was dead.

MIKE SHOEMAKER:

I realized we would need to choose a sketch to give out to the media as a clip. I remember sitting in Marci Klein's office, crying and thinking, what sketch would Chris want us to use? I picked "The Chris Farley Show" with Paul McCartney.

FRED WOLF:

My manager called me and said, "Chris Farley died." Five months later he called me and said, "Phil Hartman died." Thankfully, he hasn't had to call again.

FR. MATT FOLEY:

After we got the message, my team and I left Santa Cruz. It was a two-hour drive by truck on a dusty road back to Quechultenango. I was driving. It was a very quiet ride. We all knew that somebody in the truck had lost someone; we just didn't know which of us it was.

I finally pulled up to the parish house, we got out, and someone handed me a note saying that Chris had died; both Mrs. Farley and my sister had called. I was devastated. I had prayed so hard for him, and I had never given up on him. My sister had already booked my ticket home. I caught an all-night bus to Mexico City and flew out the next morning.

KEVIN FARLEY:

Brillstein-Grey got me a flight out that afternoon, and my manager drove me to the airport and got me on a plane. I flew into Chicago, met Johnny and Ted and Maria, my girlfriend at the time. I grabbed Johnny and hugged him. He looked like hell, like he'd come through a concentration camp. We got on a plane and flew into Madison together.

TOM FARLEY:

I drove home from my friend's office. I don't really remember the drive; I was just crying my eyes out. We had Laura's sister take the kids and we went out the next day.

JOHN FARLEY:

They had to do an autopsy, so that took a little while. Dad started taking care of all the arrangements for the funeral.

TODD GREEN:

Kevin Cleary and I flew back to Madison together. Mr. Farley called me in Kevin's hotel room, and he said, "Listen, I want all the Edgewood guys to be the pallbearers. You, Barry, Healy, Meyer, and the two Cleary boys. That's the way we want it. That's the way Chris would want it."

TIM HENRY:

Everybody had gone to the funeral home to meet with the priest and the funeral director, and Mrs. Farley asked if I would stay at the house while they were gone, just to watch the phones and be there if people came by. While I was waiting, a lot of neighbors came by, dropping off food and so forth. And of course, this being Wisconsin, several people brought over cases of beer. "Yeah, put that first twelve on the back porch so they'll get nice and cold!"

Then the phone rang. It was David Spade. He asked me to give Mrs. Farley his number and to tell her he'd called.

DAVID SPADE:

It was just very hard. Everybody takes it differently. I couldn't really talk to Johnny or Kevin; they reminded me too much of him. I talked to the family but didn't go to the funeral. I caught some shit for that, but it was my choice. I couldn't deal with it. I couldn't put myself through it, and that was selfish, but I didn't want to grieve in public. I've talked to Sandler and those guys, and they get it. They understand. I just don't like it that some people took that as meaning we weren't getting along.

TOM FARLEY:

Over the weekend, Kevin, Johnny, and I had to get Chris a shirt and a pair of socks to be buried in. We went to the big and tall store where Chris would shop when he was home; they had his measurements. We got him a white shirt, but instead of black socks, they had these red and green Ho-Ho-Ho socks with a little Santa Claus on them. I said, "I think Chris would want to be buried in these." So we bought those, and we all had a good laugh about it.

We went and delivered them to the funeral home, and they told us to take them around to the back entrance, which is where they actually prepare the bodies. That's when it really hit me again: I was delivering socks for my brother to be buried in. The whole week was just full of those moments, realizations like that.

JOEL MURRAY:

The morning of the service, David Pasquesi, Bonnie Hunt, Holly Wortell, and I ended up in a car together, driving up to Madison and telling stories. To a man, everyone in that car was saying, "Why isn't this his wedding? Why aren't we here for him to be marrying some nice local girl? What a party that would have been."

TOM FARLEY:

The funeral was two days before Christmas, and so everyone went through hell trying to get to Madison from all over. They already had holiday travel booked elsewhere and they had to change flights, and so many of the flights were already oversold. It was a nightmare.

JOHN GOODMAN:

I flew in through Chicago and the flight was late and I had to sprint for about a half mile through the terminal to make my connection—and me sprinting is not cool. For a moment I thought maybe there would have to be two funerals. Then I landed in Madison and the taxi got lost and couldn't find the church. Finally I saw this huge mass of reporters on the street, and I told him to let me out and I just walked.

JOHN FARLEY:

I'll never forget the sight of John Goodman. The parking lot had been kept empty, and this massive bank of news crews had been cordoned off way back at the street. All of a sudden, you see this pack of reporters in a startled panic as Goodman just parts them like the Red Sea, elbowing them aside and yelling "Get outta the way!" He breaks through them and here he comes, trudging through the snow with these two massive, heavy suitcases under his arms and his big beige raincoat flapping in the freezing wind. John Goodman, that motherfucker, he loved Chris. Come hell or high water he was gonna make that funeral.

TIM MEADOWS:

Lorne was flying up by himself from Colorado. I met up with him at the Madison airport and we got a car. We were running really late. The service had already started, so I didn't see his body in the casket, and I didn't really want to.

TOM FARLEY:

We had an open casket at the church. We stood there in this receiving line that just stretched on and on forever. People were coming through, paying their respects, and then taking their seats in the church. After a while we just shut the casket and had people go to their seats, otherwise we never would have gotten to the ceremony.

TODD GREEN:

All the Edgewood guys were there. It was really hard for Mike and Kevin Cleary. They'd already lost their father and a brother, and Kevin had put so much into trying to save Chris. But the person I felt really sorry for was Kit Kat. She was there all by herself, and nobody talked to her.

LORRI BAGLEY:

I didn't really know where to be, or who to be with. I was having these heaving sobs, and this woman took me and let me sit next to her in the pew. Dan Aykroyd came over to me and said something. I don't remember what it was, but it immediately put me at ease. He knew what to say, because he'd been there before.

JILLIAN SEELY:

Everyone was saying, "You had to have seen it coming." But Chris was so full of life that you just wouldn't think that he would die. People were in shock. I was standing next to Adam Sandler, and I said, "This just doesn't seem real."

"Yeah," he said, "I keep expecting him to open up the coffin and be okay."

ALEC BALDWIN:

It's sad when something like that happens to anyone, but somehow it seemed sadder when it happened to Chris. Most of the people whom I've seen go down that path, they didn't have the humanity that he had.

KEVIN FARLEY:

A lot of people showed. Sandler, Chris Rock, and John Goodman. Al Franken and Norm Macdonald. I was just blown away by the life that

Chris had lived. There was a deep melancholy in the room, but you also felt this great love from everyone. He had touched so many people. As sad as I was, I was really proud of him.

PAT FINN:

I was one of the pallbearers, along with the Edgewood guys. Just walking the casket in was tough. When you're thirty-three you don't expect to be doing this. It's something you should be doing for your great-grandfather or something.

It was also strange because the room was filled with people whose names were synonymous with comedy and laughter, and yet the room was the exact opposite.

KEVIN FARLEY:

Nobody in that room could hold it together.

TIM MEADOWS:

I was sitting in front of Sandler and Rock and Rob Schneider. At one point I started crying, and Aykroyd came over and put his arm around me. After the funeral, Chris Rock just lost it. That was the first time I'd ever seen him cry. Sandler, too. That's how it was the whole day. We were a bunch of men who never cried, who never got emotional, who never showed that side of ourselves to each other. And we all just cried and cried uncontrollably all day.

ROBERT BARRY:

Mr. Farley was by far the worst of anyone. Chris was his life. Every Saturday night he'd line up a tumbler of Dewars Scotch, pull up in front of the TV, and laugh and laugh for hours at whatever Chris did. After the ceremony, the pallbearers and the family went back to put Chris in the mausoleum. Mr. Farley had his head in his hands, and he was just sobbing. "My boy's not supposed to be gone. Not before me."

PAT FINN:

We were there in the mausoleum, probably about fifteen or twenty of us, for the priests to say the last, final blessing. And I'll never forget the sight of Mr. Farley, getting up from his chair, which was tough for him to do, and putting his arms around the casket. He stood up, just this big bear of a man, and he reached around and he hugged the casket and he wouldn't let it go.

TED DONDANVILLE:

He stood up and raised his arm and with his big, open hand he slapped the coffin twice, loud and hard. *Boom! Boom!* It echoed across the room, sending a jolt through everyone. It was like a final send-off, a father's last good-bye.

FR. TOM GANNON:

I only really remember one thing from the funeral, and that was looking at the father and thinking he wouldn't last a year after Chris.

KEVIN FARLEY:

We all knew Dad wouldn't be too long to follow. I think even he knew it. He closed down the business, paid off the mortgage, made sure all his insurance was in order. When you wake up in the morning, what gets you through the day is your hopes and dreams for tomorrow. For Dad a lot of that was gone after Chris died. He couldn't find it again. They say that happens when you bury a child. I would have long talks with him, and he was just confused about the whole thing, wondering why it had happened, asking God why it had happened. It was such a shock that it left him in a daze. For the rest of his life he just sat in his chair, staring out the window. But from that day until the day he died, a little over a year later, he never picked up the bottle again.

FRED WOLF:

I actually didn't go to Chris's funeral. My own father had had a heart attack and almost died. I'd gone up to Montana to visit him. I spent that day at the hospital, and I told him about Chris, that the funeral was going on right at that moment.

My father and I never knew how to talk to each other. He was an alcoholic, and our relationship was difficult. I didn't know him that well. One of the only really heartfelt conversations we ever had was that day, about Chris. My dad was saying how the things Chris did are so important for the world, that Chris may have been fighting these demons, but he helped a lot of people who were fighting those same demons feel better, if only for a little while. And I know that sounds sappy. It sounds like something you'd see sewn onto a quilt for sale in the window of some souvenir shop. But at the same time, there's a lot of truth in those quilts.

BOB ODENKIRK:

At the core of being funny is frustration, and even some anger, at the world. And Chris had so much constantly happening inside him that he was always being chased into that corner. He was always living inside that space, and that's why he was just funny *all* of the time. That was his choice. He made a lot of unhealthy choices, but that was the healthiest choice he could make to deal with the feelings that he had. You take some of the most intellectual comics in the world, and what's going on in their work, on a basic emotional level, is the same thing that was going on with Chris—his life was the purest expression of what it is to be a comedian.

DAN HEALY, friend:

It wasn't just that he made you laugh hysterically all the time; he did, but it was more who he was. I've struggled so many times to put into words exactly why Chris had such a huge impact on all of our lives. He had such a faith in other people. He believed in those basic things like goodness and right and wrong. When you were with him, he had this demeanor that simplified things for you. He let you take everything that was complicated in your life and just set it aside for a bit. And that was really the gift he gave us, honestly. Being with Chris reminded you that there was a time when you could still believe in all the things that he believed in. It reminded you of a time when you were lucky enough to look at the world through honest eyes.

IAN MAXTONE-GRAHAM, writer:

The week that Paul McCartney was the musical guest, someone said, "Let's do a 'Chris Farley Show.'"

Chris had done it twice before, with Jeff Daniels and with Martin Scorsese, and we all said, "Eh, it's been done. There's no new moves there."

But they decided to do it anyway. Franken and I were assigned to write it, and I was so glad that we hadn't persuaded people not to do it. It's so often the case that you write something you're not that excited about and then the performer brings something to it and you think, my God, I'm glad I was at work that day.

It played unbelievably sweet. It was so sweet that even now, ten years later, I get goose bumps just thinking about watching it. There's that one moment where Chris says to McCartney, "Remember when you were in the Beatles, and you did that album *Abbey Road*, and at the very end of the song it goes, 'And in the end, the love you take is equal to the love you make'? You remember that?"

"Yes."

"Um, is that true?"

And McCartney says, "Yes, Chris. In my experience it is. I've found that the more you give, the more you get."

And Chris is just like, *"Awesome!"*

And in that moment Chris isn't acting at all. It's really Chris, tapping into that quiet, needy part of himself. You see it up there on the stage. What you see in that sketch is the actual Chris Farley being happy that the actual Paul McCartney is telling him that there is an infinite amount of love in the world, and that someday that love will come back to him.

Epilogue

Christmas was always Chris Farley's favorite time of year, a time he made certain to be home in Madison, surrounded by family and childhood friends. But on December 22, 1997, he had come home to stay. Following the funeral service at Our Lady Queen of Peace Church, Chris was laid to rest in a mausoleum at Resurrection Cemetery, just down the road.

Although the last days of Chris's life in Chicago had been toxic and frenzied, at some point along the way he had arrested his downward spiral and paused to do his holiday shopping, picking out special presents for his parents and his siblings, handwriting personal notes to accompany each specially wrapped box. And so on Christmas Eve, only two days after burying their son, with the winter chill blowing in from the frozen lake outside, the Farley family sat around the tree in their living room and opened their final presents from Chris. He'd bought his mother two small ceramic clowns.

On January 2, 1998, the Office of the Cook County Medical Examiner issued an autopsy report in the case of Chris's death. It stated that he had died of opiate and cocaine intoxication, with coronary atherosclerosis as a significant contributing condition. Chris's body tested positive for cocaine and morphine (metabolized heroin) as well as traces of mari-juana and the prescription antidepressant Prozac. No alcohol was found in his system at the time, but his liver showed signs of significant damage from years of drinking. Blockages of fifty to ninety percent were found in his major coronary arteries from years of unhealthy eating. The report ruled his death an accident.

On May 29, 1998, *Edwards & Hunt* was released under the newly test-marketed name *Almost Heroes*. Chris's passing cast a shadow over the film, and costar Matthew Perry's own public struggle with addiction at the time didn't help much, either. The film's offbeat sense of humor failed to translate onscreen, and scenes of Chris's character acting drunk and out of control were particularly difficult to watch. Critics panned the film, lamenting the tragedy of its being the final installment of Chris's brief career. It earned a little over $6 million at the box office and quickly passed into history.

That summer, Chris was treated to one last curtain call. Norm Mac-Donald's *Dirty Work*, which featured Chris in a small cameo, was released on June 12. In it Chris played an ornery bar patron whose nose had been bitten off by a Saigon whore, providing some of the film's best laughs.

During the year after Chris's funeral, the health of his father, Tom Farley, Sr., deteriorated rapidly. Chris's death had forced him to stop drinking, but the damage had largely been done. Morbid obesity and liver failure left him severely debilitated, and soon his condition was exacerbated by a bad fall. In March 1999, he checked in to a hospital. After several days of constant vigil, Tom asked his family to go home and rest while he did the same. He died three hours later. He was sixty-three years old.

In the months immediately following Chris's death, several of his friends had made charitable donations to the family in Chris's name. Lorne Michaels of *Saturday Night Live*, meanwhile, issued a *Best of Chris Farley* home video, pledging a portion of the proceeds once again to the family. With this capital, Tom Farley, Sr., started the Chris Farley Foundation (www.thinklaughlive.com), a nonprofit organization to promote awareness and prevention of substance abuse problems. In its earliest incarnation, the foundation produced anti-drug public service announcements with past and current stars of *Saturday Night Live*.

From 1999 to 2003, the foundation hosted Comics Come Home in partnership with Comedy Central. An annual comedy event held in Madison, it featured the talents of David Spade, Dave Chappelle, Tom Arnold, Norm MacDonald, Bob Saget, and others. With the funds raised at Comics Come Home and other events, the Chris Farley Foundation works with high schools and colleges across the Midwest to develop programs and seminars aimed at educating kids on the dangers of drugs, primarily through the use of humor and strong communication skills. Today, Tom Farley, Jr., serves as the foundation president.

In late 2003, ImprovOlympic founder Charna Halpern petitioned the Hollywood Walk of Fame committee to give Chris Farley a star on Hollywood Boulevard. The organization hands out very few posthumous honors and almost none to those who pass away in less than rosy circumstances, as Chris had. But in April 2004, John Belushi was at long last honored by the organization, and Halpern seized on the precedent to lobby even more strongly on Chris's behalf. Michael Ewing, one of the producers of *Tommy Boy*, approached Paramount Studios to sponsor Chris's application. With the tenth anniversary DVD release of *Tommy Boy* just on the horizon, the right moment presented itself. Paramount helped push the nomination through and pegged the DVD's launch to the upcoming event.

On Friday, August 26, 2005, the Farley family joined several luminaries from Chris's life—Adam Sandler, David Spade, Chris Rock, Tom Arnold, Sarah Silverman, Peter Segal, Bernie Brillstein, and more—as they unveiled Chris's star, the 2,289th, on Hollywood's Walk of Fame. The tone was far more festive than somber. Mary Anne Farley accepted the award on Chris's behalf. Chris Rock declared that "every fat comedian working today owes Chris eighty bucks," and David Spade wistfully observed that if Chris were alive today, "he'd be working for Sandler, too." Chris's star is located at the corner of Hollywood Boulevard and Cosmo Street, directly in front of the theater for ImprovOlympic West.

In 2007, St. Malachy's Church in New York celebrated the second annual Father George Moore Awards. Moore was a pastor at St. Malachy's in the 1970s and 1980s and was a driving force in the efforts to save Times Square from the drugs and crime that had overtaken it. The George Moore Awards honor individuals who embody the clerygyman's commitment to community service and who have elevated mankind's spirit through their work in theater, television, film, music, or art. Chris, both as a famous movie star and as a humble parishioner, surely fit that description, and, on the tenth anniversary of his passing, St. Malachy's chose him to receive it.

On October 1, the Farleys joined Lorne Michaels, Alec Baldwin, Dan Aykroyd, and the entire current cast of *Saturday Night Live* for a special mass said in Chris's honor—with a sermon delivered by Father Matt Foley—followed by a dinner and awards ceremony at the landmark Broadway restaurant Sardi's. At the dinner, *SNL*'s Amy Poehler served as emcee, presenting a number of smaller awards to other members of the St. Malachy's community and introducing the evening's enertainment: a sketch from the *SNL* players, and young Broadway star Matthew Gumley performing "The Rose," a song Chris had often sung for the seniors he entertained at St. Malachy's social events.

In the midst of the proceedings, just before Mary Anne Farley accepted Chris's award from Lorne Michaels, *SNL* veteran Dan Aykroyd rose to say a few words. He did not go up to use the microphone and podium on the dais, but instead walked the aisles among the dinner guests, speaking off the cuff about his memories. He did a few spot-on impressions of Chris. He spoke of time spent together on the set of *Tommy Boy*, how the young star would come to his trailer and sit at his knee to hear stories about the old days. He spoke of Chris's faith, of his belief in using laughter to bring joy to those less fortunate. He spoke of Chris taking his God-given talent and turning it back out into the world to try and make it a better place. Concluding the speech, Aykroyd singled out all the actors, comedians, and other artists in attendance, and he challenged them to do the same.

ACKNOWLEDGMENTS

TOM FARLEY:

I want to thank everyone who poured their heart out in these interviews. I know well how talking about Chris can be both fun and painful, so I appreciate everyone who shared their memories and emotions in this book. I would especially like to acknowledge the following people who have provided endless help and support to me, the Chris Farley Foundation, and this project:

My beautiful wife, Laura; my fantastic kids, Mary Kate, Emma, and Tommy; my mom, Mary Anne Farley, and my sister, Barb; my brothers Kevin and John, the greatest, funniest guys I know; Fr. Matt Foley and Fr. Tom Gannon; the *SNL* family, who have been amazing to us every step of the way, especially Marci Klein, who understood Chris the second he walked into 30 Rock, and Lorne Michaels; Chris's buddies David Spade, Adam Sandler, Chris Rock, Robert Smigel, and Rob Schneider, who have all supported our foundation from the beginning; Chris's homeboys, Dan Healy, Mike Cleary, Greg Meyer, Todd Green, Robert Barry, and Pat O'Gara; Bob and Sue Krohn and the entire Red Arrow Camp family, who gave the Farley boys so much of our character and values; Marquette University and former dean of communications Michael Price, for believing in Chris and pointing him toward the stage; Madison, Wisconsin—our hometown and the greatest place on earth; the Second City, especially Joyce Sloan and Andrew Alexander—I feel like I'm home every time I walk in the door; the Second City gang: Holly Wortell, Tim Meadows, David Pasquesi, Joel Murray, Pat Finn, Tim O'Malley, and Tim Kazurinsky; Charna Halpern at ImprovOlympic, for all she's done for Chris and his lasting memory.

Humorology at the University of Wisconsin, year after year the most amazing group of young, talented, and philanthropic college students in the country; Jim Farley, my cousin, college roommate, and true friend; my good buddies Neil Lane, Nils Dahl, and John Plum; James Bonneville and Trevor Stebbins; Tim Henry and Don Beeby; Michael and Carol Lesser for helping to launch the Chris Farley Foundation; Shelly Dutch, who does more to help kids in recovery than any foundation I know; Cindy Grant, for her endless support for the foundation and all that we do; Tanner Colby, who now knows more about Chris than anyone alive (welcome to therapy, my friend).

And finally, Chris's closest friend and conscience, the late Kevin Francis Cleary.

TANNER COLBY:

I would like to thank, first and foremost, Tom Farley and the Farley family—Mary Anne, Barb, Kevin, and Johnny—for trusting me with their first, last, and only chance to do this project.

This book almost didn't happen, and credit for the fact that it did goes to the newest and greatest literary agency in the western world, Foundry Media. I owe an incalculable debt to Peter McGuigan, my agent, for picking up this ball and running with it—and sticking with it despite some rocky moments; Hannah Gordon, for bringing me to Foundry and fielding my near-daily queries and neurotic pesterings; Yfat Reiss Gendell, for her crack legal advice and perpetually sunny demeanor; as well as

Kristina Schulz, Stephanie Abou, and everyone else at Foundry who makes it feel like a second home.

On the day this book was purchased by Viking, it was remarked in the publishing blogosphere that Viking was "too good" an imprint for a book about Chris Farley, a comment I take some pride in. Chris's story is not what most people think it is or expect it to be, and I thank Wendy Wolf, a great editor and a wonderful collaborator, for seeing the story underneath and being its greatest advocate. Given her list of bestselling and prize-winning authors, it's an honor just to be stacked on the same shelf in the same office. I also want to thank Liz Parker, for proving that a good assistant can be your best friend in the whole world; Carolyn Coleburn and Ann Day, for plotting a PR campaign that every author should be lucky enough to have; Nancy Sheppard and Andrew Duncan, for the shrewdest of marketing strategies; Sharon Gonzalez, for ferreting out the last (?) mistakes and errors; Paul Buckley, for a book jacket that deserves to be framed; and Daniel Lagin, for a layout that begs to be read.

Months of collaboration were required to pull this off, and for those who helped I'm eternally grateful. I'd like to thank John and Kevin Farley, again, for lobbying where it was most needed; Ted Dondanville, for opening his Rolodex and, more reluctantly, his memories; Tom Davis, Todd Green, and Ian Maxtone-Graham, for their extracurricular help; Christie Tuite, for finding the elusive Jim Downey; Marc Liepis, for enduring far too many e-mails; Mike Bosze and Joey Handy, for their access to Broadway Video; Mike Shoemaker and Marci Klein, for access at *SNL*; Chris Osbrink and Tyson Miller at Callahan, for fielding my constant follow-ups; Julie Warner, for the same; Chris Saito, Susan Wright, and Brian Palagallo, for extra help at Paramount; Jillian Seely, Brian Stack, Lorri Bagley, Holly Wortell, Jim Murphy, and Mark Hermacinski, for their wonderful photographs; Edie Baskin, for hers; Jay Forman and Todd Levin, for poring over much longer drafts than this; Becky Poole, for doing the hard work I didn't want to do; Anna Thorngate, for a great edit; Shawn Coyne, for giving me a great start; Michelle Best, Father Baker, and everyone at St. Malachy's for honoring Chris; and all the agents, managers, publicists, their assistants, and their assistants' assistants, for helping us get the 130- plus interviews that make up this book.

And lastly, I'll always remember Mach Arom, for opening a door; Matt Atkatz, for his continuing friendship and patronage; Sheila Thibodaux and Marla Fredericks, for getting the money in on time; Richard Belzer, for being there at the beginning; Chris Meloni, for being, very simply, a great guy; Rex Reed, for his home, hospitality, and friendship; Mitch Glazer and Kelly Lynch, for their hospitality in Los Angeles; Laila Nabulsi, for being such a wonderful muse; Judy Belushi Pisano, for her inspiration and spirit; Jerry Daigle, for being a clutch player; Alan Donnes, for everything else; Mom and Dad, for always being there when I need them; Mason, Jenni, Gus, and Lena, for being family; and Ms. Emily Holland, for bringing me home.

NOTE ON SOURCES AND METHOD

The text of Chapter 1, "A Motivated Speaker," was transcribed and condensed from a speech given by Chris Farley at the Hazelden drug rehabilitation facility in Center City, Minnesota, in the summer of 1994. The Chris Farley quote at the opening of Chapter 13, "The Devil in the Closet," was taken from the article "Chris Farley: On the Edge of Disaster," which appeared in *US* magazine and was written by Erik Hedegaard. Some quotes from Tom Davis were drawn from his forthcoming memoir, *38 Years of Short-Term Memory Loss*. Other books that were helpful as general references include *Live from New York*, by Tom Shales and Jim Miller, and *Gasping for Airtime*, by Jay Mohr. Otherwise, all of the quotes and material in this book were drawn from original interviews conducted by the authors between the months of October 2005 and May 2007.

Given the confidential, anonymous nature of drug and alcohol rehabilitation, not to mention Chris Farley's nonexistent filing and organizational skills, very little hard documentation exists as to the exact dates and places of his attempts at treatment and his attendance at various recovery meetings. The facts and time lines presented here were drawn from personal notes kept by Mary Anne Farley over the course of Chris's life.

To every extent possible, the stories presented by the interviewees were checked against contemporary sources as well as the accounts of other eyewitnesses. In many instances, however, no such verification was possible. And, naturally, the opinions and recollections recounted by the participants vary wildly and often directly contradict one another. (Chris Farley was many different things to many different people; such was the nature of his personality.) We have endeavored to present all points of view—even some the authors and the Farley family do not agree with—in the belief that everyone's opinions have merit and deserve their day in court. Somewhere in this tangle of foggy recollection, iffy hindsight, and outright delusion lies the truth, and readers are invited to find it on their own.

THE -OGRAPHIES

FILMOGRAPHY

1992

Wayne's World, dir. Penelope Spheeris
    as Security Guard

1993

Coneheads, dir. Steve Barron
    as Ronnie the Mechanic

Wayne's World 2, dir. Stephen Surjik
    as Milton

1994

Airheads, dir. Michael Lehmann
    as Officer Wilson

1995

Billy Madison, dir. Tamra Davis
    as Bus Driver (uncredited)

THE -OGRAPHIES

Tommy Boy, dir. Peter Segal
as Thomas "Tommy" Callahan III

1996

Black Sheep, dir. Penelope Spheeris
as Mike Donnelly

1997

Beverly Hills Ninja, dir. Dennis Dugan
as Haru

1998 (POSTHUMOUS RELEASE)

Almost Heroes, dir. Christopher Guest
as Bartholomew Hunt

Dirty Work, dir. Bob Saget
as Jimmy (uncredited)

SELECTED VIDEOGRAPHY:
NOTABLE *SATURDAY NIGHT LIVE* APPEARANCES

1990–91 SEASON

09/29/90, Host: Kyle MacLachlan
"Tim Peaks," as Leo the killer

10/20/90, Host: George Steinbrenner
"Middle-Aged Man," as drinking buddy
"Weekend Update," as Tom Arnold

01/12/91, Host: Joe Mantegna
"Bill Swerski's Super Fans," as Todd O'Conner
"I'm Chillin," as B-Fats

01/19/91, Host: Sting
"Hedley & Wyche," as British toothpaste user

02/16/91, Host: Roseanne
   "After the Laughter," as Tom Arnold

02/23/91, Host: Alec Baldwin
   "The McLaughlin Group," as Jack Germond

05/18/91, Host: George Wendt
   "Bill Swerski's Super Fans," as Todd O'Conner

1991–92 SEASON

09/28/91, Host: Michael Jordan
   "Bill Swerski's Super Fans: Michael Jordan," as Todd O'Conner
   "Schmitt's Gay," as house sitter

10/05/91, Host: Jeff Daniels
   "The Chris Farley Show," as himself

11/16/91, Host: Linda Hamilton
   "The Chris Farley Show," as himself (with Martin Scorsese)
   "Schillervision: Secret Taste Test Gone Wrong," as angry dinner patron

11/23/91, Host: Macaulay Culkin
   "Bill Swerski's Super Fans: Thanksgiving," as Todd O'Conner

12/14/91, Host: Steve Martin
   "Not Gonna Phone It In Tonight," as himself

01/18/92, Host: Chevy Chase
   "Bill Swerski's Super Fans: Quizmasters," as Todd O'Conner

05/09/92, Host: Tom Hanks
   "Mr. Belvedere Fan Club," as Mr. Belvedere fan

1992–93 SEASON

12/05/92, Host: Tom Arnold
   "Bill Clinton Visits McDonald's," as Hank Holdgren
   "Bill Swerski's Super Fans: Hospital," as Todd O'Conner

02/13/93, Host: Alec Baldwin
   "Gap Girls," as Cindy
   "The Chris Farley Show," as himself (with Paul McCartney)

02/20/93, Host: Bill Murray
"Fond du Lac Men's Jazz Ensemble," as dancer
"The Whipmaster," as bartender

04/10/93, Host: Jason Alexander
"Weekend Update," as Bennett Brauer

05/08/93, Host: Christina Applegate
"Motivational Speaker," as Matt Foley
"Gap Girls," as Cindy

05/15/93, Host: Kevin Kline
"Weekend Update," as Bennett Brauer

1993–94 SEASON

10/02/93, Host: Shannen Doherty
"Relapsed Guy," as the relapsed guy

10/23/93, Host: John Malkovich
"Of Mice and Men," as Lenny/himself

10/30/93, Host: Christian Slater
"Motivational Speaker: Halloween," as Matt Foley

12/04/93, Host: Charlton Heston
"The Herlihy Boy House-Sitting Service," as Mr. O'Malley

11/11/93, Host: Sally Field
"Motivational Speaker: Santa Claus," as Matt Foley

01/08/94, Host: Jason Patric
"Cold Open: Giuliani Inauguration," as Andrew Giuliani
"The Herlihy Boy Dog-Sitting Service," as Mr. O'Malley

01/15/94, Host: Sara Gilbert
"Gap Girls," as Cindy
"Lunchlady Land," as the lunch lady

02/19/94, Host: Martin Lawrence
"Motivational Speaker: Scared Straight," as Matt Foley

03/12/94, Host: Nancy Kerrigan
"Pair Skating," as skating partner

03/19/94, Host: Helen Hunt
"Weekend Update," as Bennett Brauer

04/09/94, Host: Kelsey Grammer
"Yankees Game," as Andrew Giuliani
"Iron John: The Musical," as singer

04/16/94, Host: Emilio Estevez
"The Herlihy Boy Grandmother-Sitting Service," as Mr. O'Malley

05/14/94, Host: Heather Locklear
"Bill Swerski's Super Fans: Letter to Michael Jordan," as Todd O'Conner

1994–95 SEASON

09/24/94, Host: Steve Martin
"Clinton Auditions," as himself

11/19/94, Host: John Turturro
"It's a Wonderful Newt," as Newt Gingrich

12/03/94, Host: Roseanne
"A Woman Exploited," as Tom Arnold

12/10/94, Host: Alec Baldwin
"Japanese Game Show," as contestant

12/17/94, Host: George Foreman
"Motivational Speaker: George Foreman's Comeback," as Matt Foley

01/14/95, Host: Jeff Daniels
"Congressional Session," as Newt Gingrich

01/21/95, Host: David Hyde Pierce
"Little Women," as Toby Adams

02/18/95, Host: Deion Sanders
"Strange Visitors," as SWAT agent

03/25/95, Host: John Goodman
"Bill Swerski's Super Fans," as Todd O'Conner (with Brian Dennehy and Dan Aykroyd)

02/18/95, Host: Courtney Cox
    "Motivational Speaker: Venezuela," as Matt Foley
    "Gap Girls: Gapardy," as Cindy

05/11/95, Host: David Duchovny
    "The Polar Bear Pit," as himself

1997–98 SEASON

10/25/97, Host: Chris Farley
    "Cold Opening: I Can Do It," as himself
    "Monologue," as himself
    "Goth Talk," as rowdy friend
    "Morning Latte," as Gil
    "Mary Katherine Gallagher," as overweight classmate
    "Motivational Speaker: Spinning Class," as Matt Foley
    "El Niño," as El Niño
    "Sally Jesse Raphael: Giant Baby," as the giant baby
    "Monday Night Football Recording Session," as Hank Williams, Jr.
    "Bill Swerski's Super Fans: Ditka Goes to New Orleans," as Todd O'Conner

Index

O'Gara, Pat, 27–28, 31, 58
O'Malley, Tim, 74, 79, 83, 86–87,
    93–94, 260, 262, 274, 277, 279,
    288, 305–6, 309
Oteri, Cheri, 263, 295

Pasquesi, David, 74, 83, 88, 90, 319
Perry, Matthew, 252–55, 258, 328
Poehler, Amy, 330
Price, Michael, 41–43, 51–52

Quaid, Randy, 214

Ramis, Harold, 62
Reilly, Sheila, 43
Richter, Andy, 62, 64
Rivers, Joan, 73
Robinson, Doug, 107, 214, 245
Rock, Chris, 100, 102–3, 105, 109,
    114, 120, 122, 148, 243, 246, 279,
    282–83, 321–22, 329
Rosenfeld, Karen, 218
Rossio, Terry, 271–73

Saget, Bob, 329
Sanders, Deion, 196–97
Sandler, Adam, 4, 100, 102, 120,
    139, 146–47, 172, 193, 197, 205,
    211, 321–22, 329
Schiller, Tom, 100, 145, 197–98
Schneider, Rob, 4, 100, 102, 120,
    197, 201, 322
Scorsese, Martin, 161, 325
Scott, Judith, 73–74, 78, 89
Seely, Jillian, 228, 230–31, 242, 257,
    274, 283–84, 286, 301–3, 306,
    310, 312–13, 321

Segal, Peter, 172, 174–77, 180–88,
    190, 220, 269–70, 329
Seliger, Kit, 30–31
Shannon, Molly, 263, 293, 295,
    298–99
Shepard, Sam, 42
Shoemaker, Mike, 106, 111, 131,
    138, 140, 160, 192, 199, 201, 209–
    11, 294, 297, 316
Short, Martin, 100
Sills, Paul, 79
Silverman, Sarah, 157, 329
Sloane, Joyce, 74, 87, 92, 309, 312
Smigel, Robert, 100, 101–2, 108,
    111–14, 120, 126, 164, 195,
    296–98
Spade, David, 4, 100, 102, 110, 114–
    16, 120, 121–22, 135–36, 139,
    147, 158, 172, 175–83, 189, 197,
    204–6, 215–17, 222–24, 226, 251,
    263–64, 275–78, 316, 318, 327
Spheeris, Penelope, 171, 213, 217–
    18, 220–23
Stack, Brian, 56–60, 64–65
Stiller, Ben, 216
Swayze, Patrick, 106

Talley, Jill, 81, 86, 90, 92, 95–96
Timmons, Bob, 256
Turner, Bonnie, 173–74, 186
Turner, Terry, 172–74, 186

Vaughn, Vince, 62, 64, 291, 302
Venit, Adam, 107

Warner, Julie, 172, 181, 183–
    84, 188